Making a M
That Ma

Making a Metaverse That Matters

From *Snow Crash* & *Second Life* to a Virtual World Worth Fighting For

Wagner James Au

WILEY

Published by John Wiley & Sons, Inc., Hoboken, New Jersey.
Published simultaneously in Canada and the United Kingdom.

ISBNs: 9781394155811 (hardback), 9781394156177 (ePDF), 9781394155828 (ePub)

For general information on our other products and services or for technical support, please contact our Customer Care Department within the United States at (800) 762-2974, outside the United States at (317) 572-3993 or fax (317) 572-4002.

If you believe you've found a mistake in this book, please bring it to our attention by emailing our reader support team at wileysupport@wiley.com with the subject line "Possible Book Errata Submission."

Wiley also publishes its books in a variety of electronic formats. Some content that appears in print may not be available in electronic formats. For more information about Wiley products, visit our web site at www.wiley.com.

Library of Congress Control Number: 2023937908

Cover Images: © Just_Super/Getty Images, IanGoodPhotography/Getty Images, imaltsev/Getty Images, sdominick/Getty Images, IvanNikulin/Getty Images, edge69/Getty Images

Author Photo: Photograph By Brooke Erdmann
Cover Design: Wiley

SKY10047440_050923

To my beloved Brooke, who, through all my flights of virtual world fancy, keeps me fastened to the offline world with her heart.

Contents

Preface

The Metaverse is a vast, immersive virtual world simultaneously accessible by millions of people through highly customizable avatars and powerful experience creation tools integrated with the offline world through its virtual economy and external technology.

(If some or most of that sentence seems obscure to you, don't worry: I wrote this book in part to explain what it means.)

This is the story of the people who have worked to realize something like the vision contained in those words since at least 1992 and still strive to bring it to full fruition.

For at least the last two decades, they have been building metaverse platforms with nearly all the aforementioned features.

They are tantalizingly close, at last, to entirely realizing that goal.

But this preface is mainly intended for you, dear reader, who isn't quite convinced the Metaverse is even worth your time.

So if you are wavering on that topic, may I tell you at least seven things to know about the Metaverse, even if you read no further?

Most of what you have probably read or heard about the Metaverse across media in recent years is somewhat or completely wrong, often deceptively so.

- The Metaverse is not for everyone. Chances are you've seen more than several tech evangelists across various media outlets insist that we'll all soon be in the Metaverse. I can tell you from painful—but also amusing—experience that this is unlikely ever to be the case. And, no, you probably won't wear a VR headset on a regular basis, either.

- That said, it's also safe to say at least one in four people with Internet connectivity will be part of the Metaverse on some level. And the many side applications likely to spring out of the Metaverse are powerful, potentially impacting most everyone.

- At a very conservative estimate, over half a billion people worldwide already use one or more variations of a metaverse platform now, from Minecraft and Roblox to Fortnite, VRChat, and Second Life. That's about 1 in 10 of the 5 billion people across the planet who use the Internet. While you may not personally use a metaverse platform, you almost certainly have many friends, colleagues, neighbors, relatives, or children who do. (As to *why* so many of them do so, read on to the Introduction.)

- Despite what you may have heard, and no matter what its company name change from Facebook might imply, Meta is not and never has been at the forefront of metaverse development. In fact, I would love to tell you about the many fascinating ways Meta is repeating errors made by many of us over the last 20 years (despite several direct warnings made *by* some of us).

- Meta is hardly alone in repeating past mistakes. Many of the major tech and media companies and venture capitalists of the world are currently spending tens of billions building *their* conception of the Metaverse. Most of them are also making profound (and avoidable) design, policy, even philosophical mistakes that may destine their efforts to disaster.

- And because so many companies are making an assortment of tragic errors, while most government and community organizations remain largely oblivious of the technology, it's important that we understand the Metaverse, the people who make it possible and worthwhile, and what we can learn from their failures and successes.

Because more than any other technology that's come before it, the Metaverse is shaped by the user communities that thrive in it. *Making a Metaverse That Matters* is ultimately their story.

The introduction explains why we should even want a metaverse that matters. This book is told in four parts:

- **Part I, Conception**, tells the untold story of the Metaverse's origins in and around Neal Stephenson's classic novel *Snow Crash*, and the first fully realized attempt to create it, with Second Life—and what we can learn from the near-disaster that followed. It closes with the Metaverse's rebirth as an idea championed by Facebook (now Meta) and how its many missteps have confused the underlying concept.

- **Part II, Realization**, includes snapshots of several metaverse platforms that evolved, often in unexpected and surprising ways, to reach mass market prominence/mainstream awareness: Roblox, Fortnite, VRChat, and Lamina1, the platform co-created by Stephenson himself. Their successes and user communities help show us how the technology might evolve for the better—just as their shortcomings warn us how that evolution can sometimes go awry.

- **Part III, Promises and Perils**, explores the many ways that metaverse technology might evolve beyond its origins in gaming, and the upcoming roadblocks that prevent it from reaching full flower. It's here that I also address the many myths commonly held among Metaverse advocates and the technorati—but which I believe tend to take us in fruitless directions.

- **Part IV, A Metaverse Worth Fighting For**, is a vision for metaverse platforms that can continue to grow as businesses *and* as cherished virtual places for real communities, where grassroots creators can benefit from their inventiveness and artistry as much as the platform owners themselves. It is a guide to a Metaverse that has the best chance at being worthy of its highest aspirations—and in that process become the next great Internet medium.

As that last part suggests, there *is* a fight for the Metaverse's future, with the outcome far from certain.

This conflict will enmesh companies and the user communities who depend on each other, and draw the current Internet giants into the fray. It will finally ensnare whole societies and world governments, who scarce grasp the barest outlines of the alternate reality already emerging beneath our screens. *Making a Metaverse That Matters* tells that story too.

The "matters" of the book title comes with a hidden double blade. I believe the Metaverse will transform us, on balance, for the better. But it will also introduce dark old troubles in a new context and new dangers that we as a society are hardly ready to understand; I have seen too much of that side of things to avoid telling the full story.

The primary focus of this book is not on the technological and business components required to operate a metaverse platform. For that, I highly recommend *The Metaverse* (Liveright, 2022) by Matthew Ball, who has done essential work on that front.

Making a Metaverse That Matters is fundamentally about the *people* behind this technology, both as creators and as users. More than anything, their experiences explain why this concept, drawn from a relatively little-read sci-fi novel, has so much power. I've seen firsthand how the Metaverse can transform lives and enable human flourishing.

Making a Metaverse That Matters is also, finally, *my* story—one that I've been writing in one form or another for roughly 20 years, since around the start of my writing career.

In 2003, a publicist's email led me into the office of Linden Lab, the creator of Second Life, for a demo that went on to transform *my* life.

Hired as the startup's official "embedded journalist" in the virtual world, I began in 2003 to interview Second Life users as a roving avatar reporter wearing a white suit (my somewhat pretentious tribute to Tom Wolfe), impertinently asking them about everything—from virtual sex to ambitious collective art projects to savvy virtual business ventures that turned their founders into literal millionaires.

During that time, Second Life became the first metaverse platform to reach mainstream awareness. After leaving the company in 2006 to write *The Making of Second Life* (HarperCollins), I was shocked and saddened to watch as Second Life failed to realize its potential for many strange, aggravating, and tragically hilarious reasons—and feel some personal blame for what went wrong.

At the same time, I have learned from the ongoing story of Second Life, which still generally flourishes against all odds, what aspects of the Metaverse are truly compelling. So *Making a Metaverse That Matters* is also about watching the dream re-emerge and vowing that *this* time, everything possible must be done to ensure that it scales to the benefit of all.

A few housekeeping notes:

- A back Glossary includes dozens of definitions for technical or insider terms used throughout this book that might not be fully unpacked in passing for the sake of space.

- My blog *New World Notes* (nwn.blogs.com) is essentially a 20-year archive of stories and footnotes that went into *Making a Metaverse That Matters*. If you are interested in following up on references throughout, I welcome you to use the Google Search widget there to explore.

- Throughout this book, the "Metaverse" (with an uppercase *M*) is the original vision depicted in *Snow Crash* and refers to the industry as a whole that's attempting to develop a fully realized version of it. However, "metaverse platform/startup/ etc." (lowercase *m*) refers to an individual startup, company, or platform within that ecosystem.

Now, keeping in mind the Metaverse definition that started this preface, let us begin.

Introduction: Five Stories about Five Core Metaverse Concepts

As I write this in early 2023, over 500 million monthly active users inhabit online platforms that fit the broadest outlines of the definition of the Metaverse at the start of this book. That's roughly one in ten of the entire global population connected to the Internet. (As to that definition's particulars, I'll tell that story in Chapter 1.)

Most of the leading metaverse platforms are outlined in the following table:

The Metaverse Platform Landscape, 2023—Market Leaders

Platform	Monthly Active Users	Accessible Devices	Notes
Roblox	250 million	Windows, macOS, iOS, Android, Xbox One	See Chapter 4.
Minecraft	174 million	iOS/Android, Windows, Mac, consoles	See Chapter 4.
Fortnite	83 million (2021)	Windows, Mac, Android, consoles	See Chapter 5.

Platform	Monthly Active Users	Accessible Devices	Notes
ZEPETO	20 million (2023)	iOS/Android	Company reports that 60% of users are in Asia; 15% in the Americas; 15% in Europe; and 9% in MENA.
Rec Room	10–12 million	Windows, Meta Quest, iOS/Android, consoles	In April 2022, company reported 3 million MAU accessing through VR, most via Meta's Quest 2.
VRChat	7–9 million	Windows, Quest, Steam VR, HTC Vive	See Chapter 7.
Avakin Life	7 million (2023)	iOS/Android	Developed by UK-based Lockwood Publishing, which in 2020 raised $25 million in Series A funding led by China tech giant Tencent.
IMVU	5 million (2023)	iOS/Android, Windows, Mac	Company reports 200,000 monthly active creators, $1 million paid out per month to creators (Feb 2023).

Platform	Monthly Active Users	Accessible Devices	Notes
Second Life	600,000	Windows, Mac	See Chapter 2.
Horizon Worlds	200,000 (2022)	Meta Quest	See Chapter 3.

Numbers in parentheses represent dates of public statements by the platform company or from major news/industry publications. Other figures represent estimates or third-party counts from New World Notes, along with RTrack and Metaversed. consulting.

Anyone not already within this proudly geeky half-billion-sized cohort may wonder why these platforms and their largest representatives—Roblox, Minecraft, Fortnite, and so on—should have any relationship to the Metaverse. Aren't they just online games?

They are *also* online games, yes, but their potential extends far beyond that category. All of them share five core features that are integral and unique to metaverse platforms. Taken together, these features offer a new and largely better way to experience the Internet—and an advance to the kind of Internet experience that the remaining nine in ten people online have grown accustomed to.

But rather than discuss these core features in the abstract, let me tell you about five *people* whose lives have been changed by them.

Fran and the Immersive Virtual World

One day Fran, a senior citizen in Southern California, noticed it had become difficult for her to stand from a sitting position or maintain her balance while upright—the first indications of Parkinson's disease, a degenerative disorder of the central nervous system that afflicts millions around the world.

Fran was also an active Second Life user at the time, enjoying it as a fun way to socialize with her daughter, Barbara. Sometimes for fun, she'd have her avatar practice tai chi, a nice visual reference while meditating herself.

Then Fran noticed an odd thing: She seemed to be gaining significant recovery of physical movement—apparently, *as a direct consequence* of her activity in Second Life.

"As I watched [my avatar]," she told me in 2013, "I could actually feel the movements within my body as if I were actually doing tai chi in my physical life, which is not possible for me."

For a year up to that point, she sat and even slept in a motorized lounge chair.

After weeks of watching her avatar practice tai chi, however, "I could feel that my body had become stronger."

Until a day came when she was able to stand without motorized assistance.

"Now," she added, "I can go from a sitting to standing position without even using my arms to push against the arm rests. This has been absolutely thrilling for me."

Using a virtual world, in other words, seemed to abate her Parkinson's symptoms.

Fran's story first came to me through Tom Boellstorff, professor of anthropology at UC Irvine. Author of *Coming of Age in Second Life* (the echo of Margaret Mead is intentional), he's among the most well-respected academics studying the social implications of virtual worlds. Tom met Fran and Barbara offline, recorded video of Fran's physical recovery, then went on to receive a National Science Foundation grant (with his colleague Dr. Donna Z. Davis), to study virtual worlds and people with disabilities.

Though Boellstorff and Davis are anthropologists by training and not medical experts, they have a theory about the nature of Fran's recovery, and hope it can be researched further.

"We believe that Fran's experience may be similar to results in other current research being conducted with individuals with brain disorders or injury," Dr. Davis told me back then. "Where, by watching yourself—or your avatar—you are essentially retraining the mind to function."

While the implications of this have yet to be studied to their furthest potential, they are likely to be profound—especially in the face of a rapidly aging population around the globe. From what we can tell, they are made possible because this happened in *an immersive virtual world*.

Immersion is the sense of feeling so situated within a 3D virtual world, your awareness of the surroundings beyond your digital screen mostly melts away. Immersion powers the success of videogame consoles, PC games, and even 3D titles on mobile, especially titles in the category called "AAA"—big budget, action-oriented games with highly vivid 3D graphics, such as *Call of Duty: Modern Warfare*, *Red Dead Redemption 2*, and *Grand Theft Auto Online*. Each has sold tens of millions of copies, earning revenue that puts them in competition with Hollywood's most successful movies.

Immersion is also what first brought me, through many lateral moves, into the metaverse industry. I specifically credit the astoundingly influential PC game *Thief: The Dark Project* (1998) for achieving a sense of immersiveness that felt like a fundamental shift. In this story of an antihero cat burglar in a nameless steampunk city, the player progressed through careful awareness of the world, learning to stealthily blend into its shadows. *Thief* and its many successors convinced me that immersion could elevate interactive experiences beyond mere arcade games into something more profound.

The growing popularity of immersive *online* virtual worlds, first seen in sword and sorcery MMOs like *EverQuest* (1999) and *World of Warcraft* (2003), expanded my excitement; now, other people were part of a virtual world that you simultaneously shared together. Typically, these worlds are fanciful but recognizable simulations of our offline world, with mountains and oceans and cities and the like, visually appealing and varied enough that many people would want to explore and interact within them together.

"For me the foundational thing is that virtual worlds are shared spaces," as Tom Boellstorff puts it. "They are places online and that's what makes them different from email or Twitter. And you even see this in English with prepositions, where people say you go *on* Facebook, but you go *in* Roblox or in Second Life or whatever." And it's how Fran happened to come across an inviting meadow with a community meditation space for practicing tai chi in Second Life, which ended up changing her life.

Fran is hardly alone. Drawn to this "you are there" quality, a large contingent of people enjoy digital immersion, whether in single player games or shared multiplayer spaces. Steam, a top online distributor of immersive PC games, has about 125 million active users; one in five global consumers reportedly owns a videogame console boasting immersive graphics and audio capability. Hundreds of millions play 3D games on mobile; one title alone, the mobile version of *PlayerUnknown's Battlegrounds* (PUBG), attracts over 50 million daily users at peak.

By my estimate, the existing audience for immersive experiences is about one in four people with Internet access worldwide.

Nick and the Power of Virtual World Avatars

Immersiveness creates a metaverse platform's sense of social presence; avatars create the sense that you are part of that world and can be perceived by others in it at the same time.

Taken from the Sanskrit word for "godly incarnation," the avatar is your emissary in the virtual world, responding to your commands in near real time. Typically you view your avatar onscreen as if you were its angelic conscience, hovering just behind it, or see through its eyes from a first-person perspective. As you interact with other users through their own avatars, the sense of immersion is enough to create a real-time social context from the ephemera of pixels.

That effect can best be demonstrated by a surprising discovery:

One day, a graduate student at Stanford named Nick Yee wondered what kind of relationship the average person has with their avatar. To test this, he brought male and female volunteers into a lab and had them control their own avatars in the same virtual world; the volunteers could freely move their avatars around in this simulation, standing as close or as far away from each other as they preferred. If they wanted, they could also command their avatar to make virtual eye contact with another avatar.

What happened next was unexpected:

The avatars, Nick discovered, eerily imitated our unwritten rules of social distance and eye contact. In other words, these volunteers' avatars maintained the same relative distance in the virtual world as they would were they strangers standing near each other in the real world.

Our unwritten rules of gender dynamics and sexuality were also mirrored in this experiment. For instance, when avatars of two straight male volunteers talked with each other, as Dr. Yee explained in his paper on this study, "they were less likely to maintain mutual gaze than female-female dyads and mixed dyads." They also tended to position their avatars so that they stood side by side with each other while looking away—eerily and unconsciously replicating, for example, how heterosexual men tend to stand next to each other at a bar.

No one told the volunteers to behave this way with their avatars in a virtual world. Indeed, it's unlikely anyone told them about the rules of eye contact and social distance *in the real world*. Yet somehow, they felt such an intuitive connection with their avatars' perspectives that they re-created these unconscious social rules, as if these avatars really were an extension of their real-life selves.

While the results of Yee's study ("The Persistence of Non-verbal Social Norms in Online Virtual Environments") may surprise many readers, they are less likely to shock the many hundreds of millions of people who play Minecraft, Roblox, Fortnite Creative, and other metaverse-type platforms. For those of us accustomed to avatars in shared immersive spaces, this phenomenon is part of the magic: the uncanny sense that we are *really there*, in the simulated space, and that we share it with others, even when we are logging in from the other side of the world—they are also, somehow, right by our side.

The sense of avatars as people also seems to apply to the avatars that individual users control. In another series of studies led by Nick and his Stanford colleague Jeremy Bailenson (a pioneer in virtual world/VR research), they found that when a volunteer is embodied in a physically attractive avatar, they are more willing to talk with others and express more open, self-confident friendliness—in both the virtual *and* the real worlds.

Bailenson and Yee dubbed this "the Proteus effect," after the shape-shifting demigod of Greek mythology, and it reinforces the previous finding: Avatars help empower us and connect us in a meaningful way with others in a virtual world. (The Proteus effect can also be abused, often to socially disturbing effect. But more on that in Chapter 13.)

Jeff and the Power of User-Generated Virtual World Content

There once was a tall and rangy artist who wandered the green countryside of Ireland as an itinerant painter for hire, and through various serendipitous twists, eventually wound up as a UI designer at IBM. It is there that Jeff Berg's manager suggested he try a thing called Second Life that everyone seemed to be talking about at the time.

So he did, exploring the technical and artistic possibilities of the platform. Someone told him it was impossible to build a simulated wheat field in this virtual world, but with some practice, he built one, hand-drawing some of the digital textures, to make it seem all the more real.

Berg dubbed it "The Far Away," and it invited you to stroll through a golden expanse wrapped around a rusty train with tracks lost beneath the seemingly windblown grain. Second Life users, learning about the place, would teleport or fly there in an endless stream of avatars whose incongruous appearance made these settings seem even more surreal—sex vampires and robot furries and supermodels and space commandos and cyberpunk cowboys, all milling about in God's country.

Berg's virtual wheat field, in a word, became famous. He created that place and others to evoke nostalgia for the time before the Internet. He succeeded at that. Tens of thousands of people visited his Second Life installation, moved and made nostalgic for this bygone time.

And then Berg himself, in an ironic turn, also became famous. Or rather his avatar did, whom he named "AM Radio." Ardent admirers messaged him, telling him that exploring his works had saved them from suicide. Two people who met as avatars in the middle of his wheat field wound up getting married in real life. Many fans sent *him* romantic messages. Many pursued AM Radio around Second Life whenever he logged in, wandering the virtual world in a greatcoat and top hat, the way star-struck art mavens from another era might trail after a celebrated painter in Paris.

AM Radio's fame even started spilling out into the real world. Berg was ordering coffee at his local shop, only to overhear the two young women behind the counter talking about Second Life.

As she prepared his order, one barista enthused about a beautiful wheat field she had just visited there. And Berg realized she was talking about "The Far Away." Berg is shy and not exactly outgoing in real life, and this attention was overwhelming.

As he explained to me later: "I grabbed my coffee and thanked them and ran out the door."

Essential to a metaverse platform are creation and editing tools that enable users to reshape and customize the virtual world around them into user-generated content (UGC). There are thousands if not millions of people like AM Radio across many metaverse platforms, acclaimed and even dearly loved for their creativity, made possible by these tools that turn users into creators. You will meet many of them in the coming chapters.

The tools themselves vary wildly from platform to platform; in some they are simple, enabling users to, say, click and drag prefab furniture around their virtual homes. Other toolsets enable creators to customize a user experience so thoroughly that what they build is nearly indistinguishable in quality from immersive content created by teams of well-paid game professionals.

An equally important point here: On a metaverse platform, *all* content can be user-generated content, and *every* activity performed by users is by definition UGC. Even a user's avatar randomly walking around and chatting constitutes UGC; their very presence and social activity contributes to the immersive environment. It might seem trivial to describe avatars socializing and chatting as UGC, but I can assure that it is not. It's why metaverse platforms invariably have a cottage industry of virtual wedding planners, emcees, DJs, and so on who make a decent side income from their social skills.

The power of UGC has already been proven in the early '90s by the modding community—gamers who collaborate online to modify and tinker with a game's art assets and coding to create enhanced or completely altered game experiences, which they then share with each other as unofficial add-ons for the original underlying game.

Modding has changed the game industry so often, it is taken for granted that businesses worth billions of dollars can be altered by the creative work of a dedicated team of amateur creators (or sometimes, just one).

Modding led to the mainstreaming of the Metaverse itself. Summarizing wildly, it was modding that turned the sci-fi action hit *Half-Life* into a terrorists versus counterterrorists multiplayer mod called *Counter-Strike* (created by two amateur developers, Minh "Gooseman" Le and Jess Cliffe). Still one of the world's most popular games, *Counter-Strike* helped foster a massive audience for other realistic military combat simulators, including a series called *Arma*. A title from the Arma franchise was then modded into a battle royale game called *PlayerUnknown: Battlegrounds* (created by Brendan "PlayerUnknown" Greene). This in turn helped foster a massive audience for battle royale games, leading to a new gameplay mode in Fortnite—setting the stage for that game to evolve into one of the largest metaverse platforms you'll read about here.

At each of these stages, it was the creativity and dedication of lone grassroots creators and tiny teams to inspire and excite millions of gamers, altering an entire industry in the process. But even more often, metaverse artists like AM Radio create for the sake of art and expression itself.

But with art, of course, commerce is not far behind.

Gizem and the Battle to Make Virtual Money Real

Once upon a time, a girl sitting by herself in an ancient city traveled through a looking glass full of lightning and changed her life forever.

Gizem Mishi was a college student at Okann University in Istanbul when she came across a YouTube video of "Skye Galaxy," a bohemian-looking avatar with a powerfully resonant voice, performing in a virtual world to a throng of swaying fans. This was how Gizem first discovered Second Life. By the time she attended her second Skye Galaxy performance, she had learned the world's creation tools well enough to create a polka dot dress for herself—her first item of avatar clothing for the platform.

This virtual concert was transformative for at least two reasons. For one, someone in the audience messaged her about the dress, wondering where she had bought it. Gizem instantly realized that there was a massive demand in Second Life for virtual fashion. (Another message she received during the show was more personal, but that's a story for Chapter 2.)

Gizem founded a clothing line and gave it a brand name, Blueberry, offering decidedly feminine styles that she herself might wear in offline life, when hitting the town on a girls' night out. She sold these items for Linden Dollars, the official virtual currency of Second Life, which for a processing fee, a user could sell to other users for real money. (At an exchange rate of about L$250 to $1 USD—or in Gizem's case, the equivalent of $1 USD in Turkish lira.)

And while most of her clothing items were priced at the Linden Dollar equivalent of $5 USD or less, sales strongly grew, as did her community of fashionista fans (her "Berries," as she would dub them).

By 2013, Blueberry was netting $60,000 a year from Second Life content.

By 2014, when Gizem was creating virtual fashion on a full-time basis, Blueberry was making an income in six-figure range.

By 2015, when Gizem was not yet 25 years old, Blueberry was grossing over $1 million a year.

And then in 2016, the real world interrupted the growing Blueberry empire in the most unlikely way:

A faction within the Turkish Armed Forces launched a violent coup d'état against President Erdoğan, forcing Gizem into a surreal situation where she was creating attractive outfits for avatars while very real explosions and the rumble of choppers shook the walls of her home.

The end of the coup only exacerbated her problems, because in its aftermath, Erdoğan blocked Turkish citizens' access to Internet services that managed online payments, including PayPal. And so the virtual fortune she had worked so hard to amass drifted in the purgatory between the virtual and the real.

The rest of Blueberry's story will be told in Chapter 2, but I tell this part now to illustrate another key component of a metaverse platform: integration with the real world, primarily (but not exclusively) through the international monetary system.

Or to put it bluntly: The Metaverse includes the ability for creators to make money from their virtual world content.

Many traditional online games also enable players to earn real money from their gameplay. But this is rarely part of the official game itself, more often falling into the gray market category of "gold farming." For instance, where one player (typically in a poorer part of the world) will spend many hours of gameplay leveling up their character or amassing in-game wealth and resources—and then selling it on a third-party site such as eBay.

In a metaverse platform, the virtual-to-real economy is part of its intentional design and is focused around what players themselves create.

Gizem Mishi's story of selling virtual fashion during a violent military coup is fairly unique. But her success is pretty commonplace. On every successful metaverse platform, there are hundreds if not thousands of people who make a real-life living, and sometimes a small fortune, from the virtual content they create.

The emergence of this new economy built on virtual worlds is still not fully appreciated outside the relatively small circle of companies creating metaverse platforms. (Even the wider game industry as a whole has been slow to grasp its implications.) To better explain it, I'd compare it to another media platform altogether: YouTube.

Launched in 2005, the video-sharing site rapidly evolved into the world's most powerful platform for user-generated content, fostering a grassroots community of creators who embraced the video tools made available by the iPhone and other consumer-level devices.

"The nature of the platform led to really quick evolution and iteration of content, compared to traditional Hollywood cycles," as Hunter Walk puts it. Walk, part of Second Life's early founding team, left Linden for Google and helped scale up YouTube after the search giant acquired the video platform in 2006. The rapid user creativity happening on YouTube pretty quickly reminded him of what he had seen on the early metaverse platform.

"When I got to YouTube, I saw the same hyper-evolution of creativity," as he recalls. "It wasn't intentional, unlike Second Life, where it was built in. On YouTube it had more to do with the nature of the medium and the creativity community, riffing off different themes." (More on Hunter, by the way, in Chapter 2.)

More organic and interactive than traditional broadcast content, YouTube videos created by someone with enough dedication, no matter their background, are able to attract a massive audience—and in the process can create a lucrative career. The most popular YouTube stars have subscriber bases in the many tens of millions, translating into more engagement than what most network television programs attract. For Gen Z and younger, YouTube (and its fast-rising would-be successor/competitor, TikTok) has effectively replaced television.

Metaverse platforms are now making the same thing possible in virtual world spaces. In the same way that smartphones gave grassroots creators the power to create near-professional-quality videos, metaverse platforms give anyone with a laptop the power to create games and other immersive experiences that rival what heavily funded major publishers and digital studios can create.

This democratizing phenomenon is already happening. On Roblox, for instance, the most popular user-created experiences are played by more people than most of the top games on Steam and other major game distribution platforms. Just as Gen Z would generally prefer to watch hours of YouTube videos produced on an iPhone rather than bother with network television programming, the Roblox user base often prefers the metaverse experiences created by a handful of amateurs over AAA games produced by teams of professionals costing tens of millions of dollars.

Mr. Bristol Meets Millions

In late 2008 I gave a talk for my first book, *The Making of Second Life*, to a Los Angeles architecture and design group. By then, media attention over the first mainstream attempt to launch a metaverse, once feverish, had started shifting to a skeptical tone. The many companies and brands that had opened an official HQ in the virtual world were seeing scant return on their investments, while Second Life's monthly active user numbers mysteriously refused to grow. (More on all that in Chapter 2.)

So while I put as much enthusiasm into the Beverly Hills talk as possible, I delivered it despite a nagging sense that Second Life, and the Metaverse as a broader concept, would not be as transformative as many of us had originally assumed.

Then something happened that changed my perspective.

During the preshow sound check, the conference team casually asked me to show them what people did in Second Life for fun. I mentioned that many musicians performed live in the virtual world by streaming their mic and instrument through their computer, earning a side income through tips. I launched Second Life on my laptop to show them and randomly teleported into a ramshackle nightclub packed with dancing avatar patrons.

Onstage, the avatar of a tall and regal old Black man was performing resonant blues guitar while singing with a raspy voice. I assumed this was just an average Second Life user who had merely customized their avatar to seem old.

But when I went to check his real-life biography in his avatar profile, my jaw dropped.

He was, in fact, an elderly African American blues master by the name of Charles Bristol, 87 years old at the time.

"How y'all doing," Mr. Bristol's avatar said with a gravelly whisper into a booming mic piped into this Second Life bar by the virtual bayou. "My name is Charles Bristol. And I've been trying to make something of myself for all my life."

FIGURE I.1 Charles Bristol, 88, performing live in Second Life

Russ Roberts / Etherian Kamaboko

When he was born in 1921, the electric guitar did not exist and slavery was still a living memory. But somehow, Mr. Bristol would live long enough to see a Black man become president and, perhaps just as unexpectedly, see himself made into an avatar, so he could extend his decades-long music career into something called the Metaverse.

His entrance into the virtual world, I later found out, was made possible by total happenstance: A much younger neighbor in North Carolina, also a blues musician, invited Mr. Bristol to a virtual world jam session. Russ Roberts himself discovered Second Life in an online musician forum. ("They pay you to play?!") On a visit to Russ's home, Charles saw him playing in Second Life. "I asked Charles if he wanted to play online while we recorded his material."

By the time I stumbled into him myself, Mr. Bristol had been performing in Second Life for over a year. Too weary to frequently perform at real-life venues as he once did as a younger man, Charles now had this digital venue and access to hundreds of new fans around the world. He would go on to play in the virtual world for many years after that, with a Second Life fan group, Charles E. Bristol Blues Project, dedicated to his virtual shows.

That one random encounter helped keep me engaged with Second Life, and the concept of the Metaverse in general, writing about it whenever I can amid other editorial projects.

Because the truly shocking thing is this: Up until then, I had no inkling at all that Mr. Bristol was in Second Life, encountering him only by blind luck.

Who *else* was also in there?

When a metaverse platform achieves mass growth, the possibility of magical, serendipitous chance encounters like this become ever more possible; there are simply more and different people to meet in a shared, immersive space, increasingly from outside the social circles we are born into.

This teeming population also makes it possible to consider metaverse platforms as a viable alternative to traditional social media, especially among millennials and Gen Z early adopters.

I say "traditional" because metaverse platforms typically have key social networking features *within them*, such as the ability to friend and directly message others on the system. It's just that in a metaverse platform, your friendship network tends to extend far beyond simply friends and acquaintances from real life and, unlike, say, Instagram or Twitter, rarely includes people with real-world social capital (that is, celebrities and influencers).

By and large, people become friends in metaverse platforms because they enjoy their company and creativity. And these are typically connections from around the world, with often wildly diverse and surprising backgrounds.

The Metaverse offers us the chance to meet people from around the world through our anonymous/semi-anonymous avatars. And ideally, to be judged not by our real-life identities but through the creative expression and sociability that we bring to the platform.

We can see the early glimmers of this hope in recent studies on video games (effectively training wheels to the Metaverse). Even now, they are rapidly drawing attention away from social media:

In a fall 2021 report from reputed consultancy Deloitte, the authors noted that 20 percent of Gen Z consumers preferred playing video games over engaging on social media (20 percent versus 7 percent). Meanwhile, a 2019 University of Montreal study with 4,000 adolescent volunteers found that social media increased kids' feelings of depression, while gaming did not.

Why? The Montreal researchers speculate that social media depresses teens due to "upward social comparison" (feelings of inadequacy, when seeing others' social posts) and "reinforcing spirals" (searching for downbeat social media content to mirror and amplify their own depression).

Social media's potential for harm has been well documented elsewhere, including by staff of the companies themselves. Witness "the Facebook papers" of whistleblower Frances Haugen, a series of horrific revelations culminating in the company's internal report suggesting that the mere act of using Instagram causes depression in teenage girls.

Whereas with online games and virtual worlds, kids play *together* in real time, with the serendipity of multi-user experiences unlikely to inspire reinforcement spirals, and any comparisons they make to one another being less about their family's wealth and privilege, let alone their physical appearance, but to the skills, creativity, and sociability they each bring to the digital space.

These findings solidify my sense, based on years of virtual interviews, that teens and other vulnerable groups *thrive* in metaverse platforms. Shrouded behind the relative safety of their avatars, which are customized to reflect their personality or at least their current mood, they feel free (perhaps for the first time in their lives) to improvise their own identity and value system within the marionette theater that is a metaverse platform.

And as kids interact more in metaverse platforms, they seem to spend less time engaging in social media.

"Observationally, I would say that one is likely to displace the other," as Anya Kamenetz tells me. NPR's lead digital education correspondent, Kamenetz saw this phenomenon while writing *The Art of Screen Time: How Your Family Can Balance Digital Media and Real Life* and *The Stolen Year: How COVID Changed Children's Lives, and Where We Go Now*. "If they're engaged in a metaverse platform it would tend to displace social media use."

This strikes me as an intrinsic good. Since roughly 2010, as Facebook, Twitter, and other social media ascended, we have somehow learned to accept the costs and risks associated with them, tolerating an entire generation growing up while marinating in the toxic petri dish of Likes and Shares, as their parents and grandparents, goaded by invisible algorithms, also express the worst versions of themselves.

Kamenetz agrees with my own observation that in recent years, social media content has itself been substantially altered by metaverse platforms. Where once kids' social media consumption seemed overwhelmed by would-be influencer videos, many kids now instead opt to spend more time watching what other kids are creatively doing in Roblox, Minecraft, and other virtual worlds: "Game watching video is a huge interest for kids," notes Kamenetz. (Indeed: At the end of 2021, YouTube reported that videos about Minecraft had surpassed 1 *trillion* total views and were by far the most-watched content on the platform.)

Beyond the Metaverse's potential to shift our focus away from the templated self of social media (as my colleague Amber Case calls it), the goal of millions of users sharing the same immersive space offers a chance to expand their range of human connection to encompass the entire world.

"Looking back from the clearer vantage point of COVID," metaverse pioneer Philip Rosedale mused on Twitter at the height of the pandemic lockdown, "I realize that all my work, and especially Second Life, has been about trying to connect with strangers. We must find a way to continue."

He's right. First created to connect fellow students at Harvard, Facebook has always been intended as a network connecting real people who know each other in the real world; it's why the average user has a predictable coterie of acquaintances from family, school, work, and neighborhood, largely of the same age, economic class, and race/nationality.

But a metaverse platform by its very architecture makes it possible to meet people of all ages, nations, and backgrounds.

I'm always stunned to scroll through my contacts to review the people I first met as avatars: a 20-something Ukrainian who runs a popular Second Life brand but fled her home as invading Russians converged on her hometown; an Iraqi arts professor who excitedly logged into Second Life through his sputtering, postwar Internet connection from the ancient city of Babylon; a young Japanese sex worker, who in between porn shoots created in Second Life an eerie memorial to the nuking of Hiroshima; a professor at Princeton's Interdisciplinary Studies Institute for Advanced Study, one building over from Einstein's old office, who busily creates cosmological simulations in the open-source spin-off of Second Life. A priceless wealth of people I almost certainly would not have met, had we not shared the same virtual world.

This is why mass adoption is so essential to the Metaverse. Not simply because having millions of active users means more profit for the companies that create these platforms. But because it means enabling people like Mr. Charles Bristol, and still more diverse peoples around the world, a chance to meet, connect, and express themselves in a new global community.

Because if the Metaverse matters at all, it means mattering to people like him.

At the height of the latest Metaverse hype wave—starting with Roblox's IPO in March 2021, perhaps peaking with Facebook's name change to Meta—the definition of the Metaverse somehow became comically broad to the point of meaningless. And though it was derived from a classic novel by a still-celebrated working author, the Metaverse slowly devolved into whatever its least humble evangelists claimed it to be.

That is why my book began with a clear and succinct definition. There is a whole untold story behind those words, and it begins at least three decades ago. And while the full story is little known until now, the Metaverse was always, from its conception, much more than a mere cyberpunk conceit.

How do I know? I asked Neal Stephenson.

Conception

1

Crash Course—A Simple History of a Complex Idea

In my virtual office in Waterhead beside a river in Second Life, I have a shrine to Neal Stephenson's *Snow Crash*. It's a holdover from the virtual world's golden era, when the novel's publisher saw fit to produce (with Stephenson's official blessing) an 8-foot-tall monolith in which a readable excerpt of the novel is embedded.

To this day, avatars sometimes pay a pilgrimage, showing their respect for the shrine that symbolizes The Source to All This. Recently checking my Twitter mentions, I noticed that an excitable raccoon from Japan had posted a virtual selfie in front of it.

I vividly remember when I first read *Snow Crash* in the early '90s. It touched a yearning I already felt playing now-ancient computer games as a kid in Hawaii. Secure and surrounded by the sea, I found it difficult (and frankly a bit embarrassing) to sit inside and explore fantastic virtual worlds when the golden glow of constantly perfect days kept pouring in.

I'd spend afternoons outside surfing or playing beach volleyball, almost on general principle, impatiently waiting for night to come, when the sun would be outshined by the glow of cathode rays. Early milestone computer games like *NetHack* depicted a whole vivid alternate reality with simple text characters.

"*This*," I recall thinking, as I raced through *Snow Crash*, "is what we'll have in a decade or two."

Snow Crash has a unique place in the history of science fiction. Most classics of the genre do not pretend to describe the future in any literal way; they rarely articulate a highly specific technology that does not yet exist. Doubtless many people who went to work for NASA were first inspired by reading Jules Verne's *From the Earth to the Moon* as children. But that does not mean that they took the book with them to Cape Canaveral as a reference, sketching out schematics to shoot Neil Armstrong at the moon with a giant cannon.

Where sci-fi tends to shine best is dramatizing very real contemporary social anxieties through a futuristic, otherworldly context. And while *Snow Crash* succeeds at that as well, few remember the novel's rollicking satire of modern America at its most dystopian, katana-sliced-with-cyberpunk style and black-matte irony.

Instead, *Snow Crash* has the rare distinction of describing in granular terms a future technology that didn't yet exist—which then directly inspired thousands of very talented people to spend tens of billions of dollars over the span of several decades to bring that technology into existence.

Or, to put it another way: Stephenson's Metaverse is less remembered as a science fiction concept than as a product roadmap.

This is not an exaggeration: Decades before Mark Zuckerberg's Facebook-to-Meta name change announcement, influential technologists excitedly discussed grand plans to make it.

In the '90s, video game developer John Carmack (most recently a senior Meta adviser) not only brainstormed plans with his colleagues to build the Metaverse but even described that mission as a "moral imperative." (More on that curious phrasing in Chapter 13.)

"I had read the [William] Gibson canon in high school, but I had initially missed *Snow Crash*," as John Carmack affirms to me by email now. The novel was introduced to him through his partner at id Software, the pioneering game studio.

"I remember that someone told John Romero about it, and he relayed it to me, probably during *Doom 2* development."

And while Carmack doesn't necessarily credit the novel as driving his current metaverse work ("I have always been more focused on the problems of the day, while fiction is usually far into the future"), he does describe *Snow Crash* as background inspiration:

"I have read it, I think, three times at this point," as Carmack puts it, "and still recommend it to other people, so it has been a very notable book for me."

Other technologists do reference the novel more directly in their own metaverse projects. When I became a contractor at Linden Lab in the early 2000s, I immediately noticed that *Snow Crash* sat among a handful of technical guides, such as Richard Bartle's seminal *Designing Virtual Worlds*, in the startup's small library. It was even cited during Second Life design discussions (for instance, when staff were thinking through the implications of point-to-point teleportation of avatars from one part of the virtual world to another).

Virtual worlds over the years have varied widely in their particulars from what Neal Stephenson first described, evolving to work with what was technically feasible and commercially viable. But for countless companies and creators, the core of his conception has remained a lodestone.

"'Metaverse' has turned into a sort of golem," as Stephenson once mused to me in an email exchange from 2014, "capable of wandering the earth on its own, out of the purview of its creator. So I am always surprised to see where it turns up and what it's doing."

At the time, Facebook had just acquired Oculus, and the founders of that VR startup openly talked about creating the Metaverse for months. (A December 2013 post on the Oculus company blog is titled, plainly, "Onward to the Metaverse!")

"Ten years ago," Stephenson told me back then, "that wasn't the case. Anyone who wanted to use it in front of a normal audience would have had to say 'Metaverse, an idea from the novel *Snow Crash*.' Twenty years ago, they'd have had to add, 'a novel by Neal Stephenson.' Now, apparently, 'Metaverse' can stand up on its own three feet and lumber about, at least in the setting of tech blogs. That is the kind of event that many writers hope will happen at least once in their career. It is gratifying."

But the Metaverse was never just a fictional conceit for a cyberpunk novel.

Creating the Metaverse Immediately after *Snow Crash*

In fact, based on one expert's account, the first steps to actually build the Metaverse were taken by Neal Stephenson himself.

That's according to Avi Bar-Zeev, whose own footprint in metaverse-related technology is impressive in its own right. Currently a senior experience prototyper at Apple, Bar-Zeev helped develop Second Life in its early days, cofounded the mirror world project eventually dubbed Google Earth, and coinvented Microsoft's HoloLens augmented reality device.

But Avi's first job out of college was at Worldesign, a very early virtual world company based in Seattle, launched in the '90s during the first flush of media and business excitement over VR. (I'm just old enough to remember watching various befuddled national TV newscasters demonstrating the then-novel technology, getting strapped into headsets the size of motorcycle helmets.)

Shortly after *Snow Crash* was published, Avi tells me that Stephenson, a Seattle resident himself, would often hang out in the Worldesign office, located above an antique furniture store in the Ballard neighborhood.

At some point, says Avi, Neal Stephenson's visits took on a very specific end goal:

"Neal came by with his business lawyer and was really interested in, 'Could we build the Metaverse now? How much of the *Snow Crash* Metaverse could we actually build on present 1994 computers?' [Stephenson] wanted to know if it was feasible to build the Metaverse for consumers."

The Worldesign team, which was showing off VR demos it had made to companies like Disney, had a sober answer to that question. As Bar-Zeev puts it now:

"We told him it's probably not going to fly in 1992 or 1993: 'You're going to have to wait awhile.'" The computing requirements at the time were simply not feasible. "We were using $100,000 computers to do decent VR."

Again, this query didn't seem to stem from research for a new novel. In Bar-Zeev's telling, it reflected plans by Neal Stephenson to build something like the virtual world he had just written about. ("We met with him and his lawyer, so I think it was serious.")

Bob Jacobson, founder and CEO of Worldesign, warmly recalls meeting Neal Stephenson during his time running the startup, but he remembers it somewhat differently. In Jacobson's telling, his company was *already* planning to build something similar to the Metaverse, and Stephenson's vision helped catalyze their designs.

"We invited Neal because *Snow Crash* had just come out, and we needed a new dinner speaker," Jacobson tells me now. "He obliged, and I was knocked over [by what he described]."

In the 1990s, Jacobson's company created virtual world simulation projects for major organizations including Fiat and the U.S. Department of Defense.

As for creating something like the Metaverse, says Jacobson: "We already had it in mind. The reason I brought [Stephenson] along was he had envisioned it [in *Snow Crash*]."

Asked about all this in 2022, Neal Stephenson himself remembers meetings with Jacobson in the early '90s. However, he doesn't quite remember discussing practical plans about building the Metaverse. And certainly not with a lawyer.

"It may have just been a friend who happened to be a lawyer," he tells me. "It's certainly not my style to roll up to somebody's office for a discussion with a lawyer in tow."

As for any proposals by Stephenson to actually build the Metaverse shortly after *Snow Crash* came out, he puts it this way:

"I don't specifically remember what I was talking to those guys about at the time. I might need an old memory jar. It'd be fun to turn the time machine back to see what I was thinking when I was talking about it at the time, but it's always been an idea that is floating around."

On that point Bob Jacobson agrees, calling Stephenson "a spark plug" for a concept that was already emerging in the era when the novel was published.

Whatever happened in these encounters, Avi Bar-Zeev does have one regret from that time, talking with Neal Stephenson about the Metaverse:

"I wish I had advised him, or had his lawyer say, 'Go trademark this name.' Like, if he came up with the name 'Metaverse,' he should actually have trademarked it, and then we wouldn't be having these arguments as to what it'd be like."

Bar-Zeev means continued disagreements about how to even define the Metaverse. (More on that later in this chapter.)

But that takes us to another mystery:

On October 7, 1993, a year after *Snow Crash* was published, someone *did* attempt to trademark the Metaverse—on Neal Stephenson's behalf.

With a U.S. Patent and Trademark Office serial number of 74444540, the registration is for "METAVERSE," described as "interactive on-line computer communication services" and "interactive on-line computer education and entertainment services." It was filed by an attorney designating a "Neil [sic]

Stephenson" of Seattle, Washington as the trademark's owner. (I am grateful to Bar-Zeev for pointing me to this registration.)

Shown a copy of this trademark filing now, Neal Stephenson tells me that the Seattle address listed in the trademark filing is indeed where he lived at the time.

But, he adds, "I was not involved! Perhaps a fan who decided to do me a favor."

At any rate, the "Neil Stephenson" trademark filing was abandoned a year later. "Abandoned because the applicant failed to respond or filed a late response to an Office action," a note on the filing reads. (As of press time, my attempts to contact the lawyer listed in the trademark filing have been fruitless.)

Since then, there have been well over 300 trademark filings containing references to a "Metaverse." What that suggests about the legal implications for competing companies now claiming to make the Metaverse, I cannot speculate, but I suspect they're serious.

At the very least, as Bar-Zeev suggests, an official trademark that defined what the Metaverse actually is would have spared us decades of argument and confusion that continues to this day.

In any case, active projects attempting to create something like the Metaverse began arriving soon after *Snow Crash*. Active Worlds (first conceived as AlphaWorlds) launched in June 1995, quickly followed by Microsoft's V-Chat later that year. In 1996, Blaxxun—a company originally dubbed "Black Sun Interactive," after the exclusive hacker nightclub in *Snow Crash* of the same name—acquired Cybertown, a virtual world running on Virtual Reality Modeling Language (VRML), designed to extend the web browser's standard HTML into 3D. While these platforms may seem lost in obscurity, many of the communities that developed around them persisted for many years. (In 2022, The Verge reported on a poignant campaign by its most passionate denizens to revive Cybertown.)

Whatever transpired in 1993 above that furniture shop overlooking Puget Sound's Shilshole Bay, it illustrates that the Metaverse was never simply a nebulous sci-fi conception.

Rereading *Snow Crash* recently after many decades, I'm struck by the biblical specificity of its details—and by how eerily it resembles the technology and the cultural experience that actually emerged a decade or so later.

In other words: The Metaverse was not simply "coined" in *Snow Crash*.

It was effectively *designed* in *Snow Crash*.

Reclaiming the Metaverse's Definition Taken from Its Source

This 1990s history is important to tell, because despite the recent buzz around "the Metaverse," its actual conception has largely been forgotten. Consequently, many people not only believe it doesn't exist but even assert it can't even be defined.

Consider this cascade of cringey headlines from 2021/22: "No one knows what the metaverse is and that's what's driving all the hype" (CNBC); "The metaverse can't be explained" (Engadget); "The Metaverse Isn't What You Think It Is Because No One Knows What It Is" (CNET).

This is why the definition of the Metaverse that opened my book is drawn directly from excerpts from *Snow Crash*, and what Stephenson has later said about it, both of which are worth unpacking here:

It is a vast virtual world:

Hiro is approaching the Street. It is the Broadway, the Champs-Elysees of the Metaverse. . . .The Street seems to be a grand boulevard going all the way around the equator of a black sphere with a radius of a bit more than

ten thousand kilometers. That makes it 65,536 kilometers around, which is considerably bigger than Earth.

Contrary to what the novel describes, I have often seen the
Metaverse described by some colleagues as a collection or federation of discrete virtual worlds. That is not only inaccurate
according to the original source but dilutes the power of the
original conception: a *singular* virtual world where discrete areas
can have completely different environments but where the whole
is unified into the same contiguous, consensus reality, as is the
program's user interface, which is essentially a part of the world
too. This is an important distinction when discussing Metaverse
interoperability, because by definition, *everything* within the same
virtual world is interoperable on some level. (But more on that in
Chapter 6.)

Onward:

The Metaverse is accessible through VR, but also flat screen devices:

Hiro's. . . in a computer-generated universe that his computer is drawing onto his goggles and pumping into his
earphones. In the lingo, this imaginary place is known as
the Metaverse. Hiro spends a lot of time in the Metaverse.
It beats the shit out of the U-Stor-It.

. . . [There's] a liberal sprinkling of black-and-white
people-persons who are accessing the Metaverse through
cheap public terminals, and who are rendered in jerky,
grainy black and white.

That passing mention of "cheap" terminals contains more
insight than most Silicon Valley Metaverse boosters have ever
managed to muster. With it, Stephenson strongly suggests that
only the wealthy and dedicated enthusiasts access the Metaverse
through stand-alone VR headsets. Those without the time,

interest, or money for such hardware make do with low-budget terminals.

While Stephenson does suggest in his novel that the Metaverse will be accessed only by headsets, he changed his mind almost immediately; Carmack and Romero's first-person video game *Doom* was published a year after *Snow Crash*.

"It's kind of almost hard to remember a time when there weren't games like *Doom*," as Neal Stephenson said in a recent interview, "meaning games where your screen is a flat window into a three dimensional world. . . . You absolutely do not need AR and VR in order to build the Metaverse."

A quick note on the hero of *Snow Crash* living in a storage container:

When Meta began bandying about its Metaverse vision to an oblivious public, some pundits noted that *Snow Crash* takes place in a dystopian future, with democratic government in retreat as for-profit corporations and organized crime arise to replace it. In other words, they infer, people escape to the Metaverse in *Snow Crash* because material life is so horrible.

That's not quite the case.

"*Snow Crash* is clearly a dystopian novel, although it's kinda poking fun at dystopian novels," as Stephenson told *The New York Times* columnist Kara Swisher in December 2021:

"[T]he Metaverse I think is kind of neutral . . . it's just an entertainment medium, it's not inherently bad."

At any rate, calling the novel "dystopian" misses the zany, winking fun of a future where, say, a pizza delivery franchise is run by a *Godfather*-like Mafia family; Orwell this is not. And true to his word, Stephenson went on to actively cofound a metaverse company. (But more on that in Chapter 6.)

Back to the words that give us a working definition:

It has highly customizable avatars:

Your avatar can look any way you want it to, up to the limitations of your equipment. If you're ugly, you can make your avatar beautiful. If you've just gotten out of bed, your avatar can still be wearing beautiful clothes and professionally applied makeup. You can look like a gorilla or a dragon or a giant talking penis in the Metaverse.

When preparing to write this book, I read these passages from *Snow Crash* for the first time in decades and gasped at the uncanny accuracy of what Stephenson envisioned, compared to what specifically came to pass.

Some 10 years after the novel was published, I found myself in Second Life interviewing gorillas and dragons and, yes, reporting on a notorious incident when Internet trolls interrupted a media interview conducted within the virtual world by unleashing upon it a phalanx of giant flying penises. (Not talking, sad to say, though they did dance to Tchaikovsky's "Sugar Plum Fairy.") And these avatars were actually on the milder side of the spectrum, creatively speaking. I once interviewed an avatar customized to resemble a 3D version of Duchamp's *Nude Descending a Staircase*.

Stephenson's notion of avatar quality being limited by the power of a user's equipment has also come to pass in unexpected ways, especially in Second Life: As avatar graphics improved and became ever more ultrarealistic, only users with the most expensive PC rigs and dedicated broadband lines could fully enjoy the latest high quality, hyperrealistic avatars on the market.

The Metaverse has powerful experience creation tools:

Developers . . . can build buildings, parks, signs, as well as things that do not exist in Reality, such as vast hovering overhead light shows, special neighborhoods where the rules of three-dimensional space-time are ignored, and free-combat zones where people can go to hunt and kill each other.

It is integrated with the real-world economy:

"Hiro, I can't understand why you're holding out on me. We're making bucks here—Kongbucks and Yen—and we can be flexible on pay and bennies. We're putting together a swords-and-sorcery [game]. . . . "

Gaming, it's important to note here, is a core part of the Metaverse of *Snow Crash*. In some interviews, Stephenson has suggested otherwise, saying that he didn't anticipate how immersive online games like *World of Warcraft* would popularize virtual worlds and the 3D technology needed to run them.

"And so what we have now is Warcraft guilds," as he told *Forbes* in 2011, "instead of people going to bars on the Street in *Snow Crash*."

Stephenson sells himself short. Combat games are not only depicted as important in his Metaverse, but he also describes—for what might be the first time in literature—what's become a ubiquitous part of the online experience: the gamer leaderboard.

This occurs when a sweaty Japanese businessman is beaten by the hero in a duel of virtual samurai swords:

He has been cut off from contact with The Black Sun itself, disconnected as it were from the Metaverse, and is just seeing a two-dimensional display. The top ten swordsmen of all time are shown along with their photographs. Beneath is a scrolling list of numbers and names, starting with #11. He can scroll down the list if he wants to find his own ranking. . . .

Number One, the name and the photograph on the top of the list, belongs to Hiroaki Protagonist.

And I'd argue that the rise of *World of Warcraft* and other MMOs *affirms* Stephenson's vision. As any dedicated MMO player can confirm, people in them *do* tend to spend a fair amount of time socializing in virtual bars and taverns, as playing the actual game.

Back to our definition:

It is accessed by millions of users at the same time:

> In the real world—planet Earth, Reality—there are somewhere between six and ten billion people. . . . That makes for about sixty million people who can [afford computing technology to] be on the Street . . . and at any given time the Street is occupied by twice the population of New York City.

When Stephenson wrote these words, New York's population was about 7.3 million. Double that number, and the average concurrency of his original Metaverse—that is, the number of users logged onto an online platform at the same time—is about 15 million.

While no one metaverse platform has yet reached that number, the aggregate number of people online across the most popular metaverse platforms easily exceeds it.

On a related note—and an important one, as it's a common misconception, even among colleagues—the Metaverse is never presented as the *entirety* of the Internet.

The novel's very first reference to the Internet is on the hero's business card, which first lists "[h]is address on half a dozen electronic communications nets"—*then* followed by his Metaverse address. It's another way Stephenson's future eerily resembles our present: Even now, well over 50 years after its invention, when we have devices with the power of a supercomputer in the palms of our hands, we still send emails.

Nor is the Metaverse depicted as being used by everyone. A virtual world platform with 15 million average concurrent users as Stephenson describes would probably translate into, at a very rough estimate, 150 million to 300 million monthly active users. Quite massive, but very much not everyone. (Though as noted previously, the total user number across disparate metaverse platforms in 2023 is well over 500 million monthly actives.)

Even more telling, the hero's ex-girlfriend, once an early pioneer of the technology, has entirely exited from the virtual world by choice: "[She] decided that the whole thing is bogus. That no matter how good it is, the Metaverse is distorting the way people talk to each other, and she wants no such distortion in her relationships."

In a similar, equally important vein, the Metaverse of *Snow Crash* is presented as a *singular* virtual world. For this reason among many, I think it's a mistake to speak of the Metaverse as containing *multiple* virtual worlds (a commonly made misconception).

That single virtual world vision has also turned out to be the case in actual, successful metaverse platforms. With VRChat, for instance, you can jump from a Tolkien-esque castle to a space cruiser to a shopping mall from the '80s and beyond, but you are still recognizably within VRChat. And the essential interactive framework of the platform remains with you at all times: VRChat's user interface and facilities, such as your inventory and friends list, are as fundamental to the experience of the virtual world as the 3D representation of the world itself.

Returning to my definition and its *Snow Crash* origins:

The Metaverse is compatible with external technology and the economy.

Portals into the offline world, this compatibility can encompass something as simple as the "flat web" of web browsers (which is itself connected banking services and other systems) or, at the most ambitious, integration with physical devices. In *Snow Crash*, for instance, that includes a VOIP-controlled vehicle, piloted from *within* the Metaverse, from an elegant office in a virtual palatial estate:

> Each of the little TV monitors is showing a different view out his van: windshield, left window, right window, rear-view. Another one has an electronic map showing his position: inbound on the San Bernardino, not far away. "The van is under voice command," [Ng] explains. . . . "This is why I will sometimes make unfamiliar sounds with my voice—I am controlling the vehicle's systems."

In this passage, we learn that Ng, an inventor of amazing robotic devices, is actually a horribly damaged survivor of the Vietnam War, whose injuries are so profound, he is confined to a life support system. But this system is embedded within a van, and the van is also wired to its driving system—which is, in turn, wired to the Metaverse.

It's my favorite moment in the novel, and also among my favorites from all science fiction—a head-spinning revelation that not only forces you to rethink the future but what it means to be a thriving *human*. *Snow Crash* up to that point in the story is rife with edgy coolness and irony. Then suddenly we meet this minor character who's leveraged this technology to transcend personal tragedy.

"Your mistake," as Ng puts it, "is that you think that all mechanically assisted organisms—like me—are pathetic cripples. In fact, we are better than we were before."

It would be a decade later, reporting within Second Life, that this passage would also seem prophetic; I have met countless people with profound physical and mental disabilities who flourish in the virtual world in ways that would be difficult if not impossible without it.

Befitting the *Snow Crash* vision, Second Life's developer community began to take early, experimental steps to bridge the virtual world with hardware devices outside its digital realm.

Researchers at Keio University, for instance, created a brain-to-Second Life interface, so that a person could move their avatar around just by thinking—an invention, project lead Junichi Ushiba told me, inspired after a friend of his was paralyzed due to a swimming pool accident. He wanted to give people like his friend a new way to socialize. (VRChat and newer platforms also boast similar cross-reality projects.)

So back to our definition that ties these passages all together:

The Metaverse is a vast, immersive virtual world that's simultaneously accessible by millions of people through highly customizable avatars and powerful experience creation tools that are integrated with the offline world through its virtual economy and external technology.

Of the nine core features in that definition, most of the leading metaverse platforms boast seven or eight, with the most outstanding lacuna being scale of usage. While some have hundreds of millions of monthly users, none can yet boast Stephenson's average concurrent users of twice the population of 1990s New York: 15 million.

But at the time of this writing in 2023, we are close.

By the summer of 2022, Roblox, Minecraft, and Fortnite alone were hitting an *aggregate* peak concurrency of about 15 million every day. (When I pointed this out to Neal Stephenson himself at that time, he seemed surprised.) And during rapper Travis Scott's immersive 2020 performance in Fortnite, *Epic* reported reaching 12.3 million concurrent players.

This high usage among existing metaverse platforms, by the way, solidifies my commitment to defining the Metaverse as originally conceived in *Snow Crash*—and not out of literary fundamentalism or dogged loyalty to the author. The Metaverse, more or less as Stephenson conceived it, *works*.

And when Neal Stephenson first imagined the Metaverse, as he told me recently, it was an answer to this question: "What would it take content-wise to make 3D immersive graphics as broadly popular as television?"

Fifteen million concurrent users is comparable to mass mainstream popularity across legacy media. In the movie industry, 15 million+ people attending the same movie on opening night represents a rare pop culture phenomenon. In 2019, on its first day in theaters, roughly 17 million people gathered to watch *Avengers: Endgame*. (And their viewings stretched out over the entire 24-hour period of that day.)

It is rarer still for 15 million or more people to simultaneously engage with *any* medium. At the moment, only television can still achieve that. And it is TV that's the key comparison point.

In 2022, about 16 million people watched the Oscar award telecast. On the night of its premiere in 2019, 14 million people viewed the final episode of *Game of Thrones*. But lately, just a few television programs reach those lofty heights of viewership on a regular basis. (Yes, I'm speaking only of viewership of a single program across all TV, but these specific examples are so integral to popular culture, they strike me as sufficient comparison points.)

So Neal Stephenson's original concurrency figure also strikes me as the most reasonable benchmark for when we can dispense with talking about various metaverse platforms, and speak about the concept with a capital T and a capital M:

If we are to define it according to the features described in *Snow Crash*, and recognize that it has achieved the goal that inspired Neal Stephenson to conceive it, the first metaverse platform to reach 15 million concurrent users on a regular basis has the best claim at being called *The* Metaverse.

And if you are reading this book in 2030 or beyond, I have a strong sense that this threshold has already been passed.

While no metaverse platform has yet reached such heights in terms of mainstream usage, there *was* one that, in its heyday, very much reached that level of mainstream awareness. It was featured in top-rated TV shows and on the largest news sites and programs around the world.

Until, that is, most of that attention suddenly went away.

It was (and is) called Second Life. And I've spent at least the last 12 years trying to uncover the mystery of why so much potential could be so squandered—and what that can teach us about The Metaverse to come.

Especially because I share some of the blame.

Second Life and the Mystery of the First Metaverse Platform

It's November 30, 2006, in San Francisco, at the Commonwealth Club of California. It's the largest public affairs forum in the United States. Martin Luther King Jr. has spoken there, as have multiple American presidents and countless luminaries in literature, science, and business.

On this night the topic is "Online Personas: Defining the Self in a Virtual World." The panelists include the CEO of LinkedIn and Robin Harper, VP at the startup Linden Lab, developer of Second Life.

And, at the cherubic age of 22, the founder of a social network for college kids, something called Facebook.

Tech executives and Bay Area Brahmins are gathered to hear them discuss the future of online identity.

The moderator's first question, along with the panel's general framing, assumes that 3D virtual worlds like Second Life will define the future social experience online—so much so, that the panelists are even asked what kind of avatar they'd like to have in a virtual world. Mark Zuckerberg hesitates at first, then says being an avatar who looks like Cher might be fun.

No one then—not even perhaps Zuckerberg himself—could have foreseen what would transpire over the next 15 years.

It's one of Silicon Valley's greatest mysteries, and it's haunted me for over a decade:

How did Second Life, among the most well-publicized technology platforms of the early 2000s, anointed by countless experts as the coming of The Metaverse itself, fail to fulfill its grandest aspirations?

Now with the entrance of Meta, and continued interest in the Metaverse, that mystery is relevant to anyone wondering whether—as many now proclaim—immersive virtual worlds will be the future of the Internet.

If that's true, one may fairly ask, what happened to Second Life?

Because every breathless forecast about the Metaverse that you have read since 2020 was also said about Second Life between the years 2005 and 2010. Countless articles and news segments depicted Second Life as the utopian future of the Internet.

Jeff Bezos invested in it. IBM created an official corporate campus in it; Harvard and hundreds of other major schools and organizations erected virtual outposts in it. Second Life was featured in *The Office* and *CSI: New York*, with many more TV shows and movies to follow.

But it was not merely the media coverage that elevated Second Life. The very concept of the Metaverse, as embodied in Second Life, fascinated brilliant people from unexpected realms.

When he was preparing for a potential presidential run, former Virginia governor Mark Warner (now a leading senator) made a whistle stop in Second Life.

Famed inventor and futurist Ray Kurzweil confidently predicted that by 2045, we would start uploading our consciousness into virtual worlds like Second Life—and even gave a keynote address at the 2009 Second Life Community Convention.

Thomas Pynchon, the world's greatest living novelist, published a novel (*Bleeding Edge*) partly set in a "pixelated landscape" that eerily resembles Second Life—inviting speculation that the famously reclusive author was wandering the Linden Lab's world as an incognito avatar.

Celebrities, too, anonymously explored the virtual world. Comedian Drew Carey would occasionally tweet about his adventures in Second Life and Nylon Pinkney, his favorite avatar creator. For a tantalizing time (I'm told by a reliable source), a Hollywood project inspired by Second Life was planned to star Brad Pitt and Sacha Baron Cohen, with Pitt playing a character like Second Life founder Philip Rosedale and Cohen one of his trollish users.

Enthralled by all this attention, hundreds of thousands and then tens of millions of people signed up for the virtual world. As of this writing in early 2023—two decades after Second Life's official launch—nearly 70 million Second Life accounts have been created.

By 2007, Linden Lab had informally achieved fabled unicorn status, attaining a $1 billion-plus valuation based on secondary stock sales. Catamount Ventures reportedly sold 10 percent of its Linden Lab stock for $500 million (a source told TechCrunch in November 2007), suggesting valuation in the *several billions* of dollars.

Microsoft was even widely rumored to be courting Linden Lab to buy Second Life outright.

Asked about that now, Philip Rosedale says he can't recall serious acquisition talks with Microsoft but does clearly remember a senior executive with IBM saying to him, "We're just going to overwhelm you with interest. You're gonna have to basically just tell us to leave, because we'll have meetings with you all day long." By then, IBM not only had an official corporate campus in Second Life but upwards of 10,000 employees regularly using it.

"If anyone was going to acquire us," says Philip now, "it probably would have been IBM."

He does confirm Linden Lab was on track back then to have an initial public offering.

"We were getting ready for it because our revenue growth and our margins were so good. We had a sales team; we had all the right qualities for a company to IPO."

But then something strange happened, and it happened during the peak of Second Life's mainstream accolades, interest, and financial success.

The user base.

Simply.

Refused.

To grow.

Tens of millions of people tried Second Life, several hundreds of thousands every month, excited to see what the fuss was all about.

But somehow, roughly 99.9 percent of them quit, usually within the first few minutes.

At peak in 2006, the virtual world plateaued at under 1 million monthly active users, where it's roughly remained ever since.

But why? And what does the answer tell us about the future of the Metaverse?

I've talked to dozens of key insiders over the years, many of them on record for this book. (Still many more over many drinks after careening into the inevitable question, "Where did it go *wrong*?")

The explanation for Second Life's current state is fascinating, frustrating, and, at its heart, fundamentally human. Far from being a simple tale of technology, Second Life's fate is best understood with the highest ideals that drove it—and the conflicts that inevitably emerged while trying to conceive a utopia out of thin air.

I'm also convinced that we will not have a Metaverse that matters until we understand how Second Life failed in that goal—and just as key, succeeded in its own way against all odds.

And the answer to what went wrong with Second Life's grandest dream starts in the middle of the desert.

Part 1: Rise and Fall

Burning Metaverse

As I wrote in *The Making of Second Life*, the original intention was not to create the Metaverse *per se*, but rather a simulated virtual world with its own ecosystem to explore. But where earlier online worlds drew their inspiration from science fiction or fantasy, a genesis of Philip Rosedale's vision was Burning Man, the orgiastic art festival held every year in Nevada's Black Rock desert.

Philip was inspired not only by Burning Man's endless free-form creativity taking shape from the nothingness of the playa, but by the social connectivity that emerged:

"I was just blown away by the fact that I was willing to talk to anyone," Philip Rosedale told me then. "That it had this mystical quality that demolished the barriers between people. And I thought about it: 'What magical quality makes that happen?'"

To this day Philip considers this the essence of Second Life: "I always had an intense desire to communicate, wholly, to communicate in a genuine and intimate way with others."

The quicksilver alchemy of connecting strangers remains core to Philip's vision throughout Second Life's long evolution.

The very early versions of Second Life prior to its 2003 launch actually resembled rudimentary versions of Minecraft and Fortnite, and it's tantalizing to consider what the virtual world would look like, had it continued evolving in that direction.

"There was a time where Linden and Second Life were trending a little more toward Minecraft, where the physics and the visuals of everything will determine how everything works," as founding CTO Cory Ondrejka remembers. (As with Minecraft, the team had also created feral creatures that would hunt down the player.)

Also guns. Lots and lots of guns:

"We had a version that was very much what early versions of Fortnite ended up being, where you could shoot at each other, but you can also put up walls and break things."

Cory Ondrejka describes himself as the cofounder of Second Life, alongside Philip Rosedale, and he does so with some justice.

"Virtually all of the original core systems, other than the initial render, the original simulator, the original space server, all those initial versions, I wrote basically the first version as a proof of concept," as Cory puts it to me now. Much of Ondrejka's original code still exists in Second Life today.

By "cofounder," Cory Ondrejka also means how closely he and Philip worked together to build out their world.

"Second Life was very much a co-creation, and I don't think you would have gotten to where it was if either of us had tried to push it forward on our own," as Cory remembers it now. "And I think the dynamic tension of Philip and I not always agreeing and bouncing off each other and challenging each other is part of what enabled us to build such an energetic company, such an amazing product, and help drive things forward so quickly during that period."

When I met Ondrejka in 2003, he had dark hair and a way of speaking that veered between geekily animated and gravelly sardonic—a holdover, perhaps, from his early stint as a U.S. Navy officer. During the pandemic, however, his family decided a cheerful makeover to his now-graying hair was in order. So when I reconnected with him on video calls for this book, Ondrejka delivered in-depth technical and strategic analyses from under a head of rainbow-colored hair.

Developed in the early 2000s alongside Philip Rosedale and a handful of developers, these early incarnations of Second Life (dubbed Linden World at the time) came with creation tools, enabling players to instantiate building blocks—called "prims," short for "primitives"—into the world, connecting and customizing them into virtually any conceivable object, even imbuing them with physics and interactivity, through Linden Script Language (which Ondrejka whipped up over a few days).

It was these creation tools that the startup and its investors realized were the product's key features. They also set Second

Life on the explicit path of becoming the Metaverse. As I wrote in my first book:

> [While] Rosedale and Cory Ondrejka spoke to their financial backers, a projector displayed a live video feed of Linden World, projected on the wall. Other Linden staffers were in-world, running a demonstration that the investors could watch. A few of them were using the building tools the staff used to create content. And as it went on, the investor's eyes drifted away from the meeting, and to the screen.
>
> On it, one Linden staffer was building a giant, evil snowman—and another staffer was busy creating a mass of little snowmen, gathered around their titan Frosty, to worship him. This, everyone realized, was what made their world unique: To build and see the results instantaneously; to share the act of creation with others; to riff off their work, and make it larger than its individual components; to be in a collectively shared collaboration with people from all over the world. That was the uniqueness that they had stumbled upon, without quite planning it; that was the key feature that would distinguish Second Life from everything else on the market.
>
> [Only then] did Ondrejka begin to see a connection between what they were making and Stephenson's Metaverse. "People are going to build human artifacts," he realized. "And if you're going to have human artifacts, you're going to need to have people . . . which means people, which means avatars."

Indeed, by the time I joined Linden Lab as a contract writer/ embedded journalist in early 2003, *Snow Crash* had well ensconced itself as a reference point for Second Life as a product. On an early visit to the office, I noticed that the novel sat in a prominent place on the startup's bookshelf. When the developers discussed different aspects of the virtual world, such as point-to-point teleportation and virtual real estate, *Snow Crash* was often cited.

Off Game

But the rise of the Metaverse as a reference point contributed to a growing ambivalence within Linden Lab around what, exactly, Second Life was as a product.

It vaguely resembled *The Sims Online*, Electronic Arts' virtual world spinoff of the classic Will Wright game franchise. Second Life was marketed along similar lines, including a 2003 appearance at E3, the game industry's signature retail conference. Second Life even launched with a leaderboard based on user-to-user ratings.

At the same time, Second Life was always presented as an open-ended world without explicit goals, quests, or missions. ("If you can imagine it, you can do it here," Second Life's 2003-era website stated flatly. "You choose your own goals.")

"Second Life had always tried to distance itself from the gaming universe," as Richard Nelson remembers it. Nelson joined Linden Lab as an engineer in 2001 and would remain on staff for nearly 20 years. "It's fair to say among many Lindens, that approach precluded adding scores and gamifying the experience. In the early days, we saw ourselves as the browser of the Metaverse. Did it make sense to gamify the Metaverse?"

That perspective eventually became official policy. In 2005, David Fleck, Linden Lab's newly appointed head of marketing, announced in a company-wide email that thenceforth, Second Life would no longer be called a game. (Linden staffers back then, including me, often did so.)

"Yes, this was a messaging initiative that was implemented mostly for PR purposes," Fleck tells me now about making the word verboten. "The press was discovering virtual worlds and would immediately categorize SL as a 'game.'" In other words, Linden Lab faced a "'looks like a duck, swims like a duck, and quacks like a duck, then it probably is a duck' problem."

Fleck also saw "an opportunity for Second Life to attract non-gamers by helping them understand that it's a place to hang out, to be social should they want that, and more importantly, not compete for some end goal, as is typical with games."

Instead, Second Life was from then on to be described as a "virtual world" or a "platform" or both, open to varieties of use cases.

"That was to attract more creators," Fleck tells me now. "The thinking was that more content (creators) equals attract more users equals growth."

This helped position Second Life as a business opportunity: "Create content in SL and make big money—a message clearly targeting creators interested in tools/monetization (platform)."

It was also an attempt to frame Second Life as the "3D web" that external organizations could build on, creating their own immersive spaces, similar to how they made home pages. I mildly protested this direction in the group email thread, but as a freelance contractor, I had little lobbying heft.

"I'm still trying to remember exactly when did I first have that thought, you know: 'Second Life is not a game!'" Philip Rosedale told me in 2022.

Now that he's in his 50s, Philip's once-blondish hair leans toward platinum but is still cut with a rakish bounce, his boyish features faded somewhat but still punctuated by piercing light blue eyes and photogenic looks, which helped buoy his rise as a Silicon Valley celebrity. (*The New Yorker* more succinctly described his current appearance as "Danish movie star.")

Looking back, however, he says the distinction wasn't about game mechanics as such, but how he wanted people in Second

Life to engage with each other: first and foremost as other people. (Or as Kant put it, describing the best moral path, treating others as ends in themselves, not as means to an end.)

Philip again: "The point that I was trying to make, mostly, when I said, 'Second Life is not a game,' was merely to say that the nature of Second Life, no matter what it turned out to be in the long term, or no matter what it was that it would take to get a billion people in there, was going to be a lean-forward experience, where a primary part of the experience is engaging with other people who are nearby."

Second Life could not be a game, in other words, if it were to capture that transcendent sense he had of being able to meet people from all walks of life in the Nevada wasteland.

Metaversed

Floundering with little user growth after its official launch in June 2003, Second Life finally hit escape velocity when it explicitly adopted an essential facet of the Metaverse: integration with the real-world economy.

Around the start of 2004, the company announced that the virtual world's currency, Linden Dollars, could be bought and sold on the open market for real cash. And Ondrejka drove the effort to implement what was a revolutionary concept at the time: enabling users to own the underlying intellectual property rights to anything they created with Second Life's building tools.

"That was me on the phone with lawyers getting laughed at and the lawyers saying, 'You can't do that.'" But Linden Lab did eventually do that, formulating an IP rights policy that YouTube and other user-generated content platforms would come to adopt.

From this point onward, Second Life users could, and quickly did, create small businesses from their virtual world content.

This in turn grew the world of Second Life in a way that greatly amplified Linden Lab's own work on the platform.

"[A]t that point we had like, 100,000 people [playing] and we computed that," Cory Ondrejka remembers. "Ten percent of the people were actually doing awesome things in the world. That'd be like having a 10,000-person company. Because when you're a 150-person company, a 10,000-person company is unimaginably large."

Major press coverage of Second Life, often by tech reporters who were fans of *Snow Crash* themselves, began to gather momentum into 2006, culminating in a feature story on the cover of *BusinessWeek*—which catapulted into even further coverage. Strikingly, most of this overwhelmingly positive media attention was organic, generated by reporters and media outlets themselves.

"It was kind of terrifying," Catherine Smith, head of Linden Lab communications back then, recalls now. "I remember [a Linden Lab engineer] saying to me one time, 'Can you just please make the PR stop? And I'm like, 'Sorry, that train has left the station. I'm not pitching this anymore. They're all coming to us.'"

Charity Majors, an engineer who helped keep the glorious hairball of Second Life's complex backend operations running during its peak years, saw this rise of media attention play out in sharp spikes of new users.

"The main one that I remember was, of course, the episode of *The Office*."

An entire subplot of "Local Ad" (Season 4, Episode 9) was devoted to Dwight and Jim's nerdy explorations of Second Life. The show producers even interviewed Linden Lab staff while preparing the script, and so managed to perfectly capture in its dialog the fundamental dilemma of the virtual world's identity:

Jim: You playing that game again?

Dwight [with serene confidence]: Second Life is not a game. It is a multi-user virtual environment. It doesn't have points or scores. It doesn't have winners or losers.

Jim: Oh, it has losers.

Charity and other team members were in Linden Lab's own office as the show aired, awaiting the deluge.

"And there was just a flood, a hoard of people logging on and everything was blinking red," she says. "And we're just running around batting shit left and right. It was nuts."

Interest in Second Life was now so fervent and sustained, and so global in scope, Charity remembers Linden's engineering team collectively realizing over a team meal that the virtual world had effectively become too big to fail.

"One of the fun questions was, 'If Second Life ever went completely down, do you think it would ever come back up? Because, the load profile of turning things back on is what's high." Were Second Life to go offline, in other words, it would be hit by an endless cascade of frantic users around the world all repeatedly trying to log back on, overtaxing the system in the process.

By then the virtual world was thriving, with a population roughly the size of San Francisco's and a total landmass approaching that of Los Angeles.

In naked economic terms, virtual land sales and maintenance fees translated into real and rapidly growing revenue and represented thousands of Second Life users paying Linden Lab millions of dollars every month to own a plot of digital real estate—from a small homestead costing a few dollars to a private island costing hundreds to a mini-continent priced at thousands every month.

In a Chinatown restaurant around that time, Cory Ondrejka regaled me and other Linden staffers with a plan to turn Linden Dollars into an electronic currency, for use to buy *any* kind of goods and services, even the sort that you might hold in your hand.

"We recognized that here [with virtual currency] is a way that you lower friction, lower cost transactions, and do them in a very consistent and native way within the world," Ondrejka explains now. By then, it was possible for users to buy and sell Linden Dollars among each other, and some of them were already experimenting with them as a means to buy physical items like computer peripherals.

Years before Bitcoin existed, in other words, active plans were already underway to make L$ the first broadly used digital currency. Bolstering that economy, real-life companies starting with Coca Cola began to establish an official presence in Second Life, which further excited the media.

Beneath the surface of that buzz, something more rare and precious quickly took shape.

Emerging Culture, Rising Creators

The breadth and ambition of creativity in Second Life was almost immediately astounding. Looking back at it now, I see it as a microcosm of what the Metaverse in full flower could eventually be.

Inspired by Robert Heinlein's classic science fiction short story "—And He Built a Crooked House," a mathematician created a mind-melting four-dimensional tesseract house; working in her spare time, a game developer built Svarga, an island with a self-sustaining, fully simulated ecosystem; and a full-fledged roleplay community created the Wasteland, a sprawling tribute to various postapocalyptic pop culture classics.

This virtual expression wasn't confined to pixels. Logging in from Beijing, renowned conceptual artist Cao Fei erected an entire city in Second Life, sold virtual real estate deeds to it at Art Basel, and eventually brought the project to New York's MOMA. A full 14 years before rapper Travis Scott's avatar would grace the stage at Fortnite, platinum-selling artist Suzanne Vega performed live in Second Life—one of many performers to start or punctuate their careers from a virtual world venue. Helen, a multimedia producer in Colorado, would regularly transform her avatar into a dignified old woman dressed in old European finery, then hand the computer controls to her aging mother, Fanny Starr, a Holocaust survivor, who'd then tell groups of gathering Second Life users from around the world about her time in Auschwitz.

And for many creators working in Second Life, what they made also transformed who they were offline, often for the better.

Jeff Berg (whom we met in the Introduction) was among the first to gain fame as a metaverse artist. Through his avatar persona, AM Radio, Berg tells me, he was trying to evoke a sense of the sublime in the Metaverse, creating "spaces that are stable, unmoving, intangible, untouched and almost untouchable, unchanging, deep-rooted; places that might be points of reference, of departure, of origin." That's even evident in the names he gave these Second Life spaces: The Far Away (see Figure 2.1), Towards the Sky, The Quiet.

"All of my work, art or not, has a hope draped across it," as Jeff Berg puts it now. "That we remember always, despite all the wonders of the advancing technology around us, that our collective definition of who we are and the world we design for ourselves is rooted in the wonder of the sublime our hearts prefer."

As Jeff Berg became famous in Second Life as AM Radio, and as his work impacted people's lives, their response to him began to change Berg himself.

Before Second Life, he had low self-esteem at work and resisted advancement opportunities for that very reason. But now that people in Second Life were clamoring to meet AM Radio in-world, and because he felt obliged to meet them, he also found it easier to engage with people he met in the real world and assert himself more. At IBM, he tells me, he became more outgoing, more willing to take on leadership roles. Before becoming a famous avatar, that would have been impossible.

FIGURE 2.1 AM Radio/Jeff Berg in The Far Away in Second Life.

"Being AM Radio absolutely got me past a barrier," he says, "because I had to." Self-esteem and confidence thrived, and even years later, remains: "I will talk with anyone," he says. "I cannot be a fly on the wall."

Jeff's transformation echoes what I've seen in countless Second Life denizens; so much so, I gave it a name: *Mirrored flourishing*, the concept that positive contributions to the virtual world can and should have a positive impact on people in their offline lives—and vice versa.

For Gizem Mishi (whom we also met in the Introduction), the virtual world helped restructure the course of her entire life. She first entered Second Life from her flat in Turkey to attend a Skye Galaxy concert. This is where she first conceived of Blueberry, her virtual fashion brand. While Skye was singing, she also met an American man with a nondescript avatar, who mainly logged into Second Life to play in a user-run virtual football league.

"We ended up talking for eight hours straight with my broken English," Gizem tells me. "I still think it was my polka dress that lured him in."

Offline, Gizem eerily resembles the avatars she customizes to model her virtual fashion—20s, long brunette hair, full lips. She still speaks with a lilting Turkish accent. (Her name, by the way, means "mystery.")

She talked with this avatar jock in Second Life for three months more. And then Brandon McDuff, a former college football player from North Carolina, flew to Turkey to meet Gizem herself.

A year and a half later, he moved to be with her in Turkey. And then Gizem became Mrs. McDuff.

Blueberry was not her first brand, it should be said, for even though she founded it while still in college, by then she had already worked for two successful online startups, beginning at the age of 15, and despite logging in remotely from Izmir, a Turkish city off the Aegean sea, worked her way up to a founder's role at Peanut Labs, a San Francisco-based game monetization startup.

But then in 2016, a faction within the Turkish Armed Forces launched a violent coup d'état against President Erdoğan, which was somewhat inconvenient for the deadline for Blueberry's latest release in Second Life.

Amid the rumble of explosions outside and choppers striking government buildings in Istanbul, the Internet and electric power in her home struggled to stay online; Gizem's husband and her father set up a power generator to maintain her connection to the virtual world. Outside her window, bright orange tracer rounds lit up the sky.

"Places were getting mortared," she recalls now, voice drifting off. "It was really, really . . . it was something." Gizem managed to make her Arcade fashion event deadline at 4 a.m., uploading all her items just before her connection to Second Life was lost.

In *Snow Crash*, the hero's story culminates in a high-speed chase within the virtual world, a struggle over a data file transfer, while at the same time paramilitary choppers and various combatants battle it out in the real world. Metaverse history doesn't repeat itself, but it does often rhyme.

But the coup was also bad for virtual business. In the aftermath, Erdoğan locked down Turkish access to Internet services that managed payments online, including PayPal and, for a time, Second Life itself.

The virtual fortune Gizem had worked so hard to amass now drifted in the purgatory between the virtual and the real.

Linden Lab's CEO at the time personally interceded, helping create a way for her to repatriate these funds. And after all this high-stakes international intrigue, her husband insisted they move back to the United States. Gizem's mentor, Prosper

Nwankpa, helped set up a business and bank account based in America. The Metaverse is only as functional as the human infrastructure beneath it.

Which is why Blueberry is not only incorporated as a business in the United States but also has a brick and mortar office in Raleigh, North Carolina, a short drive from their shared home.

At Second Life's peak, stories like these seemed infinite and ever varied, evidence of a thriving, fully realized Metaverse culture that seemed even more vital than anything *Snow Crash* once depicted. For companies and organizations interested in setting up a beachhead in Second Life, it ratified their sense that this was, in fact, The Future.

But churning beneath this shiny surface, little noticed at first, a growing danger threatened it all.

Failure to Retain

"Second Life had been growing very quickly, but that growth had been masking retention problems," Ondrejka remembers now.

"[It] was like 2008 where the sigmoid curve, the growth started to roll off and that was unambiguous," as Philip Rosedale puts it from the vantage of 2022. "We also knew something that had been true all along, but we thought we would make more headway on, which was the percentage of people who signed up who actually stayed around for, say, a couple months, was really low. Like in the single digit percentages. And I think we always thought that we could fix that."

"People just bounced off it," as longtime Linden Lab engineer Richard Nelson remembers it. "The complexity of the user interface, the learning curve."

Second Life's user experience was only one among many obstacles, and in truth, few prospective users even managed to reach the first-time installation process.

Another Linden veteran once told me (as my jaw steadily dropped) that most of these millions of new signups quit before the actual Second Life program had even completed downloading on their computer.

It's humbling how few consumers are accustomed to installing new programs onto their PCs—and how impatient they become if they're not instantaneously entertained. As it happens, the only key consumer group which *is* accustomed to regularly downloading large new programs, especially those with 3D graphics, are PC gamers.

But Second Life was not being marketed as a game.

The few would-be users who were able to install the client and log into Second Life itself faced an even more daunting challenge: What do I do now?

Since Second Life wasn't a traditional game, with no explicit tasks, goals, or scores, the vast majority of them were too intimidated, overwhelmed, or frankly just too bored to go any further.

"When you enter Second Life, you either create content or consume content and experiences," as David Fleck puts it. "The majority of users are not content creators—they either lack the skills or have no interest in building content."

Fleck drove Linden Lab's marketing of Second Life at the time and faced the mind-boggling challenge of positioning a product with no explicit purpose.

"If you aren't creating content, you need to be interested in consuming what others have built, or you need to be ready to engage with other community members to socialize with them." But many if not most people are comfortable walking into a public space and socializing.

"Second Life is an open canvas that allows anyone to decide what the purpose will be to address their own needs. But that's like asking people in the real world, 'If you could do anything, what would you do?' For most people, that's a tough question to answer because they don't know the answer."

Second Life, in other words, confronted nearly everyone who encountered it with an uncomfortable truth about their lives that they had not yet faced. And then *charged them money* to face it.

Second Life originally launched with a subscription fee, but Fleck convinced Rosedale to shift Second Life to a freemium model, which skyrocketed new user signups but did little to improve retention.

This savage attrition was difficult to perceive on the outside. Business reporters unfamiliar with Internet metrics happily reported that Second Life had "over two million users," when that number actually referred to *registered* users (that is, people who had created an account), not monthly active users (that is, people who actually returned after registration).

Respected Internet academic Clay Shirky, among the few early skeptics, suggested this hypothesis in a 2006 essay:

> I suspect Second Life is largely a "Try Me" virus, where reports of a strange and wonderful new thing draw the masses to log in and try it, but whose ability to retain anything but a fraction of those users is limited. The pattern of a Try Me virus is a rapid spread of first-time users, most of whom drop out quickly, with most of the dropouts becoming immune to later use.

I wrote an anti-Shirky diatribe in response back then, convinced he was underestimating Second Life's growth potential. After all, if Bezos was an investor and major companies were rapidly setting up an "official HQ" in Second Life, surely this retention problem would work itself out.

I later found out that Linden Lab itself was also blinded by the problem back then. Cory Ondrejka names it as one of the core issues that could have changed Second Life's fate:

"I think Clay wasn't 100 percent right, but we weren't 100 percent right, either. And I think we could have gone harder and treated as existential the fact that people were bouncing off Second Life as hard as they were.

"And instead, I think we were [thinking] 'Well, they'll reengage, and maybe the data is a little fuzzy.'"

The company desperately flailed at staunching the loss.

"[We tried a] million different changes to the onboarding experience," Philip Rosedale remembers. "We tried, what, probably 10 or 20 different versions of the new user experience and twiddled around with different things, like how soon you met somebody else, what sequence of instructions you were taken through."

The tiny percentage of people who were familiar enough with 3D online worlds to download the client and successfully log in faced another problem: While Second Life looked like an MMO, it didn't perform like one.

Because unlike standard MMOs, the entire 3D experience of Second Life is streamed onto a user's computer. This made it possible for users to create and update their environments in real time. That also meant that reality itself would often seem to sputter, pause, or appear as an undifferentiated blob. Performance was generally egregious for people without a desktop PC and dedicated broadband line—and they were a steadily shrinking market in the era of laptops and Wi-Fi, let alone smartphones.

In the end, hardly anyone got through that gauntlet. Those tiny few who did stepped into something wonderful.

"Once you got past that hump, the possibilities were just endless, the things you could build or do. It was sticky as fuck," as Charity Majors observes. "The people who got into it, and learned to use it, and made connections, would never leave. But getting them over that hump is something where I feel like there was a little bit too much ideological purity standing in the way of our success." (More on that in the "Choose Your Own Inertia" section of this chapter.)

This growing catastrophe quietly metastasized even as Second Life was still being feted in the media, while a small but dedicated user base of some 600,000–800,000 (when you subtracted the monthly sign-up churn), the chosen few, were happily creating a thriving virtual community.

But as Ondrejka says, it was an *existential* threat to Second Life's grandest plans.

I first heard an inkling of this trouble in 2007 from an insider I deeply trusted.

"They're scared," she told me, referring to Linden Lab. "They don't know what to do."

Still enjoying the euphoria of writing *The Making of Second Life* while being invited to speak about the virtual world in far-flung cities around the world, I was shocked. (But not shocked enough, in retrospect, for her words to fully register.)

Open to Closing

Linden Lab made multiple major attempts to grow the user base. Among the first was a substantial revamp of the user interface. Long in development, informally dubbed "Viewer 2," it resembled a web browser for 3D content. (Again, *not a game*.)

"It bombed in a big way," says Richard Nelson.

In a cruel irony, it was an idealistic move by the company that largely condemned Viewer 2.

In 2007, Linden Lab open sourced the code to the Second Life viewer, hoping this would encourage the creative community to improve on and customize it, which would in turn foster more creativity.

"While it is clearly a bold step for us to proactively decide to open source our code," as Cory Ondrejka said in the official announcement, "it is entirely in keeping with the community-creation approach of Second Life."

This move did inspire the development of many user-created third-party viewers (known as TPVs), versions of the Second Life software with additional or enhanced user customization controls.

It also placed the company in direct competition with its own community.

Vexed by the user interface changes implemented in Viewer 2, the established user base mutinied, rejecting the company-made viewer and preferring a TPV that was optimized for veteran players.

This made it even more difficult to encourage new users to stay. They'd create an account, download the official software, log into Second Life, and encounter established users who were using a TPV with a completely different user interface—in effect, a whole other perceptual reality.

"People come in and the first thing [veteran players] tell you to do is download another client," notes Nelson.

By 2012, a Linden Lab engineer reported that the official Second Life client was the *third* most popular viewer among the user base. This effectively made new user growth nearly impossible.

Linden Lab open sourced its software to encourage creativity and innovation among its users. In retrospect, it's no surprise that these users leveraged this openness to serve their own immediate desires, even at the expense of the world's long-term success.

It illustrates the double-edged power of a metaverse platform: At some point, the user community's contributions to the platform become so popular and seem so indispensable, they become essential to the platform itself. Sometimes leading to painfully unintended consequences.

While attempts to grow user retention floundered, a new opportunity emerged in 2007 with the launch of the iPhone. Selling 20 million units in its first two years, the iPhone's instant popularity augured a new paradigm for online activity. By 2008, rumors began swirling that Second Life would join that transition with an official iPhone app. Surely the company realized it should?

If only that move would get enough love.

Love Machine and the Tao of Linden

Inspired to create Second Life in part by the democratizing openness of Burning Man, Philip Rosedale brought similar idealism to Linden Lab, the company building it.

"Philip, I think, had this really amazing idea, which was: I want a company without managers," as Cory Ondrejka explains, characterizing the vision thus: "'I want just a company that can scale indefinitely. And everybody just kind of does what they want, but what they want is the right thing.'

"It's why he loved ideas like the Love Machine."

While the name may evoke a glowing pink sex toy with mechanized appendages, the Love Machine actually was a computer applet inspired by *The Future of Work* author and MIT professor Tom Malone. It came out of Philip and Cory wanting a way for employees to send each other praise for accomplishing specific tasks and projects, along with a nominal gift of one U.S. dollar. Cory called it tipping; Philip redubbed it the Love Machine.

In effect, Linden Lab had taken something like the user-to-user rating and leaderboard system they gave to early Second Life players, and applied a version of that to themselves—to help run the company. In theory, the Linden Lab employees who earned the most Love would, without any bias from management, get warmly recognized by their own peers as the most important contributors. The aggregate data of all this Love (to whom and for what) would also give company leaders insights into the kind of projects considered most crucial.

The Love Machine did have its virtues.

"I fuckin' love it," as Charity Majors puts it. "Just that pattern of making it fast and almost frictionless and easy to just celebrate people and shine a light on the importance of parts of the company that don't get a lot of love—so good." After leaving Linden Lab, Charity would even go on to implement a version of the Love Machine in Honeycomb, a successful observability startup she cofounded.

Like the employees of many tech companies before the dawn of Slack, Linden staff often communicated with each other via Internet Relay Chat. To make it easier to use, one staffer automated the Love Machine, turning each Love nomination into a clickable link in this group chat. Pile-on Love giving soon became the norm.

"We'd created an incredibly powerful viral loop for ourselves," Ondrejka wrote in a 2022 postmortem. "The bummer, of course, is that it made The Love Machine way less effective."

Not all employees were highly active on IRC, so they largely missed out, while employees who *were* on IRC could see which employees were receiving the most Love: "[That] emphasized—and made public—the haves and have-nots among recipients, which hadn't been the intention."

And now with hundreds of people on Linden Lab staff participating, those nominal one dollar tips became pretty substantial rewards. Catherine Smith remembers getting hundreds of dollars in Love tips when Second Life was positively featured in the media. She also remembers a Linden Lab staffer having to walk to the company's bank to collect the latest tranche of Love awards—and trudge back to the office through downtown San

Francisco carrying $10,000 in cash. (At that point, Love was implemented into staffer's paychecks.)

In Cory Ondrejka's eyes, the Love Machine was not working as a management guide.

"Kind of like [Second Life] leaderboard stuff, it worked in a way that was self-reinforcing in ways that weren't necessarily very useful." Were people judiciously giving Love to genuinely important tasks and personnel, or caught up in the moment, promiscuously throwing their Love around?

Despite its arguable usefulness, a number of other Silicon Valley companies have adopted a variation of the Love Machine. "It's kind of amusing to see so many of them have the same quirks that Linden had," Cory notes impishly. "Google still uses a version of it today."

Cory Ondrejka now believes the Love Machine led to the final company rupture that helped seal Second Life's fate.

"The Love Machine was one of my attempts to support Philip's goal of minimal management, growth without hierarchy. It didn't work, but lots of people thought it did (or at least better than it really did), so it made [my] debates with Philip even harder."

It was easier to discount a particular proposal raised by Cory, if there wasn't enough Love to back it up. "The Love Machine rewarded people for doing things that helped you. It didn't help focus people on strategic needs."

Whatever the Love Machine's problems, they were compounded by another idealistic management principle: Linden staffers *voted* on company tasks and projects through JIRA, a software development tracking service popular in Silicon Valley but not necessarily intended for running an entire company.

This approach was expressed in the company's official principles of corporate culture (cheekily dubbed "the Tao of Linden"), as: "Choose Your Own Work."

That Tao edict had considerably more problems than the Love Machine.

"It's crazy that, you know, I was expected to vote on an engineer's project and they were gonna vote on mine," as former PR head Catherine Smith puts it. "It's kind of like the whole 'work on what you want' part of the job felt like it had no application to me whatsoever. Because I gotta deal with shit whether I want to or not."

As the company rapidly grew in size while the entire Internet ecosystem changed, that level of intransigent shit quickly became un-dealable.

The Unmaking of Second Life

Linden Lab's democratized work culture took on a different cast as the company grew to many times its original size.

"[W]hat always happens with cultures, as companies grow, is things get encoded as bumper stickers, but the context gets lost," as Cory Ondrejka puts it now. Staff were given much freedom on which important tasks they would work on, "But it was never just 'choose your own work,' it was: 'Choose your own work from the most important things to work on.'

"But as you then grow, you lose that connection back to the original idea. And so because of that, Linden at 350 people was operating in a very disorganized way. . . [It's] really rough for being able to make certain rapid moves, particularly with a lot of pressure on parts of the company, around scaling."

All this happened in the growing shadow of social networks like Facebook (launched in 2004) and Twitter (launched in 2006) and rabid enthusiasm for the iPhone (launched in 2007). In this crucial moment, Second Life could have pivoted, shifting its focus to be more integrated with social networks and increasingly toward smartphones.

But it is difficult to convey a company's existential crises through the language of Love and where work projects were voted on.

"Or put differently," Cory Ondrejka tells me, "massive pivots—massive change—needs coherent vision, leadership, and direction from the top, plus the capacity to act on change throughout the org. A Linden without Philip and me wasn't getting the leadership, so nothing the Love Machine could do would help."

Because at that point, Cory's arguments with Philip around how to grow the company grew more heated.

"I'm bashing against Philip with, 'We need to be a little bit more organized and a little bit more actually structured, even if it's just structured in terms of priorities . . . so that folks aren't trying to solve from an infinity of design space every day.'"

Linden Lab had made a virtual world that was so vast with possibilities, most people who visited it were too overwhelmed to choose what to do. And then driven by similar idealism, they had created an open corporate structure for themselves that left most of the staff similarly adrift.

Including, ultimately, the founders themselves.

Philip and Cory's clashes culminated around Thanksgiving of 2007.

"After months," says Ondrejka, "of Philip and I meeting for many hours a week, effectively in marriage counseling, trying to find a path through our disagreements."

Philip Rosedale finally sent Cory Ondrejka an email announcing his decision to fire him.

"It hurt at the time; it was terrible," Ondrejka says now. "And it was aggravating. And made me angry." He tried to exit gracefully, but at Linden Lab, "people were really unsettled."

Cory's departure from the company impacted even me, though I'd been away from Linden Lab for over a year when it happened. Invited to the company's steampunk-themed holiday party very shortly after Ondrejka's defenestration, I vividly remember seeing Philip in a tuxedo with Victorian trim, alone at the bar, sadly staring into the middle distance.

The effort of that epochal restructuring seemed to take a toll on Rosedale too; in subsequent months after Ondrejka's departure, several Linden staffers tell me he seemed detached, melancholy, "moping."

"I remember he came back from Burning Man, and I see Philip kind of put his head down in his hands," as Catherine Smith recalls it now. "And I thought, 'He's just not happy here. Now it [involves] running a big company with 300 people working there, and they were solving really hard problems. It wasn't really fun stuff anymore."

So it was not entirely a surprise when, in March 2008, Philip Rosedale announced that he himself was stepping down as company CEO, transitioning to chairman, moving away from direct company-wide management to focus on overall development and strategy.

"We didn't know how to make [Second Life] better," as Philip Rosedale remembered it in 2022. "We didn't know how to fix some of the problems we were seeing. That made me feel like maybe I wasn't the right CEO for that role, you know?" (One suspects Linden Lab's board and investors had similar pointed concerns.)

"Like our willingness to question everything was sometimes a liability because it could almost unglue everything . . . [so] I left. I felt like maybe we should try getting another CEO because that was a good experiment."

But this move left Philip and Cory's team at Linden Lab, as talented as it was, rudderless on a day-to-day basis while facing crucial, platform-level decisions.

"Philip and I had a dynamic where we pushed each other, how we disagreed about things, where we generate ideas," Cory reflects. "We were good at driving forward. So we both leave and you have different leaders who certainly brought interesting ideas and tried really hard to figure out what to do next. But it was a bad moment to stumble."

Second Life's cofounders actually departed around the peak of Second Life's financial success. In the wake of Philip Rosedale's exit in mid-2008, I calculated that the company had a run rate of $100 million, of which it was clearing roughly $40–50 million a year in profit. (A well-placed insider later confirmed to me that my estimate was roughly accurate.) Meanwhile, consumer and media interest in the virtual world was still quite high.

Flush with money and popular awareness, all Second Life needed was new leadership who could grow the user base.

Linden Lab's board sought and hired one of the most qualified people to be the new CEO. And then another. And maybe yet another.

Cavalcade of CEOs

Mark Kingdon, a digital advertising veteran, took the reins from Philip Rosedale with a clear vision for remaking Second Life's first-time user experience:

"We need to give them a really simple and intuitive interface, and as their capabilities grow and their desire to create content and own land and transact grows, we need to elegantly release those features to them, rather than hit them with 350 menu choices their first moment in-world," he told me shortly after ascending the Linden throne.

Kingdon also carried forward an ambitious partnership with IBM to make Second Life interoperable with OpenSim, an open source version of the virtual world, and also to make Second Life a viable product for hosting business meetings.

Yes, 12 years before a global pandemic would make the idea of avatars hosting corporate gatherings in a virtual world seem somewhat appealing, Linden Lab attempted selling that vision to major companies, colleges, and other large organizations.

But virtual meetings attracted few steady customers, while the interoperability project was abandoned (more on that in Chapter 8). There were improvements to Second Life's user interface, but as noted, they were actively rejected by the established user community.

After a stint of two years, Mark Kingdon stepped down as CEO in 2010.

At the insistence of Linden Lab's board, 30 percent of Linden Lab's staff were also laid off. The Second Life community created a virtual memorial to these laid-off Lindens, each of their avatar names embossed on a black marble tombstone.

It's hard to convey my own personal sense of simmering unease during this time. By then I couldn't picture a professional life apart from Second Life, surely not in an era with simple-minded Facebook games popular at the time, or rudimentary virtual worlds for kids, such as Minecraft and Roblox. (But more on that in Chapter 4.)

Second Life's floundering also felt like a betrayal of the core user base in all their quirky but soaring creativity. Would no one else stroll through the golden fields of AM Radio or listen to the velvety blues licks of Mr. Charles Bristol? And who else would emerge from a cradle of human civilization to become a self-made millionaire, following in the steps of Gizem Mishi?

I had hoped that Kingdon's successor, Rod Humble, a highly respected game designer with executive roles at Sony Online Entertainment and Electronic Arts, including work on *The Sims* franchise, would steady the Second Life ship. By then I'd become convinced that the company's unwillingness to position Second Life as a game first had condemned it as a consumer product.

But while the Humble administration did implement some game-like features in the user interface, these only alienated the established user community, driving them further into the arms of user-created third-party viewers.

By 2012, a Linden engineer reported that the official Second Life viewer was used only by "a minority" of its own customers. It no longer mattered how user-friendly the official software had become (and it had not), because it effectively segregated new users from the locals.

Tom Grant, analyst with the esteemed firm Forrester Research, even gave this phenomenon a trenchant name: The Iron Law of Oligarchy. Writing in 2010:

Second Life is an extreme case of how you can develop a very happy group of customers, and still fail miserably at reaching a wider audience. Some businesses are comfortable with that outcome, as long as the customer base stays loyal, and the business stays profitable. Most would be terrified to discover that their best customers are, in subtle ways, holding them back. I can't say for sure that the Second Life notables are the reason why the UI is still klunky, and the useful content is hard to find, but I definitely have my suspicions.

The Second Life community could have been cajoled and inspired to adapt a new user interface, but Philip Rosedale was no longer there to galvanize them. (And again, he was adamantly against a game-like makeover.) For that matter, few Linden staff from its earlier days were still with the company, and that further eroded the company's relationship with the community.

"The dedicated engineers we once had on staff when we cultivated a conducive culture were no longer in existence in the later years," Kona Gurion tells me. A longtime QA manager with Linden Lab, Kona was originally recruited to the company when he was a Second Life user (a fairly common practice in Linden's early years, when dozens of employees were brought over from the user base).

"We no longer hired as diligently and with the level of scrutiny that we did before 2011, when candidates interviewed through a varied panel of people of no less than five staffers."

The goal of that, as Kona put it to me bluntly: "Hiring people who actually give a shit about the product." But somewhere around this time, Kona suggests, creating Second Life became for many Linden staff just another job.

Rod Humble's tenure spanned from 2011 to 2013. By then, tens of millions of dollars had been spent to grow the user base.

But Second Life's population steadfastly remained some 600,000, give or take, a small enchanted city with an eccentric but charming citizenry with countless wonders behind its walls—deep in a burning desert that few dared cross.

Third Life

Ebbe Altberg, a veteran of Microsoft and Yahoo!, was appointed Linden Lab's CEO in 2014. A stocky, voluble Swede, Ebbe seemed from the start fully confident he could bring the virtual world into the mainstream.

"I've been fascinated with [Second Life] from the beginning," Altberg told me early in his tenure. "I don't mind those challenges, and I think we can fix this. I think there's things we can do that can make it broadly appealing, and then come back to the world. . . . "

Ebbe soon unveiled a key piece in that plan to find a broad audience, first put into development during the Humble era: an entirely new virtual world.

First teased in June 2014, Sansar became Linden Lab's last hope to create a modern metaverse platform that avoided all the mistakes of Second Life's past.

"We believe that there is a massive opportunity ahead to carry on the spirit of Second Life while leveraging the significant technological advancements that have occurred since its creation," as the official announcement read.

Notably, Richard Nelson tells me, Sansar was conspicuously developed without any use of the Love Machine.

Ebbe's confidence was infectious, rekindling Linden Lab's waning morale.

"We are still the shit when it comes to virtual worlds," he told his employees during an all-hands meeting. That assertion was promptly emblazoned onto T-shirts that staff would sometimes wear.

But Sansar stumbled sharply from nearly its very first moments.

Only a few months earlier, Facebook had purchased Oculus Rift, a VR startup that first attracted wild interest as a Kickstarter, for $2 billion. The sale convinced Linden Lab that VR was the next coming trend.

"There was a lot of excitement around it," as a Linden engineer told me, "and it seemed to have a natural fit to a metaverse. And if living in it is appealing, VR would be an important part of it."

But it's difficult to develop a metaverse platform that is both optimized for smartphones (Linden Lab's announcements promised a mobile version of Sansar) *and* for VR headsets, which have high demands on graphics performance.

Faced with either option, Linden Lab positioned Sansar as a VR product at launch.

In retrospect, Facebook's purchase of Oculus put Linden Lab on an ill-fated path it could not escape. Which is somewhat ironic, because a Linden Lab veteran at Facebook helped make that purchase possible. (But more on that in Chapter 3.)

But Ebbe Altberg cannot be fully blamed for focusing so fully on VR. After the Oculus acquisition, it was widely accepted wisdom in Silicon Valley that virtual reality was destined for mass market success. In 2014, Philip Rosedale himself was so bullish, he predicted there would be 1 billion VR headset owners by 2021.

"It was all hot and hip and interesting to talk about VR, so we kind of rode that a little bit," Ebbe acknowledged when I sat down with him in 2019. By then it was abundantly clear that VR headsets were selling nowhere near the stratospheric numbers that Valley elite once promised. (As of early 2023, the actual number of VR headsets on the market that can run a metaverse platform is decidedly not a billion, but roughly 20 million.)

While there was some early internal talk about enabling Second Life users to bring at least some of their content to Sansar, the technical challenges made this impossible. And in any case, doing that threatened to bifurcate the Second Life user base.

"We were always afraid of splintering the community. We didn't want to poach users [with Sansar]," Richard Nelson tells me. Instead, Linden Lab hoped to grow a new user base from Sansar, with the established SL community occasionally visiting its younger sibling.

Sansar struggled to find a new community apart from Second Life. And by the time it launched to open beta in 2017, several alternatives had far outpaced what either platform offered in terms of ease of usage and popularity.

IMVU, a virtual world with notably janky graphics and dismissed (if not ignored) by Linden Lab as an also-ran competitor when it launched a year after Second Life, now had millions of monthly active users. (Thanks, for the most part, to creating a version of the software for smartphones in 2014.)

Roblox, launched in 2006 at the peak of Second Life's success and therefore short-shrifted as a kiddie virtual world, had well over 50 million users in 2017.

Minecraft, launched in 2010 with a striking resemblance to Second Life's earliest incarnation, had by 2017 sold well over 120 million copies.

Sansar was sold to outside financial interests in 2020.

That same year, Linden Lab itself was bought.

By 2021, "Second Life" was displayed on the website of Waterfield Group, an investment firm that buys companies that earn a decent revenue and helps keep them profitable into perpetuity.

When I first visited the Waterfield site, I stared for some time with a dull resignation at where the first metaverse platform to reach the popular imagination was now displayed: as a portfolio holding listed beneath a company that serviced software for pumping oil and gas.

But the Waterfield move helped secure Second Life's longevity. Linden Lab's investors were finally satisfied with a liquidity event. (By then, some of them had been expecting this for over 20 years.) In Waterfield's care, the virtual world is likely to keep running as long as its established community keeps it profitable.

Only later did we learn that Ebbe Altberg helped make this move possible even while racked with unimaginable pain.

Richard Nelson was at the all-hands meeting when Altberg announced to his team that he had cancer. It ended in a group hug of Linden staff encircling Ebbe.

"We all really liked him, and you could see it taking a toll," Nelson remembers. "It was painful to see him fade out."

When I first met Ebbe in person, in early 2019, he was gaunt and pale but just as high-spirited and ebullient as always. The cancer didn't cause his energy or enthusiasm to flag, even as bouts of chemotherapy ground him down.

One insider told me that Ebbe's illness gave him a serene confidence in the arc of his life course. He had a world to care for, and a community to secure, even to the very end.

When a military coup in Turkey strangled Linden Dollars at the border, for instance, threatening to disrupt a Second Life creator's livelihood, it was Ebbe who personally reached out.

"I will cry talking about this," Gizem Mishi remembers now. "Ebbe himself responded, we had this two-hour-long talk and—may he rest in peace—they created a safe way for me to still work."

Ebbe ran Linden Lab when the COVID-19 pandemic hit in 2020, sending the globe into quarantine—and many quarantined people into virtual worlds, hungry to connect with others. Second Life saw a spike of old, dormant users. Ebbe ran Linden Lab when growing awareness of virtual worlds fed into renewed and rising interest in the Metaverse.

Ebbe Altberg's passing was announced on June 4, 2021.

Ebbe did not quite live long enough to see Second Life return to public awareness. But a month after Altberg's death, Mark Zuckerberg announced his intentions to turn Facebook into "a metaverse company."

In a keen irony, Facebook's name change came almost exactly 15 years to that day at the Commonwealth Club, when Second Life's Metaverse vision was hailed while a very young Zuckerberg sat to the side, almost like an afterthought.

Now Zuckerberg was being acclaimed as the Metaverse visionary, while Second Life was being remembered as one of Meta's ancient predecessors.

Now it's for us the living to ponder how this outcome might have been different.

Part 2: Postmortem

A couple key factors contributed to Second Life's failure to gain mass market.

Through no one's fault, for instance, Linden Lab had architected itself into a technical corner. In 2003, it seemed completely sensible to create a program optimized to run on a desktop computer with dedicated broadband. The succeeding years relentlessly chipped away at that assumption, as consumers shifted their overwhelming preference to Wi-Fi connectivity, and then to laptops with limited 3D graphics capabilities. And then starting in 2007, stampeded to the iPhone and later Android. In fewer than five years, Second Life seemed conceived for an obsolescent era.

"We missed mobile," Philip Rosedale openly acknowledges now. "We paid a high price for that. Just like Facebook, by the way."

Yes, around that time, Facebook was also slow to create a native mobile app of its own—but then rapidly changed course. (As we'll see in the next chapter, these moves are intertwined.)

"It was too soon," Charity Majors observes, offering a postmortem from an engineer's perspective. "Both on the server side and the client side. The technology needed in order to make the experience real just didn't exist yet. Super basic fundamental stuff you need in order to scale a platform, we had to build or invent or hack away from scratch. Which is a testament to just how incredible the caliber of engineers was that we had there at the time."

But the technical issues *per se* did not undo Second Life's mass growth, for other, similar platforms launched in the same era have gone on to grow much larger.

Hunter Walk, reflecting on his time at Linden Lab from the vantage of his subsequent years at Google and now as a leading venture capitalist, muses around similar counterfactuals:

"A different, simpler economy might have created more incentives for the audience to grow," he tells me. "I guess I would have loved to give it a go where we could have designed around, 'You need a certain degree of experience in terms of frame rate and concurrency' and then said 'What's the creation model and simulation model that allows us to maintain that density and simplicity?' More LEGO-like but still interesting."

Or, if I might rephrase that another way: What if Second Life had been more like Minecraft and less like a second life?

End Game

"Second Life not launching as a game first was a mistake, if the end goal was the largest audience possible," Richard Nelson puts it now, though he notes that that direction might have come at a serious cost, at least in the beginning:

"I think if Second Life launched as a game first, we wouldn't have had the fun wacky crowd we did get [early on] that was into the metaverse concept."

Having finally left Linden Lab in 2020, Nelson makes that point from a unique perspective: as a technical director at Roblox. (More on that in Chapter 4.)

Charity Majors agrees that Second Life should have had more game-like experiences at the start but believes the company's culture would have rejected them:

"All of the things that would make getting started catchier, faster, and more fun were things that I feel like leadership was violently against because it would have violated the vision."

Core to that vision was keeping Second Life an open creative space.

"[I]f your world really is a game, does it overwhelm everything else going on?" as Cory Ondrejka frames the challenge now. "And is that right? And with Second Life, our choice, right or wrong, was no, we don't want a singular drive to overwhelm the creativity in Second Life.

"Maybe the right answer lies somewhere in between, where Second Life really could have used things like a stronger link mechanism, a stronger sort of textual overlay; we could have done more powerful search style structures, which then leads itself to sort of other styles of leaderboards that aren't as easily gamed, and that aren't so singular in how they drive behavior."

In other words, content and activity ranking systems that SLers could enjoy as a kind of competitive mechanic, if they so choose.

I put the question to Philip Rosedale in the form of a hypothetical.

"If you could go back and make Second Life more like Minecraft, Roblox, and Fortnite put together, would you have done that? If you knew you'd end up with a very, very large user base—mostly of kids, perhaps, but also a much larger user base of adults?"

Philip doesn't quite answer in the affirmative but doesn't quite disagree:

"I think that looking back, if we had been even more focused on building tools that enabled gaming-type experiences, there might have been a very substantial lift from that," he tells me.

"My passion was always for connecting with people. And so I think that it was always important that we do that. So I wouldn't have been happy, I probably wouldn't have been willing to work on Second Life if it supported games to the exclusion of supporting expression.

"I would have wanted to stay with a lot of rich self-expression and communication, but maybe we could have done things that enabled game-like experiences in a way that would have both been satisfying to a larger audience and maybe even been a better on-ramp. So I guess I agree with you in that regard."

This cultural resistance to Second Life not being a game had real consequences that not only hurt user growth but caused Linden Lab to ignore easy opportunities—often to the irritation of the community creators who would have benefited from a growing consumer base.

Gizem Mishi of Blueberry vented about this in a phone call to Ebbe Altberg.

"I was very frustrated that I'm putting in all this work, and I feel like I hit a ceiling," as she put it to Ebbe. "How can you do this to us? We deserve to grow!"

She demanded to know, for instance, why Second Life was not available on Steam, the world's largest distribution market for PC/Mac/VR games. The *Sims* franchise was available on Steam; *Garry's Mod*, a popular UGC-driven sandbox game, became a hit on Steam, selling over 20 million copies.

But as Gizem tells it, Second Life on Steam was simply not an option Ebbe would even consider on a conceptual level.

"I am not joking, his answer word-for-word was, 'Second Life is not a game.' I will never forget him saying that."

The misconception persists today, even beyond Second Life; it is fashionable among many tech evangelists to argue that while the Metaverse may begin with game platforms, it will inevitably slough off its ludic carapace to become an immersive Internet with many multiple-use cases, completely separate from gaming.

In my view, all this misses a fundamental realization:

The very act of pretending that 3D graphics are a "world" inhabited by fantastic avatars *is itself a game*—as primal and basic a rule set as what we formulate on the fly while playing with each other on the playground as kids.

The grass is lava. Dinosaurs are here, and they want to eat us. The pixels on the display screen in front of us are actually a humanoid fox who's also an officer in Starfleet Command.

Fixated on turning Second Life into a "3D web," Linden Lab lost sight of how virtual worlds and the Metaverse itself are and must always be essentially whimsical and playful.

What's in a Name

Another core friction point was not technical or related to the UX but perhaps the most subtle and the most profound of all: calling it "Second Life" in the first place.

The virtual world's naming, led by early Linden Lab business developer Hunter Walk, seemed to make sense at the time. As I wrote in *The Making of Second Life*:

"A lot of the game worlds were verbs that described what you'd be doing," as [Walk] recalls it now. "You know . . . ever-questing! I wanted the name to be a vessel that people could fill themselves, that would be evocative of the promise of the world, and then put that responsibility upon the user to fill the promise.

"It's such a strong notion, it's such an idea: everybody wants a second life. You see more and more people with avatars and screen names," he told [Linden management]. "I think if we hit our stride we can sell this. It won't be geeky. It'll be 'Of course, why wouldn't you want one?' Because it doesn't have to be better or worse, it doesn't mean your first one is lame or great, it just means it's different, and you can be somebody different, and do something different."

His original suggestion, "Life 2," was then massaged by the team into "Second Life."

In the fullness of time, we can confirm that consumers *do* generally prefer metaverse platforms named after verbs, or at least strongly imply them: Mine*crafting*, building blocks and forts in Roblox and Fortnite, VR*Chat*-ing, and so on.

Looking back at it now, was it a mistake to name the platform Second Life?

"I don't know," Hunter Walk answers after a long pause. "It was a profitable startup, but it obviously did not fulfill the reach and potential that I hoped for. It feels right to ask in retrospect: Did that seem too geeky, describing what it was as opposed to what we needed it to be? I'm not sure a name with a different product would make a difference. . . . "

From my vantage point, calling it Second Life created a double blade of skewed expectations, alienating most potential users (especially gamers) while also attracting a group of people who did very specifically want a second life—which alienated the first group even further.

"I think that's totally true," Philip Rosedale says, when I ran my analysis by him. "The very idea that it was a second life and that it was separate from your first life and maybe that reflected mimetically or negatively on your real life.

"I didn't think about it at the time, because in my mind, I was only thinking about the *Second* Life," Rosedale says, emphasizing the first word. "I think we also thought it was going to be a temporary problem."

Adds Walk: "Maybe the way some people reacted to the name reflected on what we were prioritizing in terms of what the world would be like, and led us down the path of making a microverse and not a metaverse."

This is also true: To the extent that the name was embraced by the dedicated user base, many or most of them interpreted it to mean a kind of roleplay luxe life they want but cannot have in the offline world—which is partly why the virtual world now teems with virtual seaside mansions, high-end shopping malls, and sexy nightclubs. (This direction was also shaped by the choice of default avatars, but more on that in Chapter 9.)

Paradoxically, while the name Second Life *did* contribute to the virtual world's lack of growth, it also helped attract excessive media coverage. With their game-like monikers, no competing metaverse platforms, even those far larger in terms of users, have received anywhere near the same level of outside attention.

Without that name, observes Philip Rosedale, "[H]ow else could we have done it, and gotten the kind of fascination that we did get? I don't know that if I find a time machine [to change it], I'd hit that button. Because I don't know what other name I'd use."

Choose Your Own Inertia

Philip Rosedale created Second Life to connect people together, to enable them to communicate in a genuine way with anyone. But in the end, it may have been the breaking of in-person human connections that hobbled that vision.

In the virtual world, online communities generally come together for the sake of mutual fun and creativity; they evolve together around those goals.

In the offline realm, companies function from a panoply of interests, especially in the context of the Silicon Valley startup, where some staff are motivated by the creative challenge or even idealism, others by the chance of sudden wealth and fame. (Most, probably a mixture of those motivations.) And while California startups may boast more amenities and quirkiness than the average U.S. company, the corporate hierarchy and governance structure is generally the same.

The Tao of Linden was an ambitious bid to transform the corporate hierarchy; it sought to offer Linden Lab employees a culture that was about as creative and freeform as the virtual world they were creating. Its success, however, was decidedly limited.

"[T]he whole 'Choose your own work' went way too far," Charity Majors says now. "We had no real management. And I get that; I hate managers too. But I also feel like it contributed to a lot of our floundering and our lack of direction."

Charity believes this lack of management ultimately hurt Second Life as a product:

"Profoundly. Profoundly. We were not executing at the level that we should have. And we didn't have the kind of clear direction that we should have. There was a lot of cultiness at Linden Lab. We kind of told ourselves a story about how the rest of the world wasn't as special or as fun or as interesting or whatever."

Engineer Richard Nelson concurs: "[I]t led us to adding all sorts of potentially interesting, yet incomplete features into the product, with not enough consideration for polishing the existing feature set or building what the users really needed first. I was certainly guilty of this."

Any Second Life user should feel a glow of recognition at Richard's words: To this day the viewer software is crusted over with features and options that resemble an MMO game welded to a 3D editor duct taped to a social network crammed into an ancient television remote with hundreds of buttons.

"I think Linden learned their lesson eventually," Nelson observes, "but the reputational damage from having a fussy, overcomplicated experience for new users had already been done by that point."

Asked about that now, Philip Rosedale acknowledges the "choose your own work" principle in the Tao of Linden had a limiting effect.

"I think that, in retrospect, is not the way everybody should work," as Philip puts it. "I was imagining that everybody in our company would have the same personality, and the same way they wanted to approach their work was just comically not true."

Many if not most people at Linden Lab did not want the pressure of choosing their own projects.

"If I come to you and you can't justify what you're working on," as he puts it, "I'm gonna fire you. That's pretty Elon Musk, right?" (We were chatting around the time that Musk had taken the reigns at Twitter, immediately going on a firing rampage.) "And that, I think, is an example of where I was wrong, because it was too much to ask somebody to gather all the information and then make a high quality, highly defensible decision about everything they're doing.

"As an adult now, as a grown-up, I recognize more. My ideas were in many cases neither unique nor correct. I would say at Linden, at least, we did some interesting experiments."

Ondrejka blames disagreements with Philip around the "choose your own work" principle as leading to his ultimate defenestration from the company.

Looking back at it now, Cory believes if he and Philip were wiser back then, they could have compromised around their management differences.

"And instead, we just kept disagreeing and that's just super unhealthy, and it wasn't good for either of us, it wasn't good for Linden."

At any rate, Philip Rosedale doesn't agree that he fired Cory Ondrejka over differences in management direction.

"No, no, I don't remember that. I mean, first off, Cory's great, I've seen him over the years.

I got into conflict with him about how he and we—both conversations are valid—disagreed about how he did things, how we did things."

Philip doesn't get into specifics, but he describes it as ultimately a lack of wisdom on his part, with Second Life and Rosedale himself hitting peak media attention when he was in his mid-30s.

"I think in retrospect, I think I probably should have tried harder to understand, to listen and understand where Cory was coming from. And instead, as a younger man, I was just kind of not wanting to argue too much, and I was avoiding tough conversations. There was no one thing with Cory and I; there was no one smoking gun or something."

In any case, what is indisputably true is that Cory Ondrejka's departure set off a chain reaction at the worst possible time.

"When I left, and when Cory left, and when others left after, that definitely had an impact," Philip Rosedale tells me now. "Because we were the original ones that were really living that dream so much."

"[S]oon after Philip steps aside as CEO, that kicks off five to six years of just a ton of turnover, both really seasoned employees and managers, senior leadership," says Cory. "And all of that happens at a time of the world changing technologically. And having those two things hit at the same time, particularly with a product that fundamentally hadn't really found a true fit yet.

"I think that that really put Linden in a challenging position as a company and Second Life in a challenging position as a product . . . its evolution slowed down, just to a crawl."

Second Life still does not, as of early 2023, have an official native mobile app. The company could have created one with minimal features early on, but it would be a monumental task to create an app compatible with the core experience and retain Second Life's essence; it would demand an epochal shift in resources and corporate focus.

It would have required, in other words, the cofounders unified around that direction and leading this charge. (Assuming that the Tao of Linden had been changed to "Choose your own work—as long as it's mobile-first.")

Ondrejka also blames the rift between him and Philip on his own relative youth back then.

"I think both of us would say: I wish we'd the tools 15 years ago, the maturity, to figure out where we were willing to disagree and keep rolling forward."

Cory credits that realization to a lunch meeting he had with Philip in 2019, at Orchard City Kitchen near San Jose. They had reconnected and briefly met from time to time since 2009. But it took a decade, by his lights, "when we both had enough time to reflect."

"That was the first time I think we were both able to really see the magic we had together. Second Life doesn't get built by either of us alone."

To be sure, Cory allows now, he and Philip still might have failed to push the virtual world into the mass market.

"[But] I think Second Life would have had a better chance if we were still there."

By December 2008, within a year after both Ondrejka and Rosedale had departed, the passage in the Tao of Linden reading "At Linden Lab, you are expected to choose your own work" was quietly excised from the company wiki.

It was instead supplanted with a decidedly vague adage: "Good people make good choices . . . and vice versa."

As for Cory Ondrejka, his involvement in the Metaverse was far from over then. But that's a story for another chapter.

As for me, I should end this postmortem by bitterly gnawing on my own share of the blame for Second Life's failure to reach the mainstream. Distracted with writing my first book deal, made over-giddy by constant media requests to explain this strange, exciting virtual world, I didn't do enough to manage expectations and advocate for the changes I've unfolded above.

During the apex of Second Life hype, the platform needed a far harsher critic who could point out the many shortcomings that needed to be resolved before the virtual world was anywhere near ready for prime time. I made little attempt to become that, at least not before it was too late. Fixated on the amazing avatar stories I kept stumbling into, airing technical and usability complaints seemed trivial, an issue to be addressed by others.

And when Linden Lab management announced that Second Life would no longer be called a game, I convinced myself that Second Life was becoming, after all, "the 3D web." (Some passages from *The Making of Second Life* reflect that positioning.) For years, I'd hear dedicated users confidentially declare, "Second Life is not a game," and for quite a while, didn't have the heart to gently point out that they were mainly just echoing corporate PR messaging.

Or to summarize all this in 50 words:

Second Life failed to go mainstream because its developers didn't realize in time that a metaverse platform must first succeed as an easy-to-play sandbox game, didn't transition to the social media and mobile era, and had an open-ended management structure that could not move the organization toward those goals.

In most cautionary tales of failed utopia, the perfect society falls to utter ruin.

But this is not one of those stories. For as Linden Lab the company kept struggling and failing to grasp mass market success, another mystery was still unfolding. This one is much happier.

Part 3: Second Life Forever

As I write this, Philip Rosedale remains a key adviser to Linden Lab and the evolution of Second Life as a platform. The company, for instance, is slowly rolling out its "Puppetry Project," a new feature that enables a user to have their real movements and facial expressions captured through a webcam and other motion capture devices, then displayed on their avatar in real time.

"If you ask me what's a breakthrough area in the next five years where we could all go, 'Wow, that's a huge, huge, huge improvement,'" Philip tells me, "I would say it would be animating the face and body of avatars with a [web] camera." It might even attract a wave of new users interested in its creative possibilities for live performance and video streaming.

But the ultimate story of Second Life is being told by its virtual community, and it imparts a living vision of what the Metaverse can be at its best.

Against all likelihood, the established Second Life community keeps thriving within this glittering menagerie. An active and resilient community of some 600,000 active users, they held fast to each other and to the world long after tens of millions abandoned it.

As we'll see in succeeding chapters, the leading metaverse platforms in terms of population are, for the most part, dominated by minors, skewing heavily male, mostly people from the wealthiest nations of North America and the European Union.

By contrast, according to a 2018 demographic survey compiled by Nick Yee's Quantic Foundry, 52 percent of the Second Life user base is female, with a median age of 48.

According to 2019 data shared with me by analytics firm SimilarWeb, the virtual world was most popular for a time with people from Brazil, second only to the United States. And while we in the United States tend to take the Americanization of the broader Internet for granted, the rest of the globe may be heartened to hear that U.S. citizens in Second Life were just some 30 percent of the total.

These diverse demographics lead to genuinely inspiring virtual communities that rarely exist beyond Second Life's digital borders—certainly not in the social media realm, where activity is heavily siloed according to national origin, gender, and age.

In 2022, when Vladimir Putin's armored divisions rumbled into Ukraine, the country's cottage industry of metaverse creators was among the many overturned by infrastructure attacks that sundered them from the Internet. Among them was Hanna, the young creator of the beloved Second Life fashion brand OSMIA, who fled her city as Russia occupied it, even though she was six months pregnant.

The Second Life fashion community rallied to support Ukrainian creators like her with a purchasing campaign. And before she escaped to safe territory with her newborn child, a fellow creator kept Hannah's virtual world brand operational, so her family could still have that income to support themselves. Her friend is Russian.

Second Life is the only Internet platform I know of where it's quite common for people of different generations who are not related to enjoy each other's company, breaking through age boundaries by a shared interest in creative expression, conducted through avatars that rarely indicate real-life age.

The trans community is notably large in Second Life, with around 500 registered groups, comprising people from all ages around the world in search of a secure place to express their identity. One of them, named Kayla, encountered so much transphobia in her offline life that she expresses her authentic identity only through her avatar.

"When I found Second Life," Kayla told my blog's columnist Cajsa Lilliehook, "not only could I be expressive of my gender, but also my real personality and visual styling." Ishtar Angel, another trans community member, told Cajsa a similar story: "It was Second Life that actually helped me realize I was trans. I may be stalled in my transition, but I would not give up knowing who I am and how I feel now to when I didn't know."

As U.S. wars in Iraq and Afghanistan wound down, I started to notice that military veterans, separated by distance and social unease in real life, would informally meet together in Second Life to discuss their PTSD symptoms and other painful topics, and together start to heal. These informal avatar-based support meetings grew so rapidly and are so valuable, retired Marine Lt. Col. Jay Kopelman, director of a vet support organization, once said with wonder: "I know Marines who say that Second Life is working when nothing else has."

Its very nature as a user-generated virtual world inspires seniors like Fran Serenade to create new communities, and feel such powerful affinity with her avatar that her Parkinson's symptoms abate, inspiring academics to ponder how other seniors might also benefit from the Metaverse.

Second Life's music scene is varied enough that it can accommodate Skye Galaxy, a pop pianist in his 20s whose voice was so alluring, it brought Gizem into the virtual world, which subsequently changed her life—and also Mr. Charles Bristol, a bluesman in his 90s whose very presence as an avatar surprised me so much, I've never left myself.

Second Life's creation tools are robust enough to empower content creators like Gizem Mishi, who can build multimillion-dollar brands from Constantinople, and artists like Jeff Berg, who can craft dreamlike experiences with pixels, visited by thousands, and no matter where they are in the world, feel themselves being spoken to.

Gizem, by the way, is far from the only creator in Second Life to reach seven figures of income through their virtual content. In an informal survey I conducted in 2018, one in ten Second Life merchants surveyed stated they were making well over $100,000 a year from the virtual world economy.

Linden Lab recently confirmed to me that Second Life user creators had grossed a total of $86 million in 2021—roughly comparable (based on publicly known data) to what Linden Lab itself grosses annually from Second Life.

That last point should be stressed: Creators in the Second Life user community earn roughly as much in aggregate from the virtual world as its corporate owners. No other metaverse platform has reached anything like this level of equity with its own user base.

Jeff "AM Radio" Berg is far from the only metaverse artist in Second Life, for a burgeoning art scene remains, even boasting gallery events and installation unveilings, where the entire surrounding world is part of the expression.

With funding from the Canadian government, an artist known only by her avatar name, Bryn Oh, regularly opens the doors of her private island, and tens of thousands rush in, eager to see what latest whimsical or disturbing stories she is telling in dioramic 3D.

On the other side of the world, Japanese avant garde pianist Tia Rungray often performs before a live audience of avatars, while a visual collaborator accompanies him, one time with a flurry of abstract video images, another with two massive cubes rising up in the virtual desert.

If an implicit goal of the Metaverse is to be a microcosm of the real world and its people at their very best, as I believe it is, Second Life has succeeded at this. In the process, it has also become a microcosm of what the Metaverse can and should become on a far broader scale.

To summarize all *that* in 50 words:

Second Life continues to succeed as a niche virtual world and model for the Metaverse because its creativity tools are open and powerful, its user community is diverse, and its company shares virtual world revenue about equally with a user community whose members are free to create endless value and possibility.

While other, newer metaverse platforms boast far higher user numbers, almost none of them come anywhere close to meeting Second Life's high standards of creativity, equity, and diversity. But better platforms are possible.

Making a Metaverse that matters means making that happen.

3

How Facebook Became Meta (But Lost the Metaverse on the Way)

If the mystery of Second Life is how a company widely acclaimed as the Metaverse could fail to become that on a mass market scale, then the mystery of Meta offers us a mirror image conundrum:

How could a company with such a massive user base and near-infinite resources of money, talent, and experience also fail so thoroughly at making the Metaverse? (So far.)

And to enhance that mystery, here's another layer to consider: Meta's initial metaverse efforts were largely led and advised by veterans of Second Life.

Indeed, by the time you read these words, Meta may have officially pivoted away from its metaverse strategy. Although Mark Zuckerberg in late 2021 announced its creation of the Metaverse as so important to the company that he actually changed the company's name to reflect that, the Internet giant already appeared to be backing away from that goal within a year.

By December 2022, after months of punishing stock declines, his trusted lieutenant and head of Reality Labs Andrew Bosworth posted an announcement with the somewhat defensive title "Why We Still Believe in the Future."

Notably absent from those 1,800 words: a single mention of "the Metaverse." Not one.

With corporate announcements of that caliber usually reviewed by dozens of eyes, it's difficult to believe the omission was unintentional.

For the record, I attempted over several months through various channels to speak with Mark Zuckerberg. After a couple of preliminary screening calls with his effervescent PR team, an interview seemed to be quite possibly happening—when suddenly I was informed that Mark's schedule was "completely bananas," and "we won't be able to make interviews work."

On the very week I received that message, Zuckerberg conducted a three-hour, in-person interview about the Metaverse with controversial podcaster Joe Rogan. It felt like an intentional troll.

To be sure, I do not also have millions of credulous listeners. Then again, to my knowledge, Zuckerberg has never granted an in-depth interview with any journalist well versed enough in virtual worlds to ask hard questions about his metaverse ambitions. (And there are several who write for major news outlets.)

At any rate, I have forwarded key questions to Meta PR staff about the thorniest revelations I came across in the writing of this chapter, based on interviews with numerous insiders, on and off the record. As of press time, I have not received a reply. Which is a shame, because these sources document Meta's first lurching steps into the virtual world, and how it managed to go so wayward so quickly.

This is an important story to tell, especially because many if not most people probably still assume Meta and the Metaverse are interchangeable.

For those of us who've worked in metaverse platforms for decades, the widely held assumption that Meta *is* the Metaverse is very much a blade that cuts both ways. If a massive company like Meta is making it, it seems to follow that the Metaverse must indeed be the next generation of the Internet. By that same logic, however, any slip or stumble by Meta is taken to be a death knell for the Metaverse as a whole.

No: Speaking with many people directly involved, the story I came away with is Meta systematically ignoring decades of knowledge and experience that have gone into building metaverse platforms before its own.

This is the story of how Second Life veterans helped shape Meta's foray into the Metaverse from the very start—but then how Meta refused to heed their warnings as it all veered off course.

The Second Life of Oculus

In a very real sense, Meta's Metaverse ambitions may not have ever happened at all, were it not for Linden Lab's own metaverse plans with Second Life falling into disarray.

After Linden Lab founding CTO Cory Ondrejka exited in 2007 from the startup in bitter acrimony, he taught at USC for a time, worked for a record label, and in 2010, became Facebook's Engineering Director.

Ondrejka joined just in time for Facebook's first existential crisis, when the social network, still a startup back then, was attempting to shift its focus to smartphones.

When high-tech publications recount Silicon Valley's recent history, much is written about this move, and it's typically narrated as a moment of heroic decisiveness on Zuckerberg's part:

"That company-wide pivot—despite the bad timing, considering the then-looming IPO—is widely considered the most important move in Facebook's history," as tech news site Vox depicted this moment. "[A] recognition by Zuckerberg that mobile, not desktop computers, was the next great platform. If Facebook wanted to survive, it would have to do so by riding that mobile wave."

To the extent that this pronouncement is accurate, credit for Facebook's survival belongs in good part to Ondrejka. At Linden Lab, he had faced a somewhat similar crisis, with Second Life missing its chance to evolve into the mobile era. Now Cory made the case to lead this change for Facebook.

"[S]oon after I got there," Ondrejka remembers, "when I looked at the mobile strategies at Facebook, it was pretty clear that [the current mobile app] wasn't good enough. So I pitched Mark that we had to go build a really great native experience on mobile."

Driving all of Facebook's mobile projects before and after its successful IPO, Ondrejka and his team "took us from mobile being a real problem in Facebook to mobile being Facebook's fundamental strength."

Having succeeded at that task, Cory remembers, "Mark was like, 'Figure out the next exciting thing you want to do.'" A tip from VC Marc Andreessen led Ondrejka to Oculus, still a small crowdfunded startup in Irvine.

It's where Ondrejka saw, as he recalls, "[the] best VR demo I'd seen," on par with expensive VR technology he'd demoed at Stanford.

Ondrejka quickly lobbied Zuckerberg to experience it for himself:

"I go back up to Facebook and say 'Look, we know you need to see this.' We were spending a lot of time thinking about what platforms were coming. And while it was never VR on its own that was going to be the next platform, it felt like VR could be a part of it, because of games and because it allows you to learn so much about wearables, navigation, 3D space navigation. And it really sets you up for AR, which always felt further away."

Cory's shepherding ultimately led to Facebook's acquisition of Oculus in 2014.

As part of that purchase, Ondrejka began telling company leadership, including Zuckerberg, about the power of virtual worlds.

"All the work we did during that time was sharing some of the lessons from Second Life, sharing virtual world lessons in general, thinking about what it'd mean to have virtual world notions connected with a social network—either connected directly or near it, having VR as an interface," Ondrejka recalls.

"And really laying out that: 'Look, there is a play to be made here, once Oculus is shipping out product, and is high quality.' So that was in 2014 where I was talking [to Facebook executives] about virtual worlds as one obvious application of VR." He wrote up numerous documents and decks about virtual worlds, presenting them to Facebook leadership.

In the period around the Oculus purchase, Ondrejka doesn't recall talking about the Metaverse specifically as a project Facebook should start building—but they did reference the concept quite a bit:

"Mark and Meta are certainly free to carve out whatever way they want to tell the story," as he puts it. "But it certainly isn't one that we were talking about in that era. We were talking about virtual worlds, and certainly the word Metaverse would be used because everybody's read *Snow Crash*."

But beyond talking about the technical standards or virtual worlds, Ondrejka doesn't recall "Building the Metaverse" as an explicit goal for Zuckerberg back then:

"It certainly happened sometime between when I left [in late 2014] and when they announced it."

But he definitely presented an intellectual, aspirational framework for it to Zuckerberg.

"It was virtual worlds, whether you call it a metaverse or not, as powerful economic engines, as powerful places to apply technology, or *incredibly* powerful spaces for people to interact and collaborate—that we were talking about in 2014. I wrote all of those white papers and decks. Because look, Second Life taught us all that. And so the notion that Facebook could apply its scale to that problem? Absolutely, we were talking about that.

"Deciding to brand it all as a story around the Metaverse, that ultimately came later."

Perhaps not much later: A year after Ondrejka departed, Oculus's then-CTO John Carmack was openly talking about early metaverse plans in the works at Oculus (still a separate brand from its parent company, Facebook). In 2015, metaverse developer Joyce Bettencourt recorded an off-the-cuff chat with Carmack at an Oculus dev conference.

"I fought against us staffing up the metaverse team at Oculus because I thought that was going to be a disaster because we don't know what we're doing well enough yet," he told her. "That's always a problem with a well-funded company. It's like, 'Let's put 30 people on this problem and see what happens.'"

Carmack then mentioned that the team at Meta still wasn't clear what metaverse actually even meant:

"'Metaverse' means different things to different people, and you need clarity of purpose. And I tried to get some of that. 'What exactly do we mean?' And there was still lots of hand-waving."

If Facebook's purchase of Oculus set the company on the path to Meta, it also led to a chain of unintended, painfully ironic consequences.

As I mention in Chapter 2, the Facebook acquisition of Oculus, led by Second Life cofounder Cory Ondrejka, sparked a ferocious buzz around VR in Silicon Valley. That in turn led Linden Lab to make its Second Life spinoff, Sansar, a VR-focused product—a costly, disastrous move that ultimately led to Linden Lab being sold.

The other unintended consequence is even more painful and continues to linger over the entire tech industry.

Acquisition Bias

Shortly after the Oculus purchase was announced, esteemed academic danah boyd, a Partner Researcher at Microsoft Research, published a much-discussed opinion piece in the online business site Quartz, proactively entitled: "Is the Oculus Rift sexist?"

In it, danah brought up an earlier study she had published that strongly suggested VR tended to make women nauseous. It began when she was a grad student given a chance to try out an early VR demo:

> Ecstatic at seeing a real-life instantiation of the Metaverse, the virtual world imagined in Neal Stephenson's *Snow Crash*, I donned a set of goggles and jumped inside.
>
> And then I promptly vomited.

Hardly an obscure researcher, danah is a widely and frequently cited expert in tech and mainstream media, especially around her work on teens and social networks.

That VR can cause nausea has been fairly well known for decades—it was reported by military researchers as far back as the 1960s, who noticed it among some volunteers testing early flight simulators. However, it's often attributed to poor graphics or how the sensation of motion is displayed. Any variation in VR nausea based on gender is usually explained away by pointing out that males tend to play 3D video games more than females, and are therefore better acclimated to immersive virtual reality.

But what danah boyd discovered went deeper than that. She noted, for instance, that a difference around experiencing 3D was even observable in trans people at a gender clinic in the Netherlands—and that it also influenced *thinking about* 3D:

> [Researchers] found that people taking androgens (a steroid hormone similar to testosterone) improved at tasks that *required them to rotate Tetris-like shapes in their mind* to determine if one shape was simply a rotation of another shape. Meanwhile, male-to-female transsexuals saw a decline in performance during their hormone replacement therapy.
>
> Although there was variability across the board, men are more likely to use the cues that 3D virtual reality systems relied on. . . . I'd posit that the problems of nausea and simulator sickness that many people report when using VR headsets go deeper than pixel persistence and latency rates.

Emphasis mine, because it bears repeating: As I read it, danah's research suggests that the different responses to VR based on gender happen at the hormonal level, and therefore, may not be addressable by technical improvements.

danah ended her essay with a call for researchers to follow up on her findings around biology and VR: "In other words, are systems like Oculus fundamentally (if inadvertently) sexist in their design?" It was not a condemnation of VR *per se*, but a call for researchers working in the technology to explore her findings.

"I want folks to take what I did and push it further," as danah told me at the time. "If researchers start to investigate this issue, I'll be ecstatic."

On this point, she has not been made very ecstatic.

Few if any VR industry leaders contacted her after the Quartz essay was published, she told me; nor later in 2017, after a study published in *Experimental Brain Research* confirmed danah's findings of nausea propensity based on gender.

Reached in late 2022 for this book, danah tells me that the team developing HoloLens, the augmented reality headset owned by Microsoft, had been probing at the questions she raised.

However, she doesn't recall anyone from Oculus or Meta ever approaching her: "To my knowledge, they did not pursue any of those research questions."

I've repeatedly asked Meta about this and received no reply. In 2017, I asked John Carmack himself if the company had tested its product by gender to address the issues that danah had raised. He wasn't sure:

"I'm not involved with any of our user studies," Carmack told me then, "so I don't have any insight there." He pointed me to Oculus's PR contact, but my question to them yielded no answer.

"I mean, danah's a friend, so of course I knew about it," Cory Ondrejka tells me now. He agrees that more studies on this topic are needed:

"danah's research was super early on this one, and the opportunity for Meta has always been to have a scale of resources to be able to do much deeper research on this question," as he puts it.

"This is all still such an early moment in VR, there are tons of things we don't understand about how people react to this. If I was ever in charge of VR stuff again, I would be paying for these studies."

I cannot overstress how mind-boggling an oversight on Meta's part this is.

The company paid $2 billion for a piece of consumer-facing technology that reputable research suggests tends to make half the population literally vomit.

Then spent tens of billions more to bring it to market anyway.

Then Silicon Valley followed suit, investing tens of billions still further, an entire industry sprung up around it, nearly all of it ignoring evidence that the whole enterprise was built on sand. Usually it seems impossible to calculate the opportunity cost of unconscious gender bias, but in this specific case, the price tag approaches $100 billion.

The consumer market they got from this investment? As of early 2023, the Quest 2 has an estimated install base of 18 million—significantly smaller than the install base of the leading video game consoles, let alone the leading smartphones.

This is not to impugn the entirety of VR as an industry, I should add. Virtual reality has many proven and valuable use cases, including physical therapy, meditation, and, of course, use by some people in metaverse platforms.

Then again, if VR was developed with danah boyd's cautionary words in mind, it would likely be in a much more sustainable state. And Meta probably would not have spent billions in the hope that VR would evolve into the next great platform after smartphones.

Horizon Lines

Cory Ondrejka was not the sole Second Life veteran to shape Meta's course, for even during his time running the mobile division, he helped recruit numerous developers who worked under him at Linden Lab to join the Facebook team. Among them was Jim Purbrick, a British developer who loved the virtual world so much, he'd spend many hours of his spare time developing various game projects under an alias avatar.

Shortly after the Oculus acquisition, Purbrick joined Facebook's VR team. Management was interested in evolving the device beyond a gamer focus to support social applications.

Before Bosworth took over Meta's XR strategy, Purbrick remembers many leaders at Oculus with aspirational metaverse plans and "glorious visions" of its future—Bosworth synthesizing these into something like a workable product roadmap.

For Purbrick, this hit very different from his days with Philip Rosedale at Linden Lab:

"Philip was very much, 'Here's the awesome vision, let's go!' Inspiring people to follow the dreams and plans he had for virtual worlds and VR from years ago."

With Facebook, the tone was much different: "'This is a strategic acquisition.' Certainly when I was involved it was not like the grand vision for Facebook. It was like, 'OK, we spent a load of money on Instagram, we spent a load of money on Oculus, which is part of our long-term bet that they're doing interesting stuff for future interfaces.'"

Still, team members clamored to hear best practices from Purbrick based on his time at Second Life. Like Ondrejka, he gave many presentations on Second Life to Oculus team members.

It didn't quite take, in part because so many staffers were being shifted around so rapidly:

"The people involved were rotating through so quickly," as Purbrick remembers it. "It almost felt like you'd help people get up to speed and learn about this stuff, and there'd be somebody else [who replaced them]. So it always felt like it wasn't really enough time for people to understand what was going on."

What Purbrick says now echoes what another Facebook veteran with deep knowledge of Horizon Worlds, the company's first metaverse platform, told me in July 2021:

"With the average employee tenure being two years or so, and the need to expand teams at rapid rates, it's very difficult to make decisions and stick to a single vision because things are always changing," as they put it. "This [turnover] leads to teams at Facebook fast following on trends," they added. "You can see it when you look at Horizon and Rec Room."

A metaverse platform launched in 2016, Rec Room was made available for the Quest 2 in late 2020, just months before Horizon went into open beta. Horizon's expressive if legless avatars have a notable resemblance to those of Rec Room. However, with its powerful content creation tools and multiplatform support (it can be played on mobile and game consoles, in addition to VR), Rec Room rapidly gained a large following among Quest users.

By early 2022, according to Shawn Whiting, Head of Influencers & Partners at Rec Room, the platform had 3 million VR-based monthly active users and—in an apparent tweak at Meta—told me, "A majority of those VR monthly active users are Quest 2."

In other words, Rec Room was by then vastly more popular than Meta's Horizon—on Meta's own device.

Back to my Meta insider and the state of Horizon in 2021:

"[N]ew leaders have been coming onto the Horizon project with new ideas to be prioritized, or the development team would be tasked with re-doing a feature made years beforehand."

This surprised me then and still does to this day. Zuckerberg publicly expressed his desire to build metaverse-like technology at least as far back as during the acquisition of Oculus Rift in 2014. "One day," he announced then, "we believe this kind of immersive, augmented reality will become a part of daily life for billions of people."

His team evinced similar enthusiasm. In November 2021, developers at Blind, an anonymous community app for employees, surveyed 1,120 staffers at Meta about Zuckerberg's metaverse plans. Asked if Meta would successfully build the Metaverse, over 75 percent said Yes; questioned whether they believed, as Zuckerberg predicted, that 1 billion people would be in the Metaverse by 2030, 67 percent answered Yes.

Yet apparently this vision staggered forward without any actual sight. The open beta launch of Horizon Worlds in late 2021 enforced that sense in the worst way possible.

Soon after launch, Horizon Worlds was barraged by a slew of bad press when a female journalist reported being sexually assaulted in the virtual world, with male avatars aggressively grinding up against her own avatar almost immediately after she logged into the platform.

The violation was horrible but completely predictable. Understanding and preparing for avatar-to-avatar harassment, especially directed at female avatars, has been a recurring virtual world challenge for literally decades.

Was no one on the team experienced enough to anticipate it?

As I soon learned, however, Meta *was* warned this would happen, many times—it was a recurring theme in internal talks given by Jim Purbrick. But somehow, his warnings, recommendations, and best practice summaries were not centered:

"I was literally banging the drum at Oculus Connect two years in a row," Jim Purbrick told me with evident frustration. "I also told every new Oculus employee I met to read *My Tiny Life* in addition to *Ready Player One*, but the message didn't reach every part of the organization, sadly."

My Tiny Life is Julian Dibbell's classic account of virtual world sexual assault from *the 1990s*; yes, the problem has been well-known and documented for that long. (That same book also inspired me, as a very young writer, to consider the possibility of embedded avatar-based journalism.)

"There are a lot of griefing and bullying behaviors that [Meta] seems somewhat slow to respond to," Cory Ondrejka puts it tactfully. "And that's just failing to have learned from prior lessons."

Ingrained Identity

In retrospect, I should have known how wildly off course Mark Zuckerberg would take the Metaverse when the avatars started warning me of trouble in 2009.

That's when I began getting reports that Second Life users were creating Facebook accounts for their avatars—and Facebook the company was summarily deleting them. Some SLers received this helpfully unhelpful system message from the community management team:

"Facebook is built around real world interactions. Operating under an alias detracts from the value of the system as a whole."

The avatar deletions were not due to overzealous policy enforcement but reflected a core principle of Facebook as a corporation. When the company filed with the U.S. government to become a public company in 2012, this philosophy was emblazoned within the stock filing itself:

Authentic identity is core to the Facebook experience, and we believe that it is central to the future of the web. Our terms of service require you to use your real name and we encourage you to be your true self online, enabling us and Platform developers to provide you with more personalized experiences.

It's hard to understate how antithetical this premise is to the core concept of virtual worlds and the Metaverse since conception, where avatars are richly varied but almost always anonymous.

It took Facebook's enforcement of its philosophy, and Second Life users' resistance to it, to illustrate that point to me in painful detail.

At the time, Facebook seemed like the best way for Second Life to grow its user base, by connecting dedicated users sharing virtual world–related content with their friends network. While the social network forbade people from creating avatar-based profiles, they were perfectly free to create Facebook group pages devoted to their second life. So why *shouldn't* virtual world fans share their avatar content on Facebook?

Most Second Life users I talked to were unconvinced:

"Creating a Facebook page for your avatar doesn't seem like much help to me—the point of pseudonyms is anonymity," as Graywolf Midnight, a longtime furry avatar, put it to me. "If I create a Facebook page for Graywolf Midnight, it's very easy to find out who owns the page. That defeats the point of pseudonyms in the first place."

Graywolf, by the way, is itself a pseudonym, because—in a perfect illustration of the larger point—the metaverse user I am citing has been doxxed in real life through searches of their genuine avatar name.

Nevertheless, I kept forcefully advocating for Facebook integration back then. Until a woman who read my blog quietly messaged me and torched that notion to the ground. "You don't understand," she explained. "I have a friend in Second Life who uses it as her social escape valve, because she's hiding from her abusive husband. He's trying to find her. She can't share anything on Facebook, because he'll use it to track her down. She once mentioned playing an MMO on Facebook. Her husband figured out her username and started stalking her in the game."

Up until then, my blithe and sheltered privilege as a straight male in California (speaking of bias!) had blinded me to that reality. Not just for women fleeing abuse, but for racial and religious minorities, LGBT people, and on and on, especially those people living in parts of the world where their identity is actively hated, it is imperative to keep much of their expression and identity secret, hidden under the guise of an avatar.

Meta's confusion over avatars is best illustrated by the strangely avatarized version of Mark Zuckerberg himself—the one that went viral in 2022, with huge, childlike eyes worthy of a Margaret Keane painting.

The backlash and ridicule that followed was so fierce, it even seemed to hurt Meta's stock price. While market fluctuations are impelled by many factors, the simple fact is that Meta's share price was $181 on the evening of August 15th, 2022, when the big-eyed announcement was unveiled. By August 19—with no other obvious factor at play, beyond the social virality of Mark Zuckerberg's bizarre avatar—Meta's share price had fallen to $167.

Scrambling in response to such a storm of Internet snark, Zuckerberg hastily posted a new update to his Facebook wall, depicting a much more detailed and realistic version of his avatar, which looked even more like Zuckerberg IRL.

This follow-up confirmed that Meta really did seem to believe that, ideally, metaverse platform avatars should resemble their real-world users as much as possible.

For newcomers to metaverse platforms, this is a common assumption, enforced by mainstream press coverage, which tends to cover virtual world events involving real-life celebrities—for instance, Travis Scott in Fortnite or Lil Nas X in Roblox (more on them in Chapter 10). For occasions like a mixed-reality concert, it does make sense for the avatar to resemble their real-life owner.

But this is actually the *exception*. Overwhelmingly, metaverse platform users do *not* prefer avatars based on their real-life appearance—even when the internal tools to customize them that way exist.

This should have been clear to Meta even before the company began formulating its approach to avatars. By then, the most popular metaverse platforms' avatars were very much *not* architected to be mirror images of their users—Minecraft and Roblox with its blocky or LEGO-like avatars, Fortnite with its expressively stylized cartoonish characters—or to consider a VR-centric example, the floating marionette-esque avatars of Rec Room.

According to a survey of hundreds of thousands of gamers conducted by Nick Yee and his Quantic Foundry firm, about 1 in 3 men prefer to play as female avatars (and about 1 in 10 females choose male avatars).

Why did Meta design avatars to look like their real-life owner, when so many people don't even want avatars that share their real-life gender?

As we'll explore in later chapters, the popularity of nonrealistic avatars reflects the internal motivations of people who most enjoy metaverse platforms—especially the very young, who comprise their core user base: They are in virtual worlds where they can explore and create and *experiment* with identity, which they are still developing there, and in their own lives.

So it was a mystery how Meta went ahead with mirror-world avatars anyway. I had assumed it was the consequence of deep market research, with thousands of volunteers reviewing dozens of avatar options and customization suites.

An insider recently told me the reason was simpler than that:
"As far as looking like your real life [appearance]," they explained, "the thinking behind that was that people will be less inclined to harass others. Same idea behind only having one profile to your name, and your real name."

In other words, the developers applied *the Facebook identity model* to their metaverse platform—even though Facebook itself is rife with harassment.

"[Everybody] operating in a world of metaversal punditry comes to assume you want a single singular permanent identity and you want that singular permanent identity to kind of look like you," Cory Ondrejka observes now. "And we know from 50 years of online communities, that that's wildly untrue.

"The reality is that people have roles, people have modes of interaction. They don't want to always show up as themselves either by name or by appearance. What we saw in Second Life is that many people just put on outfits like clothing. And even in situations like experiments with IBM where it was initially thought, well, you know, for serious business to work, you got to show up wearing a business suit—not a fire dragon. And then it turns out the fire dragon is just as welcome into the business community and everything works fine."

During his time at Meta, I wonder if Cory Ondrejka had ever told Mark Zuckerberg about some of the avatars Cory created for himself in Second Life: They include a floating cartoon sun (the kind you'd see in a Betty Boop short), a Transformers-type robot that could fold itself into a jet, and the Flying Spaghetti Monster, a 3D rendition of an early 2000s Internet meme. (Long story but look it up.)

At any rate, once again ignoring Ondrejka's learnings from Second Life, Meta positioned its Horizon avatars to be "infantilized human avatars" (in Cory's words), architected to look like their owner.

Ondrejka agrees with my thesis that Meta's design decisions around avatar identity and appearance are baked into its corporate DNA:

"I don't want to speak for Mark or Meta's choices," as he puts it. "You can look at the public information about Facebook, which has been the notion of having strongly an identity that is one-to-one mapped to your real identity. And doing that helped Facebook grow to the scale it grew. I think the challenge is, it's pretty clear that [this approach] doesn't map to games, to virtual worlds, to 3D spaces.

"But they can figure that out or they won't. That's their journey to go on."

All these missteps contributed to a muddled product with an unclear purpose or audience.

In February 2022, despite running a spot during that year's Super Bowl—surely the first metaverse platform commercial to run during that event—Meta reported that Horizon Worlds and its live-event component, Horizon Venues, had all of 300,000 monthly active users.

It's difficult to overstate the paucity of those numbers. As I note in Chapter 2, Second Life still amasses nearly 300,000 new signups *per month*.

It's unclear if Zuckerberg's company is still driving a vision for creating Meta's billion user Metaverse, or how many idealists in leadership remain to shape it.

According to a survey conducted in late 2022 by Blind, confidence in the Metaverse and Meta's efforts around it had dropped sharply over the previous 12 months:

To the statement, "I believe Meta will successfully build the metaverse," 77 percent of Meta staff had answered in the affirmative. By December 2022, only 50 percent of them answered Yes.

Following Cory Ondrejka to the exit a few years later, Jim Purbrick departed Meta in 2020, near the height of its metaverse ambitions.

A key reason he did so is particularly telling: The company kept demanding that he make work trips from his home in London to San Francisco, to work on the Metaverse there.

At first he convinced his superior to let him work remotely ("We're a VR company, this should be easy!"), but the travel requests kept coming. Unable to justify the environmental cost morally, Purbrick finally bowed out. There are very few if any Linden Lab alumni who remain.

John Carmack, who has envisioned creating the Metaverse since the '90s—and has frequently and publicly chided Meta's excessively high-level "architecture astronaut" approach to building it—finally resigned his senior consultant role at Meta in late 2022.

That December 2022 Blind survey, by the way, also asked Meta staff if Mark Zuckerberg had clearly explained what the Metaverse even is. Fifty-six percent of his own employees answered No.

The Second Life of Horizons?

As of this writing in early 2023, it's still too early to write off all Meta and Mark Zuckerberg's efforts to make the Metaverse. The company could, with a few judicious moves, regain momentum on that front.

But even if they do, it remains confounding how Meta made so many painful, easily avoidable errors in its construction.

Meta can still change direction to a path that actually gets them closer to their original metaverse ambitions. But it would require radical departures from its current course.

Renowned UX designer and futurist Amber Case (a former fellow at MIT and Harvard's Berkman Center) is skeptical Meta can do so:

"That's like thinking IBM can change its character. [Meta's] such a huge company. Now, you could have a skunk works group, you know, like Wyden & Kennedy had." (She's referring to the acclaimed advertising agency that cultivated a small independent team to create highly quirky and unique brand campaigns.) "Or like a little research department where they would actually have to make weird stuff."

We've already touched on how Meta's focus on real-life identity is baked deep into its character. Amber notes how visual UX is too, taking us back to a time when Facebook wasn't the leading social network, trailing far behind one that allowed much more user creativity:

"Facebook's entire ethos, why it won over MySpace, is MySpace allowed you to do anything. It was kind of junky." She means that users could wildly customize their personal pages, even to the point where many pages were transformed into cluttered monstrosities.

Facebook, by contrast, presented users with a neat and highly constrained profile page, limiting how much an individual user could customize it, while also imposing a uniform format for how they described their background and interests—what Amber calls "the templated-self."

"Having a templated-self company make an open metaverse doesn't work. They can only make it a closed templated-self metaverse, where you represent yourself as if you're representing yourself on Facebook."

Amber makes another fascinating suggestion for Meta if it wants to improve its Metaverse plans:

"They'd have to hire a lot of trans people."

Her reasoning is immediately obvious to me; in every metaverse platform I've worked in and reported on, there's a disproportionately large number of trans people in the active user community. Indeed, as I'll explore in Chapter 7, nearly one in five VRChat users surveyed identified as trans/nonbinary, or otherwise outside traditional male/female categories. (By contrast, in a 2016 study, less than one percent of US citizens were estimated to be trans.)

"When you're trans," Amber goes on, "you're actively thinking about the shape that represents you, your outward container, and how it doesn't match your inner container. So when trans people go into VR and the Metaverse, they can be anything they want, and it's free and it's fluid. So when they're making these environments, they're much more likely to be creative and allow you to be a horse or a dragon or whatever. Because they understand arbitrarily defined identities, and that you can change them at will."

Whether or not Meta turns its metaverse efforts into an independent spinoff company that actively recruits nonbinary people, the Internet giant will definitely require confronting the sunk cost fallacy that is the Quest headset line—an impressive piece of hardware, to be sure, but still selling at a glacial pace. And which research suggests (I must say yet again) is a likely deal breaker to roughly half the population.

"Anything that is going to move the world forward, as a social avatar experience, has to be primarily on mobile," as Philip Rosedale puts it, speaking from painful personal experience.

"And I would also say that to Mr. Zuckerberg, right? Like, I got bad news for you Mark: You're not gonna want to hear this. But your stepping stone to where you want to be steps on a mobile phone. And you better figure that out."

But perhaps the key realization Meta must make is that the vision of one metaverse platform owned by Meta that somehow amasses a billion users is not even feasible.

At least that's the take of the person who helped set up Facebook to buy a VR company, and in doing so, helped put it on the path to becoming Meta.

"The notion that there is only one virtual world is a little silly," as Cory Ondrejka puts it to me now. "I think it's going to be many of those things. Some of them will share technology, some of them will share standards. . . . You would expect providers to work across some of them, you would expect things like payments stored across all of them. They might even share some rendering techniques. But fundamentally, doing mirror worlds, doing really high-fidelity real-world implementation, tends to require very different approaches to meshes and rendering than more game-like environments.

"So no, I was never pushing the singular world [at Meta] and never felt like that was a particularly strong direction."

It's true that no one virtual world could ever support all the use cases attributed to the Metaverse while appealing to all the people who enjoy immersive experiences. It's why I say the one platform that first meets Neal Stephenson's underlying goal of being as popular as television qualifies as The Metaverse.

The lead candidate to be *that*, if only in terms of raw user numbers, comes with the most unlikely origin, dismissed for years as trivial. You probably know little about it.

But chances are every single kid in your life knows all too much.

Realization

4

Kid Stuff: Minecraft, and the Rise of Roblox

User Base Snapshot:

58.8 million average daily active users in Q3 2022.

- Daily active users over the age of 13 grew by 34 percent year over year in Q3 2022 and accounted for 54 percent of all DAUs.

- Fastest-growing age cohort in Q3 2022 was 17-to-24-year-olds, which grew by 41 percent and accounted for 22 percent of hours spent on the platform.

32 million+ user-generated experiences on the platform; dozens have 1 billion+ visits.

Over 12 million developers and creators on the platform.

(continues)

(continued)

- 2.7 million creators earned Robux during June 2022 by creating experiences in Roblox Studio.

$600 million+ earned by the community in 12 months (Q4 2021–Q3 2022), up from $538.3 million in 2021.

Demographics and Activity: As of Q2 2022, users over 13 years old made up over 53 percent of the Roblox user community, with the fastest-growing age group between 17 and 24.

Roblox reports that the vast majority of the top 10,000 community developers by earnings or hours of engagement in their experiences are over 18 years old. "For example, about 90 percent of developers of the top 1,000 games by earnings are over the age of 18."

Most active users by location in 2021:

- United States
- Brazil
- UK
- Philippines
- Mexico

Data courtesy Roblox

On a cool spring afternoon in 2021, Richard Nelson finally stepped onto the tree-lined Roblox campus in San Mateo for the first time. He had actually joined the company in 2020 at the height of the pandemic, and had been working from home since then. Having left Linden Lab after a near 20-year stint as a developer of Second Life and later Sansar, this was his first time strolling the grounds that Roblox built.

It was quite a change. Where Linden Lab's San Francisco offices tended toward the cramped side, Richard found Roblox's corporate grounds to be sprawling, with a cafeteria and an on-site gym. Where Linden Lab staff would often break up the work day for impromptu chats at their desks or run Nerf gun battles through the office, Roblox employees were quiet, subdued.

But most notable, they were far more numerous. While Linden Lab peaked at some 300+ employees, Roblox's full-time staff had grown to well over 1,500 by 2021. To be amid so many people devoted to the same vision was exciting.

"I had a strong sense of déjà vu," Richard remembers now. "When I joined Roblox, I had already helped build two metaverse platforms from scratch."

On the surface, Roblox appears completely unlike Second Life and Sansar. Promoted as a game platform until very recently (for reasons I'll get into down the way), Roblox is bright, colorful, and *simple*, with blocky, LEGO-like avatars and an aggressively easy-to-use interface.

Despite those surface differences, Nelson says all three have many common themes.

"It felt like so many of the conversations around how to build a certain feature or how it might interact with user-generated content were retreading old ground. What I found over time, though, was that the small differences in the history and development of the platform can lead to completely different takes on the same problem."

Rapidly recapping Chapter 2, the development of Second Life during Nelson's early tenure was often a whirlwind of individual projects that didn't always congeal, in the hopes that a "choose your own work" philosophy would contribute to a unified whole.

"Roblox feels like it takes a more measured approach to building the product, gathering feedback from users and making sure the functionality coheres and it is easy to use," as he puts it. "It might take longer to ship, but the results are more polished."

And, by very explicit design, more game-like:

"I think the focus on game creation has given Roblox a mainstream appeal as well as a diverse and powerful toolset that is helping it expand into many nongaming areas. I really wish Second Life had focused on games a bit more.

"I mean, I really love that I got to help Linden build a platform for people to express themselves creatively and build communities, but I always wanted the platform to be so much bigger. Gaming could have brought more users in the door and also helped us focus our development of the creative toolset around well-understood solutions."

Richard is right. Then again, to this day, despite the platform's growing complexity, Roblox is often dismissed as a mere game platform for kids.

Roblox was cofounded in 2004 by David Baszucki and Erik Cassel and launched in September 2006 at the zenith of Second Life's media adulation. I remember hearing about Roblox back then only in passing. (Cassel died of cancer in 2013; Baszucki continues as CEO, known mainly among players by his user name, "builderman.") With its pokey graphics and blocky avatars, it seemed to me more like an off-brand LEGO Online than anything even vaguely resembling the Metaverse that was unfolding before our eyes in Second Life.

After all, that very same month in 2006, Second Life was being featured on the cover of *Wired* magazine while Virginia Governor (now Senator) Mark Warner was on NPR, talking about his recent whistle-stop appearance in Second Life, widely seen as an early feeler for a 2008 presidential run. What could Roblox possibly have to offer anyone under 10 years old?

As it turns out, quite a lot.

Neal Stephenson has told me that he came up with the concept of the Metaverse by imagining an Internet medium that was so compelling, it could be more popular than television. From the sheer size of its user base, Roblox has already succeeded on those terms.

When *Squid Game* became an international phenomenon in 2021, for instance, Roblox players used the platform's creation tools to make hundreds of interactive experiences modeled after the Netflix series' deadly games and locations.

When I visited one, I was promptly plopped into a re-creation of the series' infamous dorm room, where contestants await their next deadly trial. The Roblox version, however, was filled with dozens of avatars in green jumpsuits, cheerfully bouncing around the room and chatting.

Within the first month of the Netflix series' premiere, I calculated that Roblox creators had built 300+ *Squid Game*–themed experiences like these, which were visited over *80 million times.*

To put that number in perspective: There were likely more visits to *Squid Game* experiences in Roblox than viewers of the actual show on Netflix.

How did it succeed? With an active user base of some 250 million monthly users, it's impossible to tell the complete story of Roblox in a single chapter.

What follows, instead, is one thread in the narrative of Roblox's rise and what it tells us about the future of the Metaverse—both for good and possibly for ill.

Minecraft, the Metaverse Generation, and the Rise of Metaverse TV

It's not an exaggeration to call Generation Z, people born roughly between 1995 to 2010, the Metaverse generation. In 2020,

Roblox the company announced that more than half of U.S. kids 16 and under were active players.

I saw this trend throughout Second Life's rise in 2006 and subsequent years. While that virtual world's user base floundered at some 600,000 or so active users, virtual worlds designed for kids casually collected MAUs by the many millions.

Well before the pervasiveness of social media, Gen Z grew up with virtual worlds like Habbo (2001), Club Penguin (2005), and others, 2D web-based spaces largely lost to time. (And acquisitions, and layoffs, and controversies.)

The size of those virtual worlds was soon eclipsed in 2010 by Minecraft, which became a cult hit even in its early alpha stage. Developed by a four-person team led by Markus "Notch" Persson, Minecraft's blocky graphics confounded the game industry's traditional expectation for the most realistic graphics possible. ("I think the simple graphics helped make the experience feel more personal!" Persson told me at the time of launch.)

He was correct about graphics: Abstract enough to encourage kids to fill in the details of their characters and adventures with their own imagination, the immersiveness of Minecraft was kindled by its first-person perspective, and the richness of the world and its physics, and the sense of an unfolding natural world that seemed to stretch out forever.

"It's Maslow's hierarchy of needs," design guru and TED futurist Amber Case once told me, casually explaining the secret to Minecraft's phenomenal success. "Kids go into the world and their first goal is surviving the Creepers. Then they need to find supplies to build a shelter, then once they learn that, they start playing together with friends on multiplayer servers, and finally, they start using the Minecraft tools to create art." Thousands of collective art projects across as many Minecraft servers, depicting whole cityscapes and other staggeringly ambitious sculptures, up to and including a recreation of the entire known universe by a teen in San Diego, testify to their creators' self-actualization as artists.

I have seen Maslow's hierarchy play out firsthand: My niece Gloria is a dedicated Minecraft player. Where once she might have been overwhelmed by the basic task of avoiding death by nightly Creeper incursions, she was, after much play, happily focused on creating beautiful, sprawling homes for herself, even though she was still playing in die-and-game-over Survival mode. Proudly showing me her creation over a holiday visit, she cheerfully walked me through an intricate garden she made, only briefly pausing to brain an oncoming Creeper.

Originally launched as a single-player game, Minecraft gradually took on metaverse features, enabling users to control and customize their own multiplayer servers and in 2017 adding a marketplace for Minecraft creators to sell their content (generating $500 million in sales in its first five years).

And as the game exploded in popularity, players took to YouTube to upload videos of their latest adventures or creative builds, or even to make short movies from edited gameplay footage. With little or no input by the game's actual developers, the Minecraft user community made YouTube itself a de facto facet of the experience.

As child sociology and digital education expert Anya Kamenetz noted in my Introduction, much of kids' involvement in social media has shifted in recent years to watching and sharing gameplay videos on YouTube, led first and foremost by Minecraft.

In doing this, the user community brought a missing piece to the core Metaverse concept that its early visionaries missed. In retrospect, it should have been obvious:

The Metaverse cannot practically function unless it enables *time shifting*—that is, capturing real-time experiences for later access and enjoyment by its user base, and even the public at large.

Every day, wild and fascinating human dramas emerge in the heat of real-time gameplay in popular MMOs and virtual worlds, but few outside those who experience them firsthand would even know that they'd occurred.

Working on their own, the user community changed that. Turning to third-party streaming video, they created a kind of grassroots, public access news network for the Metaverse. I strongly suspect Minecraft and other metaverse platforms would not be as large or as active, were it not for streaming video.

As it gained traction, the Roblox user community would follow in this path. But where multiplayer Minecraft is restrictive by design (you can access player-run servers only by permission, and the worlds are generally fiefdoms isolated from each other), Roblox offered young gamers a single world with unlimited experiences and many millions of fellow players to directly engage with.

Unsurprisingly, much of Roblox's rapid growth occurred during the pandemic, with schools shuttered and playgrounds empty.

"The immediacy of young people interacting in real time with their friends [in Roblox] using voice and playing made it a lot easier to have meaningful interaction while playing a game together as opposed to just voice chat," Kamenetz tells me.

And like most virtual worlds, Roblox has an internal social network integrated *into* the game experience, with functions for friending other avatars or just following them. These connections, along with badges and other earned achievements, are displayed on a player's page on the Roblox website—effectively a Facebook for avatars.

It is not just integration with social media that has helped make Roblox successful. It's even presented on the Web to appear like a kind of streaming video:

Individual user-made Roblox games (later rebranded as "experiences") are depicted on a web page of the official site, where teaser images are displayed alongside a giant green play button, almost as if it *were* a YouTube video. Clicking it, however, launches the actual Roblox software, or for first-time users, starts the download/installation process in the background. The world only launches, in other words, when the user is tantalized enough to enter. They are not presented with an entire overwhelming platform, as with Second Life, but a single simple game/experience to start with.

It's an elegant solution to an eternal challenge among metaverse platforms: bridging the average user from casual interest to immersive engagement, which usually requires a full client download. (Recall again how a vast majority of Second Life's first-time "users," inexperienced with the downloading and installation process, usually quit before it was even finished.)

How Blocky Avatars Encourage Creativity

Someone should finally say something in praise of Roblox's simplistic avatars. In fact, it's actually a default avatar identity that wasn't intended to be what users would generally use but still went on to become a popular choice (and by default, is deeply associated with the Roblox brand). It has its origins in a very early version of Roblox, which began as a software tool for teaching and experimenting with physics.

Whether Roblox developers intended it or not, these blocky avatars, abstract cubistic humans at best, offer a liberating power to players that's not fully appreciated.

Virtual world researcher Nick Yee, who co-led the ground-breaking studies on the mirroring power of avatars known as the Proteus effect (see Introduction), concurs: "With Roblox and Minecraft in particular," Yee observes, "you see a lot more creativity when [players] aren't sociologically encouraged to be obsessed about their hair, because they can't."

The kids who play through them think less about what these avatars' appearance says about who they are in real life and more about how they can express their interests and personality. Monitored offline by their parents and other elders at all waking hours about their appearance and behavior—how they are dressed, whether they are smiling enough, how disruptive they are being, and so on and on, into their teen years, when their peers join in on this endless scrutiny—kids finally have a chance on these metaverse platforms to simply be, and do. More realistic avatars would have only introduced heightened peer scrutiny *into* the virtual world.

Freed from these offline expectations, Roblox's player base can focus on the creativity of their peers.

And the hunger for user-created experiences is voracious: Adopt Me, a user-made roleplay pet care game experience on Roblox created by a small team of grassroots creators, regularly attracts peak daily concurrency numbers in the low to mid-six figures—making it roughly as popular as some of the most successful games on Steam, such as Electronic Arts's *Apex Legends* and the latest installment of *Call of Duty®: Modern Warfare* from Activision, titles costing well over $100 million each to produce (let alone market).

Presented with these numbers, a common rejoinder among colleagues in the game industry is that Roblox games are simplistic and low frills, and therefore only popular with very young kids. There is some truth to this, but as the company adds new features to the development tools, this stereotype will rapidly change.

It's already changed quite a bit: In 2020, Roblox user "Homemade Meal," who works part-time as an effects artist for a game studio, created Tunneler, an award-winning experience inspired by the brain-melting video game series *Portal*, in which you escape from a series of locked rooms through the use of a teleportation gun. Mr. Meal was able to create a similar experience with the Roblox SDK, and it's remarkable in its sophistication.

"When people think of Roblox, they typically think of a game where a bunch of kids play with simple basic blocks," as he put it to me. His goal with the *Portal* tribute was simply to prove the platform's power—and freely offer it to his fans in Roblox.

Tunneler has so far been played over five million times. At retail, the two *Portal* games have only sold about four million copies each.

Portrait of the Artist as a Young Jamaican Woman

Known as "LAGurlz" in-game ("LA" for short, from here on out), she calls herself the first Black female developer to hit the front page on Roblox's official site. While not an official title, it sure seems plausible.

"The only big female developers are Fierzaa and Callmehbob," LA points out, "so I know for sure I'm at least the first Black female to hit the front page. The demographic of Black female devs on Roblox is basically nonexistent." (The demographics of Roblox creators in clothing design and other in-game UGC are more varied, she allows, but she hopes the company can do more to foster more diversity among fellow experience developers.)

"[Roblox the company does] encourage diversity for sure," she adds. "But since coding already, and tech, is such a male-dominated industry, it's just kinda the way things are. But I do wish Roblox had more initiatives to get more underrepresented communities interested in game development.

"I've had so many Caribbean people and Black people come congratulate me and tell me how it's inspiring to see a Black developer hit the front page. And it's really sweet to see, but sad how there aren't more."

LA first discovered Roblox as a 10-year-old girl from Jamaica who a few years earlier had moved with her mother to be with her stepfather in a small Virginia town. But her parents subsequently divorced; her mother struggled to provide for the family. ("My mom has worked so many jobs, I can't even count how many there were.")

LA was about 11 when she had an epiphany and logged into the platform's developer site. "I was looking at the Devex rates out of curiosity and saw how you were able to convert 100,000 Robux into real money. . . . Back then 100,000 Robux was so much to me." The Developer Exchange is where creators cash out their virtual currency for real money, and given the exchange rate at the time, she estimates that was about $250.

At 18, with the success of her first game, *Throw People Simulator* ("just a meme-y game about throwing people around a map, into black holes, really anything"), LA cashed out her Robux for the first time: $14,000.

She gave her mother a solid cut of those proceeds. And on a recent Christmas, she cashed out enough Roblox earnings to buy extravagant gifts for her family.

"It was actually the first time my mommy has ever gotten a gift on Christmas before, so that made me feel really good, how everyone was super happy."

It also shifted her mother's perception of what her daughter was doing, not simply wasting time when she should be focused on schoolwork.

"I think she really started to get it and take it seriously when the money started coming in. She understands I make games, so she tells everyone I run a video game studio, but I still don't think she fully understands what Roblox is or how it works."

LA does, in fact, co-own a game company: Double Bandit Studios is a registered LLC. Her work partner is known in Roblox as "Intrance."

"It's funny because I absolutely hated him at first," LA remembers. "He came off as someone who just didn't care about anything but his work and his projects. I remember I'd DM him good morning and he'd respond nine hours later." She laughs at the memory. "I've blocked him at least four times."

She reconnected after noticing he'd got into her game and bought one of her shirts.

In the first two years as a couple, their relationship was exclusively online, as they'd not yet met in real life. (They were both 20 years old when I interviewed them in 2022.) "We called every single day until the day we met up in person."

They finally did meet on Intrance's way back to the East Coast from a Roblox accelerator internship in California. It went rather well: "My mom really liked him and actually let him stay with us for three months until we moved out together."

The Roblox game experience they created together, Starving Artists, is bright and cheery, dropping players into a sunny courtyard with a circle of art kiosks they can choose. The creators managed to script an entire drawing and painting system *within Roblox*, so that players can create simple images within the virtual world—and then try and sell them to passersby.

"Once we released it, it basically just went viral! Within a couple days of releasing we were hitting 40,000 concurrent users. It was such a unique concept, so players really liked it."

I have to wince at that number when she gives it to me: For Second Life, 40,000 is often *the entirety* of the world's concurrency; on Roblox, it's just for this one game experience.

FIGURE 4.1 Intrance and LAGurlz in their Starving Artists experience in Roblox.

And while there are some quirky indie games about artists on Steam and other platforms, I can't think of any that immediately attract that many players at once. Then again, very few mainstream commercial games are that popular, let alone so instantly.

The most compelling hook of Starving Artists, however, is the ability of players to not only sell their pictures for Robux to other players but also then resell them to other patrons.

"We've had art sell for 1 million+ Robux."

That's roughly $10,000.

When I get over my shock, something occurs to me:

"Did you two kinda create NFT art in Roblox that aren't really NFTs?"

"A lot of people call it an NFT simulator," Intrance agrees. "We've been considering incorporating it into a web3 platform too."

FIGURE 4.2 Roblox's "Starving Artists" art auction.

LA and Int show me some of the most successful drawings made by their players, and the best are quite impressive cartoons—as high quality as many of the NFT artworks that actual adults recently paid millions of actual dollars for.

In 2022, Starving Artists earned a Builderman Award of Excellence, selected by CEO David Baszucki himself, given out at the annual Bloxy Awards in San Francisco. To maintain their anonymity, LA and Int did not attend in person but sent in a Thank You video:

"Growing up in Jamaica," LA said in it, "there weren't many opportunities. But Roblox allowed me to turn my dreams into reality. And I hope I can inspire others to do the same."

At press time, Starving Artists has been visited nearly 270 million times, with 7 million monthly active users—well over twice the entire population of Jamaica.

Despite or because of all this success, they're not interested in becoming employees of Roblox the company, even though they'd probably be offered salaries of some $200,000/year along with amazing benefits and relocation costs to California.

"We'd rather just be doing what we do now," as LAGurlz puts it. "Making and being in control of our own games and projects, and if we make a game big enough, then we'd hire a team to help us out.

"And honestly with the way Roblox is going and the potential this platform has, and even from our experiences with it, that $200K could easily be a million a year if not millions from just doing our own thing."

The Trouble with Children in the Metaverse

Roblox's success is also its most keen vulnerability: It is over-whelmingly popular with children.

Like any Internet platform frequented by minors, it is also a frequent target for child predators. Even beyond that critical concern, the heavy presence of children introduces a whole host of limitations and controversies.

Starting with Roblox's metaverse ambitions. In October 2021, still flush from its successful IPO six months earlier and grand proclamations by Baszucki that his company was indeed building the Metaverse, updates to the platform rules included an odd addition:

> We value friendly debate about issues and topics that matter to Robloxians. However, to maintain a civil and respectful environment, we prohibit the discussion or depiction of: Current candidates running for public office, including their slogans, campaign material, rallies, or events . . . [s]itting real-world elected officials. Roblox is a safe space for meeting online friends, chatting, and collaborating on creative projects, but we prohibit content that seeks or portrays romantic relationships, including: Animations of kissing, hand holding, or other romantic gestures . . . [e]xperiences that depict romantic events, including weddings, dates, and honeymoons.

The ban against real-life politics effectively blocked a key bridge from the Metaverse to the offline world. The prohibition against virtual romance, even of the most wholesome variety, excises a whole reason people find metaverse platforms appealing, even essential: avatar-based romantic relationships that often carry over into the real world and which are certainly an important part of the virtual world. (Virtual wedding planners are a whole cottage industry on most metaverse platforms.)

If Roblox's user base demographic becomes more centered around teens and young adults, presumably some of these restrictions could be lifted, at least in experiences that are not accessible to kids. The company reports that over half of its daily active users are over 13, and that its fastest-growing age cohort in recent quarters is 17-to-24-year-olds, accounting for 22 percent of hours spent on the platform. Roblox's strategy for maturing its user demographic depends on enhancing its graphic engine and development capabilities and enabling more sophisticated experiences, which hopefully will in turn attract and retain older users. (More on all this in Chapter 11.)

But the biggest challenge for Roblox the company is probably this one:

How to manage the reality that on Roblox, children are quite literally creating monetizable content for a for-profit company.

It is why in 2021, while most of the mainstream media was still attempting to explain what Roblox even was, an independent game journalist uncovered a far more fraught story. On his popular People Make Games YouTube channel, freelance UK reporter Quintin Smith explored how Roblox monetized its user creators—most of whom are minors—with mechanics that he depicted as grossly exploitative.

XR security expert Kavya Pearlman bluntly describes it as "child labor."

A Roblox spokesperson strongly disagrees with that depiction.

"We don't agree with that characterization of Roblox," they told me in a statement. "The core of the Roblox vision and philosophy is that we support as much creation as possible throughout the community. 'Respecting The Community' is one of our core values at Roblox, and we are proud of the positive difference that building on Roblox has made in the lives of many within our developer community. We work hard every day to continue to create an even better environment for them and all of our users."

I leave it to the reader to evaluate that statement related to the characterization.

Whatever the case, it's a mystery that the topic hasn't been discussed by the U.S. Congress or the White House as yet.

Roblox happily boasts that roughly one in two children in the United States plays Roblox, and many of them are surely sons and daughters of major American politicians. Indeed, Donald Trump's own son Barron is widely rumored to be an avid Roblox player named "JumpyTurtlee," playing games like Rage Runners in a White House bedroom while down the hall his father raged, attempting to win the somewhat more difficult game of Happy Fun Time Insurrection.

"We haven't had a mishap, a terrible mishap happen in virtual reality or in metaverse technologies," Kavya speculates. "Until that happens, a bunch of the support from Congress is not going to happen."

Even beyond the question of children creating monetized content for Roblox the company, another, larger question looms: whether Roblox can share more of its revenue with its user creators who make the platform possible. As of this writing, Roblox user creators make only 30 percent of the sales they collect from the experiences they create, with Roblox the corporation claiming the rest.

Creators like LAGurlz and Intrance are impressively successful, but the hard economic fact is that creators only begin to see decent revenue if they can attract players in the many millions.

For that reason, very few Roblox creators earn significant income.

It was Philip Rosedale who first pointed this out to me. In Roblox's S1 stock filing, a passage states that only 1,050 community developers earned over $10,000 per year from their Roblox content.

"I asked the team at Second Life to [research] exactly the same number—how many people in Second Life are making over $10,000 a year? And the answer was 1,600 people. So more than Roblox by a good bit."

That's notable in itself. It's even more so when you recall that Second Life only has about 600,000 monthly active users, compared to Roblox's more than 250 million. Yet somehow, Roblox's creative community is making much less revenue to benefit a much larger user base. (Linden Lab only takes roughly 20 percent of sales from its Second Life user creators.)

Through a spokesperson, Roblox defends the 70/30 split this way:

"A Roblox developer on average takes home about 29 cents per $1 spent by a user in their experience on Roblox—this is *after* all expenses tied to building, storing, testing, and maintaining an experience have already been paid. Unlike platforms that only provide a venue to find and download content, Roblox allows developers to express themselves creatively—immediately and for free."

The spokesperson also noted continued improvements to benefit developers, including a January 2023 lowering of cash out minimums, from 50,000 Robux to 30,000 Robux. (Another common complaint, since 50K in Robux equals $175 USD, an astronomical amount for most creators.) "By lowering the amount of earned Robux needed to DevEx, more developers may be able to convert earnings into cash to reinvest in themselves, their studio, and their community."

Part of this disparity, in fairness, is due to Roblox's dependency on the App Store and Google Play for their large user base, most of which accesses the platform via mobile—a benefit Apple and Google make the company pay dearly for. (As it does with Epic's Fortnite, a whole other spectacular, courtroom-thrashing drama in itself.) Roblox the company now describes its user-made games as "experiences," apparently to avoid the stricter scrutiny Apple places on games in its App Store.

These issues will likely come to a head in the next few years. Kavya Pearlman recommends that Roblox the company be more proactive around them, if only out of self-interest:

"[Roblox] should change their business model immediately to go from code for engagement and code for profiteering to code for well-being.

"It is counterintuitive, but it is a long-term winning game. Because yeah, sure you can keep a bunch more people and children in the game by getting them addicted. But you could flip this and say, 'Hey, we are the most trusted company, and we are restructuring, reorganizing so that you could send your children to school in Roblox. You can trust us to parent them. Because we literally consulted scientists; we have studied the impact on children's brains and [have found] the extent of technology that you should expose them to.'"

"So that's what they could do. They could actually take a leadership position on safeguarding the children, and they would totally win the game."

Her suggestion is plausible. Without much effort, Minecraft: Education Edition has been downloaded over 50 million times; teachers around the world use it as a powerful teaching tool for math, programming, and beyond. A Roblox with an emphasis on well-being could become a successor to that audience while also growing its own consumer base.

In the immediate term, however, Roblox's future is most challenged by the relatively recent rise of a competitor in what's effectively a battle royale for the future of the Metaverse. But that's for the next chapter.

Getting Started in Roblox

Creator notes:

Intrance, cofounder of Double Bandit Studios, creator of Starving Artists:

"My advice to creators who want to get started would be to figure out what aspect of development you're most interested in, such as 3D modeling, environment design, programming, UI/UX, graphic design, etc., and learn as much as you can about it. Then you can find a small studio or team on Roblox that's looking for your skillset. That'll allow you to contribute to projects without needing the funds to hire a team yourself.

"Once you meet other passionate developers who have complementary skillsets, you can then work on your own projects. Lots of developers on Roblox are willing to work on a project in exchange for a percentage of any potential revenue generated by the project. And don't be afraid to fail!"

As for finding other developers, Int recommends searching Twitter via the hashtag #RobloxDev, and the Talent Hub on Roblox's site.

Because so many Roblox creators are minors, it's recommended to confirm a prospective collaborator's adult age before working together. ("Most of the larger studios that hire developers full-time require you to be 18," Intrance notes.)

As for the *kind* of experience to create, popular genres are one route, but Int argues that the user base is large enough to encourage experimentation:

"There are a few tried-and-true game models that players are familiar with, such as tycoons and simulators. But the beauty of Roblox is that any game has the potential to become popular. I can't count the number of times we've seen a game become popular and think, 'I never would've expected players to play that.' Building a community is fairly easy once you have a game with enough players."

As a way of driving interest even before the game is ready, Int recommends posting progress screenshots. "[That] really helps grow a loyal audience to look forward to your game."

Roblox developer notes:

For developers interested in following Roblox's approach to metaverse platforms, Roblox senior engineer Richard Nelson has these insights into the workflow:

There are several things about the release process at Roblox that are worth emulating. We follow a regular cadence of shipping a new release every week. This makes it faster to get new features and bug fixes in our users' hands. We combine this with the discipline of using "feature flags" for all functionality, which means we can immediately disable any new code we ship if it turns out to have problems. This safety net is incredibly valuable in that it allows us to avoid most emergency releases and keep the platform stable and reliable.

I also think there is a lot to be said for a dedicated creation tool targeted specifically at the portion of users who want to create, like Roblox Studio. One of the immediate benefits as compared to the Second Life approach is that it allows you to streamline the client interface for non-creators. It also makes building a dynamic experience a lot easier, as you don't have to worry about objects changing state underneath you as you edit (like that physical object that rolled to the bottom of the hill).

That also means Roblox Studio doesn't enable multiplayer dynamic creation like Second Life, a trade-off he acknowledges:

"I loved the experiences I had collaboratively building with friends in Second Life, and there is something magical about being able to jump into build mode mid-conversation to demonstrate something or just mess around."

Notes for parents of underage Roblox users:

I asked Roblox if there are any upcoming changes in 2023 and 2024 that will address parental concerns about the platform. A spokesperson sent me this statement:

We have a safety-first culture at Roblox and work tirelessly to maintain a platform that is safe, civil, and welcoming for all. That includes zero tolerance for behavior that doesn't meet our Community Standards and a robust set of safety features, including rigorous, industry-leading chat filters that prevent users from sharing documents or links to third-party sites.

Today, more than half of our daily active users are over 13, with our fastest-growing cohort being the 17–24 user group. As our audience grows, we introduce age recommendations so all users can make informed decisions about the content they interact with. These age recommendations are grounded in our mission to connect a billion people with optimism and civility. We call them "Experience Guidelines," and they were informed by child development research and industry standards.

Over time, our discovery systems will recommend experiences that support age appropriateness and safety. Based on these age recommendations, parents will be able to use our new Parental

Controls that restrict account access by age recommendations, ultimately deciding and managing what is appropriate (thus playable and recommended) for their children.

While we continue to guard the safety of our users, we want to empower them with the freedom to make their own informed decisions.

5

Battle Royale for the Fortnite Metaverse

Official Fortnite User Base Snapshot, Early 2023:

- Roughly 50 percent of time spent in Fortnite is in creator-made experiences developed by the Fortnite community and third-party brands.
- As of 2022, Fortnite has 400 million registered accounts.

Data courtesy Epic Games

Years after the avatar known as AM Radio had moved and inspired the user community of Second Life, the avatar's real-life owner, Jeff Berg, received an intriguing invitation to see a new art installation in another virtual world.

By then, nearly all of AM Radio's works had gone away from Second Life, largely dematerialized due to the high cost of virtual land.

In the interim, Berg had lost another essential, more tangible part of himself: his marriage. And as he and his wife grew apart, they also moved across the country. Their teen son Cary went to live with his mother on the East Coast, while Berg himself remained in the Midwest.

So when Cary reached out to his father, it was through an Xbox that Berg had bought for them to play together online.

One night, Cary casually IMed him: "Hey check this out."

And so Berg did.

Cary had re-created some of AM Radio's most beloved Second Life works in Fortnite Creative.

There they were on a Fortnite island on an expansive desert lined by soaring mountains, beneath a gold and purple sky. A radar array pointed out into nothingness; an ancient farm house stood alone in the wasteland, where rocking chairs were tossed and frozen in midair. A rusty but soulful train lay abandoned in a wheat field.

A decade or so after they'd dematerialized, Berg's son had diligently worked to re-create many of AM Radio's most famous Second Life creations, including "The Faraway," in Fortnite Creative.

"I knew they were deleted and I thought that was a shame, so I wanted to have them in Fortnite," Cary simply explained.

Since most of AM Radio's works no longer exist in Second Life, Cary had to delve through ancient YouTube videos to find reference images.

FIGURE 5.1 "The Faraway" of Second Life re-created in Fortnite Creative by AM Radio's son

"He stayed up all night and surprised me with this Fortnite island build," Berg told me, amazed, moved—and also impressed by the power of the Fortnite creation tools.

Cary later moved to the Midwest to attend school there, and to live with his father. Virtual worlds continue to keep them connected, even when they share the same couch.

"He and I are gaming together right now," Berg told me one evening. "GTA and Fortnite."

AM Radio laughed. "It's good to have him here. But here we are, playing games tonight."

Besides being a bridge between father and son, Fortnite and Second Life share strands of the same DNA. An early prototype of Second Life, dubbed Linden World, had a heavy focus on combat alongside in-game creation.

Cory Ondrejka and his developers at Linden Lab showed Tim Sweeney, CEO of Fortnite creator Epic, a demo of Second Life at the Game Developers Convention in 2004.

FIGURE 5.2 Jeff "AM Radio" Berg with his son Cary (ion right)

As Ondrejka remembers the presentation, Sweeney was impressed by how Second Life users could dynamically create together and told Cory and the team that he wanted to make an Epic game with that kind of functionality, which would expose more of the Unreal Engine's tools to players.

"Of course you want collaboration, of course you want people to be able to work together and create things," Cory tells me. "So Tim got it right away."

About a decade later, Epic Games' Mark Rein showed Ondrejka a prototype of Fortnite that blended ideas from various Epic Games, Second Life, and Minecraft into a unique new experience.

Fortnite originally started out as a very different experience from what it is today, and no one would have described its first version as a metaverse platform. It was originally a multiplayer tower defense game, with players working together to build a fortress that could fend off oncoming beasties.

As discussed in the Introduction, PUBG: Battlegrounds (a user-made modification of another game) had popularized the "last fighter standing" multiplayer gameplay mode of battle royale. Rapidly rejiggering, Epic's devs added a new play mode, Fortnite Battle Royale, as a competitor. Launched in 2017, it quickly became epochly popular.

Not only did it incorporate building into gameplay (you could instantiate barricades and other strategic elements into existence during a match), but unlike PUBG, it was aggressively charming and whimsical, with stylized cartoon avatars, a lack of blood, and an immediate zaniness. (To start a Battle Royale match, you are airdropped onto the island in a colorful party bus.)

While the Battle Royale gameplay is frenetic and fun, the players pretty early on expressed their desire for an experience that was more of an open-ended virtual world, where combat was only one of the activities. Very soon after launch, players began organizing temporary truces so that they could party and dance together in the war zone.

As that happened, Fortnite drove another breakthrough in the realm of hardcore games demarcated by 3D action and fast reflexes. While typically the province of young males, Fortnite began attracting a significant percentage of female gamers. In 2018, CNBC reported that the mobile version of Epic's game was more popular with girls and women than males. This was partly due to Fortnite's emphasis on socialization and customizable, non-sexualized avatars, but also because the combat gameplay is not simply shoot-'em-up, encouraging creativity instead.

"It's not that women don't like shooting people in the face," as Nick Yee of QuanticFoundry once told me, citing his firm's extensive gamer surveys, "it's that they feel typical shooter presentation is drab and boring and use guns in the most dull way possible." And while Fortnite *does* come with guns, there are also booby traps and the ability to create new structures to assist in combat.

The game's overall wacky tenor also contributed to its appeal among all genders and beyond hardcore gamers; it's not uncommon to charge into battle against a humanoid banana, a blue llama, and official versions of various movie/videogame characters. Even before any talk of the Metaverse cropped up, Fortnite was already satisfying Stephenson's prerequisite for highly customizable avatars.

Jumping off from Battle Royale's popularity, Fortnite gradually took on still more metaverse qualities with the late 2018 launch of Fortnite Creative, giving players not only the power to create structures during combat but to completely customize their own game island, and then share it with other players.

Unlike Second Life, where the early closed beta combat game aspect gave way to a fully open sandbox virtual world with very few game mechanics, Epic focused first on making Fortnite fun and massively popular—and then gradually introduced creativity features that enabled players to create their own game models.

"[W]hat they've done, and it's super interesting, is this notion of overlaying these very non-game-like things and just plopping them into the game," Ondrejka observes. "They spent years ramping the storytelling up in Fortnite. It started very slowly and very gently and then it expanded and expanded and expanded to the point where then you can do a concert and have it work."

My strong sense overall, talking with members of the Fortnite Creative community, is that Epic hadn't originally anticipated outside brands considering the platform as a real-world marketing space, and assumed it would be more akin to a standard modding mode for gamers. And also, as a publisher from the traditional AAA game industry, that Epic is still holding a tight rein on the platform to protect its brand, even if that means falling short of the Stephenson ideal.

"It's insane," as one creator put it to me. "They want to be a part of this Metaverse, but they are limiting what can actually be done. If you're really wanting a true Metaverse, then more brands should be able to be in a space, whether [Epic] wants to support it or not."

But that was my sense in 2022. By the following year, everything changed.

During the 2023 Game Developers Conference, Epic announced the direct integration of Unreal with Fortnite, enabling multi-user, multiplatform live editing, and Fab, the Epic equivalent of the Unity Asset Store. And where once it was difficult for Fortnite community creators to earn substantial revenue from their custom-made islands, Epic announced it would pay out 40 percent of net revenue from the platform's Item Shop to community creators, based on the popularity of their experiences. Fortnite's evolution as a full-fledged metaverse platform was now nearly complete.

"We can set aside the crazy hype cycle around NFTs and VR goggles," Epic's Tim Sweeney explained then. "These technologies may play a role in the future but they are not required. This revolution is happening right now."

Inside the Alliance

In 2020, Joseph Robinette Biden became the first winning presidential candidate to enter the Metaverse by way of Fortnite Creative. In the Build Back Better with Biden map, players got a chance to help clean up his island or go on a Kamala Harris–themed speed run, where players would race through the map, trying to collect Kamala's errant Chucks lying about.

Unlike traditional Fortnite, Biden's map had a notable lack of guns or traditional video game–type gameplay. On the plus side, it did have an ice cream shop.

Biden's Fortnite experience garnered quite a lot of social coverage (both enthusiastic and mocking) and was directly funded by his campaign. To build it, the Biden team reached out to Simon Bell and Mackenzie Jackson, cofounders of Alliance Studios, one of the very first small businesses to emerge around creating content for real life brands in Fortnite Creative.

As with many of their other major clients, the Biden campaign contractually swore them to silence about the project, so Alliance is not allowed to mention how successful it actually was (or was not) as a campaign promotion.

"We're legally not even allowed to bring it up in conversations," as Mackenzie told me in a video call. "Because you brought it up, I can then confirm that, 'Yes, we created that.'"

I'm actually not surprised by the enforced silence; while some politicians may show interest in the Metaverse, we're still at a point where the general public (let alone the opposition party) would consider Fortnite to be a mere game, and a fairly violent one at that.

Launching Alliance among a Community of Creators

Simon and Mackenzie started tinkering with Fortnite Creative shortly after launch, when it was basically still a simple level editor.

They met via a third-party site that featured user-made Fortnite Creative maps (www.fortnitecreativehq.com). They were both uploading their own maps there at the time and wound up joining a creative team to create new ones.

"We became friends and hung out every night, working and making our maps and testing each other's work, and so that's how we met." Nine months later they met in real life, which was no mean feat; Simon is based in Australia, and Mackenzie, the American Midwest.

They describe Alliance Studios, founded in 2019, as the pioneers of brand experiences in Fortnite Creative—but acknowledge that it's a role that fell in their laps from the maps they were at first making for fun.

FIGURE 5.3 Mackenzie Jackson's Fortnite avatar "MackJack" and Alliance's Doritos map

"It was demand that got us into the brand space, with brands approaching *us*. We've never had to go out and look for work in that space," Simon tells me. When I speak with them, they are completing the launch of a branded experience for rapper The Kid LAROI, an immersive experience wrapped around a game, an interactive story, and prerecorded videos of the pop stars streaming on the virtual walls.

They are hardly the only grassroots creators who've wound up creating content for major brands. The Alliance team estimates that about 1,000 Fortnite creators make some kind of income from their virtual world, and then about 100 who are like them: making an entire, full-time income from their Fortnite creativity.

The Limits of Fortnite Creative as a Metaverse Platform

Alliance's first client map, for the e-sports team 100 Thieves, was sponsored and branded by Uber Eats and Rocket Mortgage.

The idea with that campaign is that players could claim a $5 discount code by participating. But how would they actually redeem it from within a virtual world?

Simon's idea was pretty ingenious: *build* the QR code inside Fortnite like it was a massive sculpture or ancient ruins.

"You know, using black and white blocks, placing them together into a QR code and then generating that and giving it to a brand. . . . [Players] can point their phone at the screen and scan the QR code that I created."

Despite this being an impressive breakthrough, Epic's legal team quickly nixed it as a potential security danger. (It is easy, to be sure, for this same technique to be abused by others for phishing scams and various shenanigans.)

There's a lesson in this.

"Epic didn't really have any policies in place for brand and experience in the beginning," says Mackenzie. In the early days, it seems as if Epic was racing to keep ahead of the creators.

That also means that there's still no direct way of connecting Fortnite activity with the external 2D web—a necessary feature for a full-fledged metaverse platform. Not to mention a pretty essential feature for outside brands.

"My hope," Mackenzie tells me, "is that Epic is going to understand that if they really want this whole Metaverse to exist, there need to be a lot less rules. There needs to be more in the player creator's hands as to what we're allowed to do and how to really truly bring the spaces to life and connect them [to the wider Internet]."

Simon is sympathetic to Epic's position and how tightly it controls *what* brands show up in Fortnite.

"They want to protect their platform as well. There's particular brands they don't want in the space . . . we've got other brands that are coming in third party that creators are working with; we've got the freedom to put that onto the platform and then we're seeing some really off-kilter brands coming into the space.

"We want to nurture an ecosystem. We want to make sure that the player doesn't have a spoiled experience. If it still goes with this rat race mentality, it's going to leave a bad taste for the players [where they] just get brands slapped in their face."

(We spoke, by the way, in late 2022, before the announcement of Fortnite Creative 2.0, which greatly expanded the platform's creative capabilities; still, as of press time, web and mixed reality integration options seem to remain lacking.)

The other danger is limiting Fortnite *only* to brands (and pop stars, and movies, and so on) that appeal to a narrow demographic of teens and early 20s. For Fortnite as a metaverse platform, the Age Cliff looms. (But more on that in Chapter 11.)

Advice for Brands

Having met and worked with dozens of major real-life brands, Mackenzie and Simon of Alliance have advice for creating a successful experience.

Simon notes that many brands come to them with a very specific creative campaign in mind, even if it doesn't fully leverage the potential of the platform.

"Partner up with teams similar to us or with us," Mackenzie advises, "and trust our experience to let us create a game that players are going to enjoy that's also going to represent their brands."

The Fortnite activation can't be a stand-alone experience, however, which would only limit its reach and impact:

"[Brands] need to be looking at it as a piece of a larger puzzle . . . how can we tie it to any kind of IRL event, or tournaments, or elevated beyond just what we made?"

A fan of creating adventure game experiences in Fortnite Creative, Simon acknowledges that that genre is not actually the best genre for brand experiences, because once played, a player never returns. Better to create a full-fledged multiplayer game experience where players are competing against each other or themselves, so there's a reason for them to keep returning:

"So to get into that space, you need players to be consistently playing your map, and not just one or two. You need thousands and thousands to be consistently playing your map, meaning that a game that starts and finishes and has no reason to return to isn't going to do so well."

Advice for Creators—Especially Women

The Alliance founders (alliancestudios.gg) are bullish on job growth for developers in Fortnite Creative. The trick for newcomers is not only mastering the creative tools, but self-promotion.

"We're gonna need to be hiring more people," as Mackenzie puts it. "So if you're a creative individual and this is a field that you're interested in, get in and start creating and get yourself seen, you know, get community events that are happening, post on social media, post on Discord—we should be able to see your work to see if you're somebody we might even be interested in picking up."

Fortnite Creative Discords to get started in:

- Fortnite Creators
- FCHQ Creative Community

On Twitter, the main hashtag to show off your creativity to teams like Alliance is #CreatedinFortnite.

Mackenzie is one of the few women professionally working in Fortnite Creative (by her estimate, there are fewer than

10 women among thousands of community developers), so I asked her what advice she would give other women interested in pursuing a profession like hers.

"If you are passionate about being creative, then jump in and get a feel for what the possibilities are. Most importantly, focus on the supporters. As a female in this industry, there can be a lot of toxicity and discrimination. It's not always easy, but set aside the emotions surrounding the negative and just focus on the positive."

Another guideline might be to find the right team members who'll support you. In Mackenzie's case, her Alliance comrades rallied to support her after a surgery with serious complications confined her to the hospital for over two months. They spoke with her every day over Fortnite voice chat.

"This all happened during COVID-19, so I was unable to have any visitors." Her business partner, Simon, bought her the Fortnite edition of the Nintendo Switch, she tells me, "which I used in the hospital until I purchased a laptop to continue working while in the hospital. I worked [in Fortnite] every single day, and I would, hands down, say that they were a massive part of helping me heal."

6

Neal Stephenson Enters the Metaverse—Lamina1, Blockchain, and the Utopia of Ownership

I was already deep into its writing when this book took a sharp left turn, or maybe a full 180: Neal Stephenson himself announced, 30 years after the publication of *Snow Crash*, that he was becoming an active participant in the creation of the Metaverse.

His new company was Lamina1. And as cofounder Peter Vessenes explained in a June 2022 announcement:

[Lamina1 is] the base layer for the Open Metaverse: a place to build something a bit closer to Neal's vision— one that privileges creators, technical and artistic, one that provides support, spatial computing tech, and a community to support those who are building out the Metaverse.

In a keen irony, the Lamina1 announcement received less media attention than it might have at other times. By then, "the Metaverse" was garnering so much coverage, many people missed that the actual creator of the Metaverse was now also involved. Up to and including (as a subsequent premiere white paper announced), designing a virtual world himself:

> Under active early-stage development, Neal Stephenson's THEEE METAVERSE promises a richly-imagined interactive virtual world with an unforgettable origin story. Built on the Lamina1 chain, creators will come to experience Neal's vision and stay to develop their own.

It later emerged what the title of that project actually meant: Once the foundation of Lamina1's blockchain, SDK, and payment systems had been laid down (more on those below), Neal Stephenson would himself lead the development of the Metaverse as he first imagined it in *Snow Crash*. But that was long down the road.

"[It] was clear in late 2021," as Stephenson wryly explained to me on a video call in the summer of 2022, "that I was going to spend the next year answering emails and phone calls and messages about the M word anyway."

After my 20 years of a writing career that sometimes feels like a long footnote to *Snow Crash*, it's jarring to finally speak face-to-face with Stephenson for the first time. His trademark goatee, something you might picture a steampunk dirigible commander wearing, has turned almost completely silver since the '90s.

"So," he continues, "I just made the decision that I would basically put my novelist career on hold for this calendar year and see what I could do to try to make something of the opportunities that have emerged from all of this."

This was not Stephenson's first foray into the business of metaverse-related development; as we saw in Chapter 1, he apparently made some initial inquiries (mostly lost to history) into actually building some version of the technology in the 1990s, shortly after *Snow Crash* was published. In 2012, he unsuccessfully attempted to crowdfund *CLANG!*, an online sword-fighting game that would have realized something like the Metaverse-based blade duels from that novel. In more recent years, he was "chief futurist" at Magic Leap, a heavily funded augmented reality headset startup that promised consumer marvels. (And after several false starts, pivoted to become an enterprise-focused product.)

Similarly, I'm told Stephenson's role at Lamina1 is not a figurehead position simply to attract investors and media, and goes far beyond just brainstorming company branding and drafting the company's white papers (though he's involved in all those things). Stephenson even participates in regular developer standup meetings, and helps work through technical blockers. "Neal's a coder so he talks a lot with the engineers," as Lamina1's Casey Halter puts it.

So cofounding Lamina1 is a decision he did not make lightly, Stephenson tells me. Up to then, he has held back from being involved in many other Metaverse projects:

"Interest in the Metaverse has been kind of slowly building for decades," as he put it to me, "and there have been various opportunities that have come my way from time to time to work for some company or other that's trying to do something there. And I was kind of reluctant just because I didn't want to throw my weight behind any one particular interpretation of it."

That finally changed in 2021.

"When suddenly, everything was Metaverse all day all the time. And the idea that we're working on it with Lamina1 feels to me like it's kind of more foundational; it's not one particular interpretation, or product, it's kind of a base layer of functionality that anyone ought to be able to use to build experiences. And so, as such, I sort of felt like I could get involved without seeming to officially throw my weight behind this company or that company, this interpretation or that interpretation of what [the Metaverse] is supposed to be."

As that suggests, Stephenson's vision is to turn Lamina1 into the revenue backbone of many multiple metaverse projects—and serve the community of creators who make it all possible.

Imagining the Metaverse-as-a-Service

Lamina1 aims to be a Metaverse-as-a-Service for creators working across various metaverse platforms—a play on the unwieldy Valley acronym SaaS, for software-as-a-service. (Salesforce is probably the most well-known company in that category.)

"What we're trying to do is kind of lay down payment rails," as Stephenson told me. "In order to kind of get from where we are now, to the situation where the Metaverse is a global communications medium, like TV or radio or whatever, we have to have experiences that people enjoy having. And by and large today, the people who know how to create those experiences work in the game industry. And some of them are happily employed, some are less happy, some are making good money, some are kind of struggling indie developers.

"But the bottom line is that there needs to be a way for people who devoted their careers to acquiring skills with Maya or Blender or Unreal or Unity or any of the other tools that are part of the tool chain—a way for them to extract some compensation if they are involved in making an experience that people enjoy and are willing to pay for."

The Unity Asset Store and other platforms already make something like this possible for creators, but Lamina1's approach is to give creators access to "smart contracts"—the web3 world's somewhat strange name for mini-applications that exist on the blockchain—to track royalty payments around a designated virtual item.

This will lead, Stephenson argues, "[to] what we hope is the creation of what [VR pioneer] Jaron Lanier calls 'value chains,' which is a way that a number of people could contribute to the creation of an experience and each derive some kind of compensation for their work."

As an example, consider a cool virtual car made for a metaverse platform. The external chassis may have been created by a 3D modeler, while its physics and interactivity were added by a scripter; a UX designer might later add a heads-up display and player controls, so it's actually drivable. Even though the car itself might be bought as a single object, each creator who contributed to the final vehicle—in the Lamina1 model—gets a cut of any sale.

So essentially, Lamina1 hopes to become the leading service to track, credit, and pay creators in the Metaverse.

Redefining the Metaverse with the Metaverse's Creator

My conversation with Neal Stephenson inevitably led me to a question I've been tangling with since the start of this book. Or for that matter, since 2003, when I began writing about a metaverse platform *inside* a metaverse platform.

And now I was finally able to ask the very source for the answer:

"When I define the metaverse, I adhere as closely as possible to what you described in *Snow Crash*, because so many startups have been directly inspired by it. But I've been curious, 30 years later, what's your own working definition?"

Stephenson's face flickers on the video call.

"In a weird way I don't need one," he begins, deadpan, "since I'm the one who coined the term."

But having said that, he continues:

"I would say the basic idea behind the Metaverse from 30 years ago is still applicable and is basically: What would it take content-wise to make 3D immersive graphics as broadly popular as television? And so my main concern at the time I wrote the book was that the hardware [back then] was incredibly expensive, and still slow."

That started changing with the 1993 launch of the first-person shooter *Doom*, just a year after *Snow Crash*'s publication, creating a burgeoning market for immersive, interactive 3D content.

"The World Wide Web was launched basically the same year," Neal notes. "And so those kinds of developments created a big consumer demand for computers that can show graphics, first two-dimensional and then three-dimensional graphics. Almost everyone now has got some kind of device that can render at least simple three-dimensional scenery."

And with that shift in place, Stephenson can paint his contemporary vision of the Metaverse, which remains more or less unchanged from a generation ago:

"I still stick with the basic conceit, I guess you could say, of the Metaverse in *Snow Crash*, which is that [immersive experiences] should be linked in a kind of spatial arrangement. It's what is lacking in the World Wide Web—you've got this web of hyperlinks all over the place that jump you from one site to another, and there's not really a kind of spatial organization that ties it all together. I think there should be a spatial way of tying it all together. So I think that's another kind of fundamental aspect of the Metaverse."

As we explored in Chapter 1, this "spatial arrangement" is a single virtual world, "a black sphere" geographically larger than Earth, including fantastic "special neighborhoods" where the rules of three-dimensional space-time don't apply.

"And stuff that's almost too obvious to mention," Neal continues. "Multi-user on a massive scale. Interoperability is kind of implied and kind of necessary, and just certain constraints as to scaling and physics. So gravity is pointed down, avatars are all kind of the same size, so that the thing just kind of makes sense and hangs together as a three-dimensional construct."

That suggests to Neal Stephenson that the Metaverse should be a single shard, but he is still thinking through those details:

"[L]et's say I build up an experience somewhere in the Metaverse that turns out to be incredibly popular, and a million people show up. Well, I can't fit a million avatars in the space, my servers maybe can't process that much data. So what do I do with this problem of too many people showing up? I could have something similar to the fire code in a physical space—'Sorry, we can only have 100 people in this room'—something like that. But that would really place a severe limit on the ability to generate revenue from this popular experience."

What Stephenson is discussing remains a core challenge for every platform ascribing to be the Metaverse. Thirty years after conception, it is still technically daunting to display many dozens, let alone many hundreds or thousands, of 3D avatars in the same contiguous virtual world space, such as a large virtual concert or a political gathering.

It's a phenomenon Stephenson mentions several times in *Snow Crash*. As a seasoned technologist, he had an awareness, even back then, of the daunting challenge of concurrency. Since it would be computationally impossible to collision detect millions of online users walking on the Street together, he notes in the novel, "avatars just walk right through each other."

With those limitations in mind now, he suggests a compromise:

"[M]y guess is that the Metaverse as a whole is a one-shard proposition, but that in certain areas that are extraordinarily popular, we just can't fit everyone in—that there has to be some sharding or something equivalent to sharding."

If there's any reason to be skeptical about Lamina1's own plans for the Metaverse, they largely lie in this irony: By the time Lamina1 announced its cryptocurrency and blockchain-driven metaverse technology, several platforms inspired by *Snow Crash* had already attempted similar projects—some to great fanfare, but mostly with commercially dubious results. And because Lamina1's prospects probably depend on cryptocurrency and other web3-based virtual worlds succeeding, it's worth knowing more about the footsteps Neal Stephenson must follow.

So before returning to my flickering Internet chat with the author, a brief flashback follows. With any luck, it might vaguely remind you of a short historical digression from—well, from a Neal Stephenson novel.

A Brief History of the Cryptoverse

Whether you are reading this in a near future where Bitcoin and other cryptocurrency is remembered with a shudder as an utter economic disaster, or if crypto is still considered a groundbreaking, transformative technology, know this:

Like most things metaverse-related, crypto pretty much started with Second Life.

"Created" by "Satoshi Nakamoto"—quotes being necessary in both cases, since its originator remains anonymous to this day—Bitcoin and its would-be successor Ethereum were not originally conceived as virtual currencies for metaverse platforms. But as noted in Chapter 2, Linden Dollars of Second Life were ultimately intended for use in purchasing real goods and services.

As explained in a June 2021 news article on Bitcoin.com aptly titled "A Look at How Second Life's L$ Helped Kickstart Bitcoin's Value," Linden Dollars helped drive up the value of the cryptocurrency shortly after its inception in 2009, when purchasing Bitcoin with standard fiat cash was nigh impossible. "Bitcoin had a fascinating relationship with Second Life users because L$ could be exchanged for fiat, which gave BTC an alternative fiat gateway in the early days."

For a while, there were even in-world ATMs where Bitcoin could be purchased for Linden Dollars, and vice versa. Oculus founder Palmer Luckey once recounted to me, entirely bemused, a time when he purchased Bitcoin from someone who insisted that they meet each other as avatars in Second Life to finalize the transaction.

Without Second Life, in other words, it's quite likely Bitcoin and crypto in general might not have achieved enough escape velocity to enjoy the market euphoria they went on to attract.

This origin story is important to keep in mind. Because while it started in Second Life, the virtual world could not also offer a good answer to a question that also remains to this day: What can you actually *buy* on a regular basis with cryptocurrency?

For over a decade, Bitcoin enthusiasts have floundered about for a convincing answer to that question.

Linden Dollars, by contrast, are valuable because an economy of some half a million people use it to purchase Second Life–based goods and services from community creators. L$ is regularly used more often for daily transactions in the virtual world than Bitcoin is across the entire real world: Roughly 400,000+ per day in Second Life, a rate rarely exceeded by all BTC transactions across the entire planet.

And then an answer to cryptocurrency's usefulness as currency finally emerged: to buy content from yet *another* virtual world.

Launched in August 2017, Decentraland appeared years before the latest Metaverse hype wave. Announced as an open standards–driven social VR world, it was unveiled with the fervor of a 21st century land rush, with plots of land offered in exchange for Ethereum—1,000 square feet for the ETH equivalent of USD $24.

Within seconds, the founders had sold $25 million worth of nonexistent (not even digitally, at the time) plots in Decentraland.

"[It] will finance the development of the protocol, the tools and services that developers will use to build on top of Decentraland," cofounder Ari Mellich proudly told me at the time. "And for the first time in virtual world history, each purchaser of a Decentraland plot could well and truly claim that plot to be their property."

He meant as opposed to Second Life and other virtual worlds where land may be buyable and sellable by consumers but only on the indulgence of the platform's actual holding company (which usually imposed rules to these sales or even forbade them in some cases).

"[T]hey literally OWN the land, unlike in centralized virtual worlds," Mellich claimed to me, "so there's no entity, not even ourselves, who can take away ownership, modify their content, or suddenly decide that their content is not theirs anymore. That's the power of the blockchain and decentralization. . . . People are used to having their virtual worlds created by a company. In our case it's an open community that builds collaboratively."

Stephenson's *Snow Crash* envisions Metaverse land distribution as being operated by a trust fund similar to Network Solutions, the private company contracted by the U.S. government to manage domain registrations in the web's early days. In the novel, the consortium also develops the network architecture underlying all this virtual real estate. This is perhaps the only significant way in which subsequent metaverse platforms have differed from their fictional conception.

Except, that is, for Decentraland.

But when whispers of real estate gold (however virtual) reached the ears of those who trade in real financial assets, they came calling. In early 2022, J.P. Morgan erected an official "lounge" in Decentraland—as bland and perplexing as you might imagine. And with that imprimatur and other buzz-generating events, a metaverse real estate boom was born—eerily paralleling the Second Life real estate boom of 2005–2006.

With every Decentraland announcement, Second Life déjà vu echoed through seemingly every major news periodical. As if the earlier boom had never happened—or no one in these outlets remembered it:

- Investors Snap Up Metaverse Real Estate in a Virtual Land Boom (*The New York Times*, November 2021)
- Metaverse Real Estate Piles Up Record Sales in Sandbox and Other Virtual Realms (*The Wall Street Journal*, November 2021)
- Virtual Land Prices are Booming, and Now There's a Fund for That (*Bloomberg*, March 2021)

In the end, however, it was a feather in a cyclone of howling avarice.

As the media clamored in 2020–2021 around the latest news hook from Decentraland and The Sandbox, another entry in the blockchain-based metaverse niche, neither of them gathered steam in the only way it ultimately mattered: attracting actual users.

By October of 2022, Decentraland was only tracking 7,000 daily active users, game-industry analyst Lars Doucet informed me when I checked back in on the world's status.

"Everybody who is still playing is basically just playing poker," as Lars put it. "This seems to be a kind of recurring trend in dead-end crypto projects—like people turn the [project's] Discord into a meetup place for poker games. Kind of an eerie rhyme with left-behind American cities where drugs come in and anyone who is left is strung out at a slot machine parlor or liquor store."

As of this writing, no full-fledged metaverse platform organized around the blockchain has succeeded in terms of mass growth. Or really, hardly any growth at all.

The same can be said of NFTs, touted for their purported ability to confer ownership across all platforms, including the Metaverse, with smart contracts that designate royalty payments when a particular NFT is sold by one user to another. At their supposed peak in early 2022, analytics firm Chainalysis found that fewer than 360,000 people owned NFTs.

An insider has told me the NFT ownership number is higher, but not by much. And this is judging blockchain on its own purported objectives, setting aside the crypto implosion of late 2022, when the cratering of FTX amidst criminal charges for the CEO seemed to convert the entire industry into a value-hemorrhaging sinkhole.

Why?

"I think they put the cart before the horse," I told Charlie Warzel of *The Atlantic* in early 2022. "If you put out a speculative offering, like a new coin that gains people entry into a digital world, people might show up, but I don't know why they'd necessarily keep coming back. On a basic philosophical, human level, a thing is only valuable if a group decides it is. These crypto metaverses put the speculation before the community."

I note all this not to categorically condemn blockchain—I know at least a few good and smart technologists who still find potential value in it—but to set the stage for Lamina1's entry. Because at the moment, that stage is covered in blood and fire.

Which takes us back to my call with Neal Stephenson.

Lamina1's Theory of Value

It's odd to be in a place where you're not fully convinced by a new approach to the Metaverse proposed by the creator of the Metaverse, but here we are.

"Let me ask what is I guess a devil's advocate question," I put it to Neal Stephenson. "The blockchain hasn't really worked for any other metaverse platform, and there's been several. The key factor, far as I can tell, is that creating a value to virtual land as the first and foremost principle leads to just rapid real-estate speculation, but not really community. And so there's not this flywheel of user-created content that we've seen in Second Life and other platforms.

So how do you think Lamina1 will succeed as a blockchain-facing tech?"

Stephenson pauses for a moment, then answers from a philosophical height:

"Why are dollars valuable? Because you can buy regular stuff with them, stuff that you actually need in the real economy. People do speculate in dollars, there are currency speculators, but it's a small fraction of the number of people who engage in dollar transactions every day. And you can make similar comments about real estate in the real world. But why is it valuable?

"Well, it's valuable because hopefully, people are using it to do interesting things. Again, there are people who speculate in real estate, who buy property because they think that the value is going to go up. But at the end of the day, the value is grounded in something—a real economic value that is happening on different patches of land.

"So I think that the same is true of virtual real estate and cryptocurrency, that the value is going to arise—in the case of real estate—from the use of that real estate to, as you say, build communities and create experiences that people enjoy having. And if people enjoy having those experiences, then that suggests to me that they'll pay for the privilege. And so now you've got a real economy that's using tokens to pay for virtual goods and services and compensate the people who made those. And it doesn't prevent speculation, you can never prevent people from engaging in speculative activity."

And unlike other blockchain-oriented metaverse startups, Lamina1 will not itself be built on crypto speculation:

"This is not a company that is going to fund itself by putting out an Initial Coin Offer or something like that," as Stephenson puts it. "We're seeking investment through normal tech investor channels. And when it comes time to establish a market for real estate, we want that to be based on, again, something more than just pure speculation. That's why we're focusing on creating tools and foundational utilities that content builders are going to need. Because if they don't show up and begin to populate the Metaverse with interesting experiences, then there's no "there" there. And the only thing that's left is speculation."

Setting aside my own pronounced skepticism around the blockchain, I went in search of a web3 expert who could parse out Lamina1's white paper and value proposition. Devin Abbott is a developer and colleague who—after a successful stint as a mainstream Valley entrepreneur, selling his first company to

Airbnb—became a passionate if nuanced advocate of the block-chain and other web3 concepts.

Royalties, Devin pointed out, are not part of the original specs of NFTs. By 2022, we were already seeing the rise of NFT marketplaces that explicitly ignored the NFT royalty stipulation in their smart contracts. So Devin saw some value in what Stephenson and Lamina1 were proposing, that royalties would be stipulated at the code level:

"Conceptually I agree with the premise [of Lamina1]," he told me. "Blockchains are a good solution for global payment processing, especially for digital goods, so it makes sense that this will grow to encompass game assets."

That said, he went on, much of what Lamina1 seems to be creating might seem redundant to web3 developers. As he put it: "It's already easy for a web3 dev to write a smart contract that supports attaching assets and splitting payments like what [Stephenson] describes. Without diving deeper I'm not sure what value he's bringing to what already exists."

Devin Abbott suggests something like this may first happen on smaller, niche metaverse platforms with people who already own NFTs. "If I want to build a metaverse game and cut costs to get something that kinda works, I can connect my wallet with a platform/engine that supports different assets." From that, he argues, grassroots developers might follow suit, making those assets easier to support and transfer, creating a feedback loop where such content is compatible with larger and larger metaverse platforms.

If any of that happens, these indie developers—and for that matter, Lamina1—may find themselves going up against serious competitors.

In the summer of 2022, the Roblox Corporation announced a job opening for a senior engineer who could "help Roblox Marketplace to be web3 ready and support billions of items and transactions to happen both on the blockchain and Roblox." It would be strange if the creator of the Metaverse found his startup losing out to a much larger metaverse platform, but that is a quite possible outcome.

A Literary Arc to Lamina1

I have often wondered over the years how Neal Stephenson, having written over a dozen novels, feels to be barraged so often by questions about *Snow Crash*, a much earlier work that's not his most literary in the classic sense (it began as a graphic novel), mainly pestered about the Metaverse piece that's actually just part of a much larger whole. For instance, who talks about *Snow Crash* character Sushi K, an Asian rapper who tours the United States to great acclaim? What seemed like a comically impossible hypothetical back in the '90s is now, in the era of KPOP global dominance, a standard everyday phenomena.

As Stephenson tells it, Lamina1 will not only reflect *Snow Crash* but echo many of his other books and the ideas contained in them, written throughout his career—often inspired by the technologists who were in turn inspired by him:

"After I wrote *Snow Crash*," as he puts it, "I got to know people in the tech industry who had read the book and who had been working on projects like Habitat . . . and they had figured out long ago that you couldn't build these kinds of virtual communities without, basically, other people's code running on your hardware."

Habitat was a pioneering virtual world developed for LucasArts in the late '80s by F. Randall Farmer and Chip Morningstar. In the updated acknowledgments to *Snow Crash*, Stephenson credits the first use of "avatar" in this context to Habitat.

"So they've gotten really interested in the problem of how do you do that without letting them take over your computer," he continues, "and then began to look to cryptographic solutions as a way to create that kind of controlled execution environment. And so crypto entered the picture very, very early, when people began to think in a serious engineering way about virtual communities. And that led pretty soon to thinking about cryptocurrency."

So Lamina1 draws from roughly *all* of Stephenson's major novels.

"If you look at *The Diamond Age*, that is a book whose entire plot makes no sense unless you assume the existence of a world-wide network that can transfer money anonymously. So now the girl in that book, Spence, and Miranda know each other through a virtual environment for years, but they have no way to establish each other's real-world identities, because of this anonymous system. The whole plot story basically revolves around that.

"*Cryptonomicon* is obviously about cryptocurrency. It's about a different kind of cryptocurrency than what we have now, because it was published 10 years before the blockchain came into existence. But nevertheless, it's about that. *The Baroque Cycle* books are all about the origins of money, currency, and payment systems [and] why money has value.

Finally: "In *REAMDE*, that's explicitly about a video game in which real world money can be used to carry out financial transactions and about the kind of various complications that arise from that. *Fall* is kind of in a sense a sequel to *REAMDE*, to re-engage some of the same characters, and sort of takes that to the wildest possible extreme."

The influence of Stephenson's writing on Lamina1 even includes his 2021 environmental thriller, which has little to do with the Metaverse:

"*Termination Shock* deals with climate change, and one of the things that we're engineering into the Lamina1 chain is carbon negativity. If you're running a node you need to be able to demonstrate that you've done it in a way that doesn't create a net increase of carbon dioxide in the atmosphere.

"So that's kind of soup-to-nuts to answer your question about how my books relate to what we're doing now [with Lamina1]. It seems like a reasonable, natural next step."

When we first talked in the summer of 2022, Neal Stephenson and his team expected the main net of Lamina1 to be running by late 2023, around when this book is to be published.

"So it'll be a real functioning currency token system," he told me then. "And we'll be rolling out tools that people can actually use and then we'll have to be able to say more about some of the first party projects that we're working on." Including, hopefully, his secretive but oddly named virtual world, THEEE Metaverse. (Talking with an insider, my sense is it's an ironic placeholder title; with so many other parties claiming to be making The Metaverse, it's Stephenson's snarky reply that he himself is making the one where "The" deserves so much emphasis.)

So as this book goes to press, it is far too early to know what will become of Lamina1 in the greater landscape of the Metaverse. But for painfully obvious reasons, no survey of the technology is complete without situating it somewhere central. (For the latest updates, consult this book's Afterword.)

I should also add another irony: In all my interviews with quite a few Gen Z metaverse platform creators, none of them have mentioned having read *Snow Crash*. Many only knew it by reputation. (*Ready Player One* is somewhat more known, but largely due to the Steven Spielberg adaptation.)

Asking them about Stephenson's novel itself only elicited awkward pauses. I felt an embarrassing tug across the X to Z generational divide. Bringing up *Snow Crash* felt a bit like asking them if they had heard Nirvana's *Nevermind* all the way through. How do you do, fellow metaverse kids?

For that matter, few of these metaverse platform creators even consider what they do to be "working in the Metaverse" *per se*, preferring instead to specify their platform of choice.

This strikes me as a positive milestone. In the 1990s, "the information superhighway" was a pervasive metaphor to describe the Internet. Now that we are all hurtling on that digital *autobahn* all the time, the term is scarcely remembered (and certainly not needed).

In a similar way, Neal Stephenson's Metaverse plans and ambition to build THEEE Metaverse paradoxically face a market where his ideas have already become so influential, inspiring so many massively popular platforms, that his success as a business founder now competes with his success as a novelist.

On that theme, it's an additional irony that Neal Stephenson's novels greatly influenced the rise of both the Metaverse *and* cryptocurrency, but it very much remains to be seen whether these two concepts belong together in the same platform. (More on that in Chapter 8.)

And in another final twist, the success of Laminal and THEEE Metaverse might depend on the long (long, long) awaited adaptation of *Snow Crash* for the screen—recently planned as an HBO series but now in the hands of Paramount Studios.

When that does finally happen, as Neal Stephenson notes drolly, computing technology has become so advanced over the decades, it's no longer even necessary to depict the Metaverse in *Snow Crash* with 3D graphics.

"[T]oday if we were to watch a 1995 adaptation of *Snow Crash*, we would be immediately pulled out of the story by the obviously substandard graphics from 27 years ago," as he puts it.

"[W]e've kind of reached the point where it's not clear that you would even use computer graphics. I mean, you could film actors playing whatever role and just claim that they were photo-realistic avatars."

Or to put it another way: Neal Stephenson conceived of the Metaverse as something that might one day be as popular as television. For his own metaverse startup to stand the best chance to succeed, the Metaverse might first need to be depicted on TV.

CHAPTER

7

VRChat and Finding Furry Anime Utopia

Chris "Strasz" Hornyak was only a casual VRChat player at first, randomly exploring the platform with his spouse, both wearing VR headsets while at home in the same room, adventuring in the virtual world while trying not to whack into each other in real life.

Then COVID-19 came calling. During the lockdown, Chris tells me, "Exploring VRChat effectively became our way of going on dates."

VRChat became something more transformative to Strasz, a longtime virtual world enthusiast and MMO gamer, when he descended by elevator into a massive virtual rave in a basement space with glass and metal floors:

"And I remember going into this environment and everybody was dancing, and I was shoulder to shoulder with people, and there's like lights and music playing and everything was going on and I got so overwhelmed," as he describes the experience now. "Everyone was dancing and swaying, and I kept expecting to feel their elbows bump mine, I kept expecting to feel their body heat. I completely felt like I was there and I've never gotten that elsewhere."

It also connected him to the Metaverse in a direct and profound way. "I read *Snow Crash* growing up and I wanted to visit the Black Sun so bad and it was the closest I ever felt to having that experience."

While it may come as a surprise to anyone who assumed Meta would shape the future of the Metaverse, its purest contemporary incarnation so far resides in VRChat, a small startup first bootstrapped by a tiny team that does not even call what they're creating a metaverse platform. (But more on that later.)

By my estimate, based on user concurrency and other variables and sources, VRChat has over 5 million monthly active users, occasionally climbing toward 10 million around the holiday season, when there's an influx of new VR headset owners.

While VRChat has received far less media attention than Meta, it trounced the Internet giant on its own territory. In 2022, Meta could only count some 200,000–300,000 monthly active users in its metaverse platform, Horizon Worlds.

But the true kicker is this: Owners of Meta's Quest 2 headsets *overwhelmingly* prefer playing in VRChat over Meta's own virtual world.

This preference became so pronounced, it actually helped nudge Meta into raising the price of that headset. Senior adviser John Carmack said as much at a 2022 Meta conference: "[S]ome of the most popular apps on Quest are free apps, VRChat and Rec Room, that we get no revenue from at all . . . sitting there at the top of our ranking list in many cases."

In other words, Quest 2 owners were not buying enough premium content from Meta but instead using their headsets for free-to-play metaverse platforms that *directly compete* with its own virtual world.

When Philip Rosedale speaks to me about VRChat, he ranks it as parallel to Second Life in terms of ambition, achieving an experiential leap that complements his career goal of deeply connecting people across the Internet.

"VRChat has a lot of very, very powerful properties," as he puts it. "Most importantly—most importantly—you can use your hands when you talk to somebody, and you can see your [avatar] body when you look in the mirror with somebody. I think that's just earth-shatteringly good."

Simulating a mirror's reflection in real time is computationally challenging, and it's one of the many marvels VRChat made possible in its virtual world. Rosedale is not only talking about the technical breakthrough but how that effect creates a bond with one's avatar and people in the same shared space as you. "That idea of standing and looking at a mirror when you're next to somebody else, that's a really interesting modality for experience."

None of this success, however, was preordained. For the first couple years of its existence, VRChat seemed nothing like the best new metaverse platform on the Internet, but rather, an also-ran VR social app fated for obscurity and abuse by the worst Internet trolls.

This is the story of how the best contender in recent years for "The Metaverse" crown succeeded in the most unlikely way.

Knuckling Under

Cofounded by game industry veterans Graham Gaylor and Jesse Joudrey, VRChat is not officially called a metaverse platform. (At least not yet.) But it very much emerged from that well of inspiration.

"I backed the Oculus Kickstarter in 2012 with many of the same motivations as others," as cofounder Graham explains. "I'd read *Snow Crash*, *Ready Player One*, and all the typical VR enthusiast books and was excited to jump into VR for the first time."

Back then, Graham spent many of his hours chatting about VR and related topics on Reddit.

"One day I had this revelation: Why are we doing this on Reddit when we could be doing it in VR? I quickly built a prototype, posted the download link on Reddit, and we immediately had a small community spring up."

That was in 2014. In its first few years, that small community remained as such. In September 2017, VRChat was attracting a maximum of 105 users from Steam over a 24-hour period, and the all-time concurrency high for the year was 115 people total.

"[VRChat] has a steep hill to climb," I snarkily blogged at the time. And quickly consumed those words.

Three months later, VRChat *catapulted*.

As the platform approached New Year's Eve in 2018, a number of popular YouTubers discovered it, learned its creation tools well enough to make rudimentary content, and began streaming video from VRChat itself, broadcasting their smartass antics to hundreds of thousands.

What followed next conveys many lessons in the launching of metaverse platforms, some of which are still being learned, including:

- Metaverse communities will instantly convert pop culture fandom—from TV, movies, video games, and beyond—into content.

- Video streamers, especially on Twitch and YouTube, exert enormous power to turn viewers into players. For better and worse.

A slew of avatars made to resemble "Ugandan Knuckles," an Internet hell spawn meme with more than a little racist connotation, invaded VRChat, followed by a wave of viral videos.

A crush of new users followed, and as the world entered 2018, VRChat was peaking at *20,000* concurrent users.

At the time, I expected this to be a passing blip of interest, as coteries of Internet trolls, finally bored, went off to search for other easy targets. After all, that very thing had happened to Second Life through its phase of peak media attention, with trolls from the 4Chan message board and other acrid wings of the Internet regularly exploding the grid with self-replicating Mario confetti, giant dancing dildoes, and suchlike.

But then a strange thing happened:

VRChat usage kept growing. And evolving.

"Shock value memes like the Ugandan Knuckles thing are only interesting for so long, but stuff like building a social community or a social circle, those are the things that make people stay," as one veteran VRChat resident put it to me at the time.

"Really, though, we didn't see that large of a jump in trolls during that incident," VRChat's founders tell me now. "Most of the people coming in were amused and were looking to see what was going on; they weren't really trying to troll or disrupt things . . . at least not in a malicious way."

In any case, Graham and Jesse want to assure me that the Ugandan Knuckles viral moment was *not* the chief cause of VRChat's user growth.

"A lot of people tend to think that specific moment was a stroke of luck for us—when in reality, fostering a community that could create anything (and spread it like wildfire) was very much part of the plan," as they put it to me. "Obviously, we couldn't have known that specific meme would've taken off like it did, but that's okay—that's part of the magic. We want to let people create and share the content that works for them.

"VRChat is all about UGC—that's what makes it such a different platform. Everything is created by the users, and we try our best to give them as much freedom as possible. That was the case before that particular meme, and it's certainly the case after."

As VRChat's growth continued, another surprising trend emerged.

In 2019, the company reported that 30 percent of its daily users wore an HMD.

By 2022, however, the founders tell me that ratio had reversed, with *70 percent* of active users wearing HMDs.

Graham and Jesse attribute that to Meta's debut of Quest 2 headsets in the interim. "They offered users a (relatively) affordable way to get into VR. While we were (and are) still experiencing PC-based growth, that of course has lots of limitations."

VRChat, in other words, has effectively become one of the few killer apps of consumer VR, with daily usage outstripping hit VR games like *SuperHot* and *Beat Saber*. (Ironically, Meta bought the developer of the latter game for $2 billion.)

Core to this success was a feature that VRChat's creators implemented around the time when Knuckle-flavored trolls were running roughshod in the community.

Game of Trust

As part of its user safety tools, VRChat founders Graham Gaylor and Jesse Joudrey and their team created the Trust System, with a series of ranks in ascending order of karmic credibility:

- Visitor
- User
- Known User
- Trusted User

Each rank is instantly identifiable by the color of the avatar's name tag floating above their head, with the highest rank of transcendence, Trusted User, emblazoned in royal purple.

"The Trust System was meant to solve a problem that we were having early on during our time on Steam," Graham and Jesse explain to me. "In short, people were uploading stuff, often before they really understood how to develop or create content for VRChat. This led to disruptive avatars, broken worlds, and unhappy users.

"That's always the biggest challenge with UGC. You want to give people complete creative freedom, but obviously, at a certain point you need to tweak things for the sake of quality, safety, and stability."

The Trust System also gave new users a kind of game mechanic that encouraged them to return many times to the virtual world—and in doing so, appreciate the people and platform within it.

Where most game systems mainly reward repeated (if not mechanical) activity, the implicit challenge of VRChat's Trust System "game" is to prove oneself to be a consistently positive person and a valuable member of the community.

"Letting people spend some time hanging around VRChat (and learning all the unspoken social rules that are present here) lets them understand the platform better," the founders explain, "which means that they could be thinking more of the community when uploading content."

The system also confers a sense of status to established VRChat community members that first-time visitors can quickly notice.

"[New users] would look out for people that had more experience that relates to User and above, because it was a good sign that you knew the social customs and VRChat," as Strasz puts it.

The Trust System was an important function for VRChat gaining escape velocity in terms of organic growth. Now that it has, the system has become a kind of leveling mechanism for new players. Where traditional MMOs might have newbies level up by killing various numbers of rodents and such, VRChat rewards new users for spending time exploring the virtual world, expressing themselves, and connecting with others.

"People come in and [say], 'Okay, I want to make a world, I want to make an avatar,' and then they see, 'Oh, I have to be this user [level]'," Strasz explains. "So then they socialize, they bounce around a little bit and make friends. That does have a good benefit because it means . . . they're going to be interacting with people that also do those things."

By making trust an explicit goal, VRChat quickly became a social space for newly minted owners of virtual reality headsets. VR enthusiasts who initially bought a headset to play games now devote most of their time in VRChat to being with other people.

Strasz credits this trend to a yearning for a "third place"—sociologist Ray Oldenburg's term for spaces that are not home and not work, such as a local park or pub, where people connect for fun, enjoyment, and creativity.

"It's been going away, especially in the United States. There's not a lot of places people can go and hang out, meet people, meet friends, and a lot of places that, post-college, you can go to and be like, 'I'm going to meet people and feel like I'm hanging out with them rather than it just being like a Discord call' or something like that. And I think that's what makes VRChat so sticky."

Unlike the neighborhood sports bar, however, what emerged (and continues to emerge) from VRChat is a third place that could exist only in the digital world. Miraculously, wackily so.

Communities Create Community

One day, a 20-something Persian-Canadian videographer from Toronto was wandering the world of VRChat when he stumbled upon a sexy anime girl who turned out to be a drunk Finnish man engaged in an existential argument with a small purple dinosaur.

"We as a species," the Finn slurred, "we have frickin' invented this shit. . . ."

"But I'm not human," the dinosaur demurred.

"That's OK," the anime girl replied, poking her green light-saber at the baby T-Rex for emphasis. "You're still a mind."

The young Canuck hit Record and uploaded this Camus-but-blotto convo to YouTube. It subsequently changed his life.

Hilarious, surreal, but also somehow poignant, it rapidly went viral.

"That's when it really clicked in to me how crazy talking to someone from across the planet in VRChat actually was," the Canadian says now. As a videographer, he had shot Toronto street protests and guerilla interviews with activists.

"I didn't expect to be doing VR interviews," he tells me. "However, as it grew I realized it had potential, and I wanted to take it more seriously."

And so began the career of "Syrmor," who effectively became VRChat's first embedded reporter.

Up until then, most VRChat videos were mainly rude memes and coarse trolling. Syrmor's videos, by contrast, are whimsical and moving.

In VRChat, Syrmor interviewed a bullied kid with ADHD and social anxiety who explained, while wearing a Kermit avatar, how being in the virtual world helped him express who he really is. Syrmor riffed with a man dying of ALS confined to a wheel-chair in real life, who visited VRChat with the help of his attendants, and chatted with Syrmor about taking magic mushrooms at pagan festivals while riding a sports car as a mushroom-shaped avatar in VRChat. Syrmor quizzed a chatty penguin who unburdened himself, speaking about his offline life as a military contractor who witnessed the gory aftermath of an airstrike he helped conduct. "And the first time I saw that was the first day of the job," he told Syrmor, tiny flippers flapping for emphasis, "and that was a 'holy fuck' moment. Like what the fuck am I doing?"

Syrmor met people of all ages, from around the world, with tragic and horrible and occasionally sweet secrets to share. And just as I experienced in my own embedded journalist years in Second Life, Syrmor kept coming across an endless parade of people eager to tell their real stories through the safety and distance of their avatars.

After his early interviews with combat veterans in VRChat, other retired military personnel began contacting Syrmor, wanting to unburden themselves as well.

"I just started getting a ton of emails from veterans who wanted to talk," he tells me in VRChat one day, as we wander a surreal re-creation of a shopping mall from the '80s. "I feel more and more people are seeing VR as a legit way to discuss what's on their chest, or to feel like they're getting their story out there."

Syrmor's experiences with vets here match mine in Second Life—as I touched on in Chapter 2—strongly suggesting that metaverse platforms continue to create possibilities of catharsis

FIGURE 7.1 Syrmor greets an alien in vrchat

for lonely or suffering people unable to express the truest sense of themselves in their offline lives.

A squat black and white cartoon cat in VRChat, Syrmor chortles when I tell him his YouTube channel devoted to VRChat interviews now has more subscribers than the YouTube channel of *People* magazine, and simply says, "Nice."

It is also true: With well over 1 million followers, Syrmor's YouTube channel has more viewers than many legacy media brands.

He's not alone. As with any other successful metaverse platform, there are hundreds if not thousands of YouTube and Twitch channels devoted to VRChat. A dozen or more have viewerships approaching Syrmor's reach, most devoted to random virtual adventures or technical tutorials, some of them just as thoughtful. It's where I first met Chris "Strasz" Hornyak, who got his start creating long-form videos attempting to express the eldritch uniqueness of VRChat, sometimes citing Foucault along the way. When a virtual world community becomes active and deep enough that people in it start citing postmodern philosophers, it's probably long past time to take it seriously.

In a 2021 survey I conducted jointly with Syrmor and his massive user base of VRChat fans, 59 percent of VRChat users were 20 years or older, with 14 percent stating their age as 31 or older; two out of three were male, but (very notably) the remaining gender split was almost exactly equal between females (17 percent) and those who selected "trans/nonbinary/other" (17.5 percent).

Asked what they most love about VRChat, respondents overwhelmingly selected "Community."

A Community Endlessly Creating

Any extended visit I've made into VRChat feels like I'm diving into a sea of stories, endlessly flowing together, all full of longing for human connection.

One day I wandered into a bucolic, forest-shrouded dog park, watching a bizarre menagerie of avatars play fetch with an assortment of adorable, AI-powered virtual canines. The dogs were actually created as a project funded by Dr. Brenda Freshman, a professor at CalState Long Beach, with an aim of studying how VR experiences like this might benefit isolated senior citizens. But since the park was open to the general VRChat public, many visitors began trickling in, often there as a way of recovering from the grief of losing a pet in real life.

Her colleague on the project casually mentioned a phenomenon he noticed that seemed just as striking: Many VRChat users were logging in mainly so they could be in the virtual world with others while they slept in real life.

I boggled at the idea that people around the world, most of them strapped into VR headgear, would actually crawl into bed so they could sleep alongside other people scattered around the globe. But searching through VRChat's world list, I found dozens of places where "sleep" was mentioned in their description; randomly teleporting into one, I found myself in what seemed like a cozy home in a Japanese fishing village at night beneath a gentle rain. And sure enough, all around me, I could hear avatars peacefully snoring through their microphones.

Another day I met "Yumi," a young guy living somewhere in Germany who felt too out of shape and shy to hit his local nightclubs—but then discovered he could dance in VRChat. His surprisingly agile moves were tracked by his full VR body rig, then replicated on his avatar (an adorable anime girl in pigtails), causing nearby VRChat users to gather and cheer, turning him into a resident celebrity and social media star.

"I would have never danced this much in my life EVER if I didn't decide some months ago to buy VR," he told me. "I feel a lot more confident in myself since then."

As creators grew more confident with the platform's tools—VRChat is deeply integrated with the Unity 3D editor—they began building entire interactive experiences, full-fledged games, even mixed reality projects.

It's how I met with a semi-anonymous inventor in Japan ("Micchy" in VRChat) who was busily creating a serial communication bridge between VRChat and Raspberry Pi, so that he might achieve a modest goal: Control an 8-foot tall *Transformers*-type robot in the real world—*from within VRChat*. (Ng the inventor from *Snow Crash* only drove a van from within the Metaverse.) In ways like this, VRChat's developer community is experimenting with mixed reality projects that connect the virtual world with external technology—the last and most challenging feature to qualify as the full-fledged Metaverse.

I also met "Jar," a steadfastly anonymous programmer who gave up her technical programmer day job to make social games full-time in VRChat. She created and launched a survival co-op game world called *Murder 4*, and within 8 months, it had been visited nearly 8 million times; her two most popular games typically attract 2,000 to 4,000 concurrent players at any given moment. This might not seem like much, but it competes in usage numbers with even the top selling VR games made by professional studios. At peak, for instance, *Murder 4* has more online players than typically enjoy the hit title *Beat Saber* on Steam.

Meta, I should again note, bought the developer of *Beat Saber* for $2 billion. To create content on its own platform, VRChat the company has paid Jar roughly zero dollars.

As Jar's VRChat games became popular, so did she, with a growing fan base intrigued by her mysterious avatar name and distinctive appearance, which resembles a shadow in humanoid form, with white hair and a jeweled mask.

Before the advent of metaverse platforms, it was rare to find game developers who had a close and active relationship with their fans. But like most other VRChat creators, Jar holds court in her own Discord with her most avid supporters, a server with the tongue-in-cheek name The Cult of Jar. ("I like to think the name is slightly satirical because there are some creator-centered communities online that come across as cult-like.")

Jar's VRChat games generated a community of players who play often and support their creator. Nearly 1,500 of them contribute to her Patreon, giving her a solid full-time living.

"I feel so much more liberated," Jar told me once. "Being able to do what I actually enjoy doing during the day is working wonders for my personal well-being. Like a kid in a candy store, I have a huge list of ideas, and I get to choose whichever ones I am most passionate about."

I met "Merlin," a VRChat community member who created UdonSharp, which compiles code written in C#—a very commonly used programming language—into Udon, VRChat's official scripting language. By doing so, he enabled thousands of C# programmers to quickly join and contribute to the VRChat creative community. And he did it all on a voluntary basis to serve other VRChat creators, even while unemployed, living in large part off donations from VRChat users.

Merlin's efforts in turn unleashed successive waves of innovation in VRChat, such as "Udon Tycoon," a user-made game reminiscent of the classic PC game *Roller Coaster Tycoon*, but in VR *and* in a multi-user virtual world, with new building tools built on top that enabled players to create and save their own roller coaster tracks with others. Played by tens of thousands of VRChat players in its first week of launch, it evinced more engineering and design ambition than most corporate-funded VR games.

Cultivating an extremely open development platform capable of attracting such a wide range of applications, however, comes with its own unique problems. And in mid-2022, VRChat's connection to its community was tested as never before.

EAC and the Ironic Challenge of Metaverse Community Management

The crisis erupted in the summer of 2022 with the introduction of Easy Anti Cheat (or EAC), a program that blocks modified versions of VRChat. As the official announcement explained:

> Every month, thousands of users have their accounts stolen, often due to running a modified client that is silently logging their keystrokes as well as other information. These users—often without even realizing it!—run the risk of losing their account, or having their computers become part of a larger botnet.

User rage immediately spiked. A portion of their anger was understandable, because some mods blocked by EAC included accessibility features, such as text captions for deaf users and contrast for colorblind users.

But the collective protest that followed threatened the health of VRChat itself, with many thousands of vengeful users bombarding its listing on Steam with bad reviews. VRChat's aggregate review score on Steam dropped in days from Very Positive to Overwhelmingly Negative.

"The EAC situation was a tough one," founders Graham Gaylor and Jesse Joudrey acknowledge to me. "We knew that EAC was always going to be a hard sell, to say the least. EAC mostly addresses something that isn't entirely visible to all users. This led many people to believe that we were doing it for some nefarious purpose. Of course, we weren't! Our Trust & Safety and Security teams were pushing for it knowing the burden mods were having on our team and users."

This is not uncommon for metaverse platforms: The vast majority of users, being positive members of the community, see little of the platform's dark side, and so when a restrictive technical change is made, imagine the worst. These platforms' success depends in great part on community management teams fostering positivity while also squelching the worst bad actors and most offensive content. But because that content isn't seen by most users, the community can respond to an imposition like EAC with paranoia and outrage.

"The sheer number of people losing their accounts due to mod use was staggering," as the founders put it to me. "Not to mention the number of harassment reports we received explicitly due to people being attacked by malicious mod users."

They still had to confront the other conflict this unleashed: anger that genuinely valuable mods—for instance, to help users with visual impairments—were also being banned.

"We knew, though, that not all mod users were malicious—many were just there to add in quality-of-life fixes or functionality that we'd yet to implement in VRChat. It was one of those things that had to be done, but we knew that no matter when we did it, it'd be a rough time."

As the community protest raged, the founders reviewed the feedback and started prioritizing the legitimate user-mods that would be lost due to EAC:

"We knew that we'd lose some trust with the community, and we wanted to prove to them that we were still the same company and that we still wanted to make VRChat the best platform possible for our users. We prioritized feedback focused on accessibility, and then organized teams to blow through as many tasks as possible.

"We got lucky in that some of the most requested features were stuff we already had prototyped—we just weren't ready to release them yet. But with the pressure, we polished them up and sent them out, essentially in these live beta releases that let people try the new features without being locked to a beta server."

In a month or so, the VRChat team raced to put out over 40 new features. The community response to EAC was so jarring, VRChat's founders even enhanced their system of interacting with the community:

"[We] revamped our communications process completely," as they put it. "We started doing weekly developer updates, as well as implementing video developer updates. We don't ever want the community to get surprised by something like that again, and so we're trying to loop them into the process as much as possible."

This approach has proven to be successful in other platforms. While it's probably impossible to prevent all mistrust and paranoia among community members, it's important to engage deeply with the most dedicated users. That way, they can become advocates to the rest of the community.

While the introduction of EAC did cause a rift with the user base, I noticed an entertaining irony at the time: The "protest" by some VRChat users over the company's ban on modified clients had all the indications of a vociferous but small subgroup, rather than a broad community uprising. Indeed, VRChat's user concurrency levels showed a substantial *increase* of users after the protest started.

This, by the way, is another sure sign of a successful metaverse platform: community members so passionate that they'll launch a coordinated protest against the company—but never log off from the actual platform.

VRChat Swallows the Internet

At a certain point, irked and alienated by the barrage of virtual genitals that beset much of Second Life, an inventive husky dog named Graywolf Midnight departed that virtual world in search of new digital lands. Specifically, a land more attuned to his VR headset and his furry avatar.

"VR finally let me actually jump into the body of the avatar I had been working on and constantly tweaking for over a decade," as Mr. Midnight explained to me. (We first met him in Chapter 3, when he groused about Facebook's policies on real names.) "Which is what Second Life had always been trying to simulate but was never quite convincing enough, since you are just looking at your avatar on a monitor; you aren't actually embodying it."

Embodiment is crucial to "furries," the Internet-driven subculture devoted to roleplaying as humanoid cartoon animals, the kind you tend to encounter at a theme park. Many furries describe themselves as feeling uncomfortable in their own real-life body and prefer imagining themselves as these fanciful creatures.

All of this may seem marvelously odd and even worthy of ridicule, but seeing that many if not most furries tend to be Internet savvy and work in tech, I often say this: Do not mock furries, for a furry is almost certainly keeping your company's servers online.

And making your metaverse platforms viable. Furries dominated Second Life's developer community for years, creating quirky and amazing experiences in that virtual world. Midnight was one of them, using the internal scripting system to re-create famous effects from classic video games in Second Life. Graywolf also perfected his avatar (at least as much as the world would allow): a silver-furred Siberian husky who walks upright on hind legs.

Six or seven friends made the exodus with him from Second Life to VRChat, but as a testament to the generational divide in metaverse platforms, Midnight rarely meets other users who are SL veterans. "Most people in VRChat, if you mention Second Life," as he puts it to me, "will have the typical, 'Oh I've heard of that, didn't it die?' response that you've probably heard before."

Graywolf's experience was not isolated but part of a broader immigration trend into VRChat. At launch, VRChat's default avatars were mainly standard attractive humans. Within a few short years, however, furries and anime characters (mostly of the schoolgirl variety) came to represent a near-plurality of the user community.

"I often call VRChat an Internet culture melting pot," Strasz tells me, "made up of a bunch of distinct Internet cultures that usually don't rub shoulders, and they all have been interacting in this space. And that's made something that's really fascinating to stand and watch."

As Strasz recalls it, a Japanese community member figured out how to customize VRChat's standard human avatar into an anime-style character. Tutorial videos of this went viral within the online message boards and Discord servers of the far-flung anime community. Many of them piled into VRChat. "I think for the furry community, it was the same sort of deal. As soon as a couple of furries popped up, and, you know, everybody else did."

A longtime community member before becoming a VRChat employee, Strasz tells me he's surprised to see how this shift of the population has been welcomed by the startup.

"The thing that always amazed me is that the company does not really try to put its finger on the scale when it comes to the community," as he puts it. "I think a lot of virtual worlds make this mistake of trying to say, 'We want this demographic or we want that demographic.' It doesn't play out that way. And for a lot of companies, they see it as a failure."

Second Life is a notable example here. The early Linden Lab team was quite welcoming and impressed by the creativity of the virtual world's furry community. Indeed, when a JIRA proposal was posted to send CTO Cory Ondrejka to speak at Furcon, the annual furry convention in San Jose, every single staffer voted on it. As the original Linden Lab team faded away, however, newer staff evinced growing discomfort at so much aggressive tail wagging. (Especially as widely shared screenshots of furry sex in Second Life began to taint the brand.)

By contrast, says Strasz: "VRChat goes with the flow, and it's very much like, 'Oh, we have these people, cool. Alright, what do they want? What can make them happy?'"

The Lure of the Market and the Future of VRChat

For all of VRChat's creative energy and explosive user growth, one notable feature remains conspicuously missing: user monetization of their own content through a virtual economy. At the start of 2023, none yet officially exists.

In its absence, an *informal* economy has rapidly grown. I estimate well over 1,000 VRChat content creators earning revenue from the content they created; some from custom-made avatars sold on sites like Gumroad (sort of an Etsy for digital content), or like Jar, from creative donation sites like Patreon.

Even more financially successful are creators like Syrmor who shoot videos in VRChat, uploading them to Twitch and YouTube; VRChat-focused channels that boast 500,000+ subscribers are easily able to earn a very good full-time living, in the six figures or more, from Google ads and direct sponsorships.

In early 2021, VRChat the company announced the ability to sell user-generated content in-world as coming soon. As of publication, however, VRChat had yet to fully follow through on that promise—despite the growth of VRChat's creator economy.

"VRChat has not rolled out its long-promised user-to-user economy," I pointed out to the founders recently, "even as many VRChat creators monetize their work via Patreon, Gumroad, etc.

"So why the delay?"

"In short: getting it right," Graham Gaylor and Jesse Joudrey tell me. "We really want to have a creator economy—it's absolutely one of our biggest priorities. Helping find a way for users to show creators how much they love what they're building is absolutely crucial for us."

Their caution is well placed. In Second Life, the arrival of an economy where L$ could be exchanged for US$ drove enormous outside interest, but it also accelerated the shift into hyper-consumerism. Where once stood collaborative art projects across the virtual world, shopping centers and weekend-long sales events quickly came to dominate.

VRChat's founders seem fully aware of that dynamic:

"[We're] very cognizant of the impact an economy could have on the community. Creators would obviously be impacted pretty heavily, but so would regular users. In many ways, introducing an economy can be incredibly destabilizing. Suddenly, creators have obligations and considerations they didn't previously have. Socially, users might feel compelled to behave entirely differently due to where they've spent their money."

When I last talked with them on this topic, VRChat's founders seemed to still be thinking through the implications of unleashing an official economy on its community:

"[There's] not just one way to introduce an economy into a social platform," as they put it to me. "Almost every platform does it differently, and there's a reason for that. What can you buy? How do transactions work? There are almost endless variables we have to consider.

"When we roll out a creator economy, we want to make sure that it's done right, and that our community is happy with it. The last thing that we'd want to do is implement a system that they feel lukewarm about—or worse, ruins what makes VRChat so special."

Therein lies the secret to VRChat's success to strong user growth and a very dynamic and diverse creative community:

"We've built VRChat with them. A large chunk of our team is made up of VRChat users. Many people—most, I'm sure!—were active, engaged users way before they were hired."

VRChat user "Merlin," for instance, who created the much-used C# scripting compiler I mentioned previously, was eventually hired by the company to do contract work, and then brought on as a full-time developer. Up until then, he was unemployed, living in large part off the Patreon donations of the VRChat community who supported his work on the scripting compiler.

"Overall it doesn't feel very different in my case," Merlin told me about corporate life at VRChat Inc. "I knew a number of the people I am now working with from being friends with them in VRChat."

"It's not just a product for us," as Graham and Jesse tell me. "It's a home. It's a refuge. We're not just building an app; we're building the app that we all hang out in after work or on the weekends."

VRChat's most pressing scaling challenge may be another one that eerily parallels Second Life: The very name implies it's for a relatively niche category—in this case, of people who want to, well, chat in VR. That's an immediate growth limiter, even beyond the limiting factor of VR itself. (As I've frequently mentioned, the fact remains that virtual reality tends to make many, or most, females nauseous.)

I expect to see expansion of VRChat to other, non-VR platforms starting in 2023, such as consoles and mobile. But doing so may also segregate the community by device ownership—many VRChat worlds are optimized for some devices but not for all of them. As I write this, however, the company is introducing a Groups feature that may enable new communities to arise around shared interests, and may help keep them connected across technical barriers.

So far, as you might have noticed, all this happens while VRChat the company makes little or no mention about being a "metaverse." That's by conscious decision:

"We don't really find metaverse to be a dirty word—and we aren't afraid to say that VRChat is, in a way, a metaverse," the founders explain to me.

"At the same time, though, we think that 'metaverse' also doesn't entirely capture exactly what VRChat is and what makes it special. This is especially true with how popular the phrase got during late 2021 into 2022. A lot of things were describing themselves as 'the metaverse,' and it started to feel a little less precise. In other words, the term felt diluted by then.

"In short, while VRChat could be described as the Metaverse," as Graham Gaylor and Jesse Joudrey put it, "it's probably better described as simply VRChat."

Getting Started

Content creators interested in establishing a brand in VRChat might first want to gain proficiency with Unity, and then with VRChat's SDK. Star creator Jar goes into some more specifics:

"If you download the VRChat Creator Companion, you can use the Client Simulator feature, which lets you play your worlds in Unity easily without having to upload to VRChat. If you are working on a basic game, this is really useful. If you are making a slightly more complicated game, there is another tool in the VRChat SDK that lets you run multiple VRChat windows on one computer. I use this all the time to playtest my games . . . with clones of myself. It's faster than getting your friends to come join the world and help you play."

But even more key than any particular technical tip, the true starting point is becoming part of VRChat's culture and community:

"For someone that wants to create content, there's an old Internet saying: 'Lurk more,'" as Strasz says. "And I think that's really part of the key. I find that a lot of people from outside of VRChat don't normally understand the culture, and they get it wrong.

"If you're an individual, get in and just spend some time [there]. For companies, have someone on your team just literally spend an hour or two every day looking around [in VRChat], interacting with people and poking around, finding communities and talking."

Star VRChat YouTuber Syrmor, standing beside me in the virtual world's '80s mall, peering up through his roly-poly cat avatar, offers similar advice, albeit more snarky:

"You have to be embedded, and spend hours in public worlds interacting with random people, and see what's going on, and what the [current] meme is. 'Oh this week everyone is into clown women.' Why? No one really knows why but you're on ground zero of this phenomenon."

Promises and Perils

VR, Interoperability, Web3, and Other Metaverse Myths

Twenty years of metaverse advocacy journalism is bound to leave a mark. Or quite a few, actually—bruises from watching many much-cherished ideas around the concept beaten down by the laboratory of life. Some of these myths somehow still persist, even as shiny new hobby horses arrive, both leading entire companies, organizations, and people down rough, unreliable paths.

Some well-trodden metaverse myths worthy of debunking (or at least roughing up a touch) include:

Myth: VR is essential to the Metaverse

As I note in Chapter 1, Neal Stephenson himself walked back from this notion almost immediately after *Snow Crash* was published. At any rate, the black and white display terminals that poorer denizens use in the novel hardly resemble VR as we understand it now.

It's still less the case in the actual consumer market. As of this writing in early 2023, the install base of the top-selling HMD, Meta's Quest 2, stands at an estimated 18 million. That's a decided niche when the Metaverse's addressable market must be targeted to all the world's Internet users—over 6 billion people.

VR headsets first enjoyed a flush of mainstream coverage in the early '90s. Since then, every factor that supposedly limited their mainstream appeal has been addressed. We were told virtual reality sales would strongly grow once they were affordable— but although they are now less costly than video game consoles, sales are still anemic. We were told mainstream acceptance would happen once there was enough content and HMDs were more lightweight—but even as hundreds of VR software titles are added to the market every year, and the headsets themselves become much lighter with every model, sales remain steadfastly slow.

Beyond the dearth of sales lies an even greater unaddressed problem: evidence that VR is not considered enjoyable by roughly half the population.

As I cover in Chapter 3, my colleague danah boyd (now a researcher at Microsoft) published a landmark study suggesting that women and girls tend to process 3D graphics in a way that often causes them nausea. A subsequent study published in 2017 by Experimental Brain Research—trenchantly entitled "The virtual reality head-mounted display Oculus Rift induces motion sickness and is sexist in its effects"—found similar results. (And this is even setting aside the simulator sickness a majority of people report from simply interacting with 3D graphics on a *flat screen*.)

XR expert Avi Bar-Zeev, a developer at Apple, shares danah's core concerns around VR, pointing to general physical differences—beginning with women's IPD, which stands for interpupillary distance.

"Literally the distance between your eyes," as Avi explains. "The IPDs of women on average are smaller than men's. So if the IPD [in the HMD] is wrong, that is enough to cause discomfort by itself."

A Metaverse that is unwelcoming to women is not a Metaverse worth fighting for.

At the same time, while VR is not essential to the Metaverse, it can still be *important* to it. We see this most vividly in VRChat and Rec Room, where those who own a VR rig tend to gain social cachet because their body-tracking equipment allows them to be far more expressive through their avatars—enabling, for instance, live dancing or even juggling through their avatar, with their real-world body movements mapped onto their avatar.

Cory Ondrejka, who spearheaded Meta's acquisition of Oculus' VR technology (see Chapter 3), succinctly put it to me this way:

"I think metaverses, virtual worlds, they don't need VR. Virtual reality is just a different interface into them. But when you're in a situation where VR is comfortable and is what you want to be using, wow, you can create amazing experiences."

This points to VR's likely future in the Metaverse: a totem for some of the most creative and dedicated members of the virtual community.

Which takes us to a related myth:

Myth: The Metaverse must incorporate augmented reality

Augmented reality (AR or sometimes XR for "extended reality") is also often proposed as an inevitable companion to the Metaverse. Why only offer people a virtual world, the argument runs, when we have the technology to add a layer of data over the real world that's viewable by an AR headset or a smartphone?

Attempts to incorporate AR into a virtual world, however, have met a reception that's at best questionable. As I write this in early 2023, Niantic, creator of the wildly successful AR mobile game *Pokémon GO*, is pressing forward with plans to launch a "Real-World Metaverse."

One small challenge to this: no proof anyone actually wants it. *Pokémon GO* remains the only massively successful augmented reality game on the market, both in general and for Niantic in particular. (The company's AR-driven follow-up, *Harry Potter: Wizards Unite*, despite mass market brand recognition, fell far short in terms of active users.)

Worse, none of the visions painted for AR in the Metaverse address the unresolved social pushback that XR owners get in public, as they ignore people around them to check the data stream on their headset screen—or worse, point a live camera at them without prior consent.

Snow Crash, I'm obligated to note, does not depict AR or XR as part of the Metaverse, even though the hero's "gargoyles" headset is revealed to have AR capabilities once the Metaverse is switched off. He even uses this function to navigate a dark passageway in real life.

Decades before Google's "Glasshole" scandal in 2014, when the search giant's first foray into AR headsets was rejected as creepy even in technophile San Francisco, Neal Stephenson wrote this about wearing an HMD in public:

"[I]t's not pretty. In fact, it's so ugly that it probably explains why gargoyles are, in general, so socially retarded."

Myth: Web3 is part of the Metaverse!
(Or vice versa.)

This freshly painted myth has persisted since roughly 2021, when hype over the cryptocurrency, blockchain, and NFT speculation bubble reached an apex. It somehow persists even after (a helpful November 2022 CNBC report informs me) investors lost *$2 trillion* on crypto ventures and assets in that year alone.

More key, web3 does not provably add any substantial value to a concept that's existed for over three decades, and has hundreds of millions of users to show for it. As explained in Chapter 6, several web3-centric metaverse platforms have failed, despite heavy publicity and interest by major brands, to gain substantial user traction.

Further, web3 solutions cause new problems for a metaverse platform without adding any value. Richard Bartle, the game industry's most respected expert on virtual worlds, recently wrote an essay on my blog where he recounted his futile attempts to explain this to web3 advocates.

For instance, responding to the common idea that virtual items can easily be stored as NFTs on the blockchain:

> If I sell you my NFT sword in-game, there has to be a blockchain check to make sure I haven't already sold it to someone else out-of-game. The longer the blockchain, the more time it takes—it could be seconds; worse, you can't lock the blockchain so that the sword can't be sold in the window between the game's verification that you own the sword and its transference in-game to another player.

> This objection was brushed aside by saying that non-blockchain databases can handle that.

> Well yes, they can, easily so—so why the need for a blockchain?

Web3 features *can* be implemented with metaverse platforms, and we see interesting potential (and so far, *only* potential) in some limited cases, such as Upland and Neal Stephenson's Lamina1. But as of this writing, web3 gains far more by trying to associate itself with the Metaverse than vice versa.

Myth: Photorealistic human avatars and world graphics are the Metaverse's end goal

There is actually no proven relationship whatsoever between the popularity of a metaverse platform and photorealistic graphics. Despite this, a wealth of metaverse startups and platforms frequently announce new plans to roll out ever more realistic environmental graphics, and ever more eerily human-like avatars.

The very most popular platforms, Minecraft and Roblox, are intentionally low-fi, mainly immersive through their physics and responsiveness. Their whimsical avatars are similarly abstract.

This likely relates to their core user base: people in their teens and preteens, who are often still uncomfortable and unsure about their own real-life identity and appearance. This seems even more acute for teen girls and young women, still negotiating the social expectations and judgments around their real-life presentation; presenting them with a lifelike, photorealistic avatar to customize is effectively asking them to take on even more social expectations and judgments.

We also have something of an opposite proof point.

At launch, Second Life avatars were human by default but not ultra-realistic. The internal prim creation tools encouraged the construction of avatar attachments (robot helmets, furry tails, and so on), which led to a wide variety of avatar types and creative environments to explore.

The arrival of mesh in Second Life, in 2010—high-resolution 3D files created in offline software and then uploaded into the virtual world—greatly changed this dynamic.

Nick Yee has already spoken in Chapter 9 about the community moderation issues that realistic human avatars provoke: Preference them in your virtual world, and all the hidden and not so hidden prejudices of our offline world come along with them.

Thanks to mesh and other graphics enhancements, Second Life avatars and environments now look as detailed and as vivid as those from top AAA games (for those lucky enough to own a powerful PC). However, this rise in visual quality has contributed little to actual user growth.

But by enabling ultrarealistic avatars, especially through mesh-based body attachments, mesh quickly altered the virtual world's culture. Within years, the virtual world's economy came to be dominated by ultrarealistic avatars; the overall creative culture changed, accompanied by the rise of environments most suited to them—glamorous beachside homes and nightclubs, beautiful locales that resembled real-life tourist destinations and locations for the latest reality TV show.

As Second Life's economy snowballed around quality mesh items, so did its culture. While avatar fashion and virtual housekeeping were always a crucial part of the virtual world, the creative tools also attracted a cohort of creators and tinkerers more interested in using the platform as a multi-user game development space and all-purpose sandbox space.

By and large, however, tinkerers of this type faded in prominence within the larger community, overwhelmed as it was by new fashion releases and shopping extravaganzas. (The tinkerer community still exists but is less prominent in the community.)

My takeaway: Putting an emphasis on graphics quality, as opposed to physics and interactivity, will tend to shape a virtual world's creative culture around aesthetics at the expense of other qualities, while having negligible effect on user growth.

Myth: The Metaverse must interoperate across the Internet

This myth is so pervasive, and so misguided in many ways, it deserves a deeper plunge.

Interoperability continues to be a grail quest for many metaverse evangelists, partly spurred by the flawed assumption that the Internet should *become* the Metaverse. The World Wide Web is interoperable, the argument roughly goes, enabling us to leap from one website to another; so too must the Metaverse be.

In my chat with Neal Stephenson (see Chapter 6), the Web metaphor seems exactly what the Metaverse should *not* be:

"[Immersive experiences] should be linked in a kind of spatial arrangement," as he put it. "It's what is lacking in the World Wide Web—you've got this web of hyperlinks all over the place that jump you from one site to another, and there's not really a kind of spatial organization that ties it all together."

And as I explain in Chapter 1, the Metaverse was never envisioned as the totality of the Internet. At its heart, it is a virtual *world*: dynamic, real time, immersive, with a base consensual reality shared by a community of active users within it. Analogizing this to the Web—flat, relatively static, and asynchronous—misses this essence.

The Web analogy, as I mention in Chapter 2, is among the many factors that caused Second Life to lose its growth momentum; updating its user interface to resemble a 2D medium grafted onto an immersive real time experience only contributed to new user confusion, and an open mutiny by veteran users. You can click from one web page to another; you cannot right-click a mountain or copy/paste the sea.

The Web experience is more or less the same between different web browsers because they stream the same underlying content. The user interface of a virtual world, however, is effectively *part* of that world and cannot be altered substantially from one user (or world) to the next.

While many advocates will strenuously disagree, metaverse interoperability *for the most part* seems like a solution in search of a genuine problem. Or to put it in the form of a question:

"Is your vision of the Metaverse really just Steam with a few less steps?"

Because the interoperable vision, usually described as a network or federation of many virtual worlds that users can teleport to, is really not too different from what consumers already have with Steam (or Xbox Live, or the PlayStation Store, and so on). Experientially, we *already* travel from one virtual world to another on these platforms after several clicks and minutes of loading time. Beware a vision of the Metaverse that offers to replace this with something only slightly better.

Veteran MMO game designer Damion Schubert likens the interoperability vision to an ambitious but naive startup attempting to create virtual cars that somehow work in wildly different online racing games such as *Forza*, *Wipeout*, *Need for Speed*, and *Mario Kart*. Each of these game experiences imbue the virtual cars within them with unique physics, game mechanics, and interactivity that simply does not translate.

"You could 'solve' this, of course, by coming up with a Uniform Car Standard," says Schubert. "That way, all the cars across all games handle stats, decals, spinning wheels, damage, and everything else the same way so every car works everywhere. But these games are chasing very different audiences. All of them would be way worse if they were more similar."

Some colleagues argue (without much evidence) that there's a deep hunger among consumers to bring their main avatar and its possessions across many virtual worlds. But this assumes that we want a permanent identity that always follows us, even to the many places where we'd prefer to be anonymous or different for myriad reasons, including privacy and boredom.

Beyond these challenges, UC Irvine's Tom Boellstorff notes that many (if not most) conceptions of metaverse interoperability very conveniently advantage leading Internet companies that want to track a user's virtual world data and connect it with their behavior on the Web and across the real world through their mobile devices.

"That is about their ideas around surveillance and marketing that assume that everyone wants interoperability, and interoperability can mean lots of different things," as he puts it to me.

What is also forgotten by interoperability advocates is that *it's been tried before.*

At the peak of Second Life's success in 2008, Linden Lab partnered with IBM to develop and showcase early stages of interoperability, enabling users to teleport their avatars from SL to OpenSim, an open source spinoff of Second Life. Intel and other top tech companies and organizations also contributed development resources.

"Interoperability is a key component of the 3D Internet and an important step to enabling individuals and organizations to take advantage of virtual worlds for commerce, collaboration, education, operations, and other business applications," an IBM executive announced in the PR push. "Developing this protocol is a key milestone and has the potential to push virtual worlds into the next stage of their evolution."

Exactly the opposite happened. The real evolution went into the mass market growth of decidedly noninteroperable consumer game platforms like Roblox and the rest. The project driven by IBM—one of the world's most profitable technology companies—floundered and rapidly lost steam, bogged down by governance issues around IP rights and security. Perhaps more pressing, interoperability attracted little interest from everyday virtual world users. (As for OpenSim, it exists to this day, but as a very niche platform mostly supported by a few thousand educators.)

Veteran metaverse developer Adam Frisby blames the project's failure on Second Life. (After a successful stint as a Second Life land baron, Frisby helped spearhead the OpenSim interoperability project.) Because from a developer's perspective, as he puts it, "The Second Life ecosystem is good for running SL but not for running anything else . . . at the lowest level it has the Second Life grid baked into it."

"Technically it did work; bugs notwithstanding, we could port data across boundaries," says Andrew Sempere, who at the time was a researcher at IBM. "But if you want to observe the rules of Second Life digital rights management and economy, you can't take your avatar with you. This is *way* more important than many people thought—your identity is you—and if you look like you but are forced to look like some horrible janky box on another platform, especially if you have invested a lot of time into your appearance, you're never going to cross that boundary."

And from a consumer perspective, since OpenSim looked and played like Second Life, the core audience who were attracted to it were people already familiar with Second Life. And since those people expected experiences they were already familiar with from Second Life, a black market for popular avatar enhancements and other items quickly sprang up in OpenSim.

A similar problem exists with interoperability efforts even now. Since there is no unified Metaverse user experience that is broadly appealing to every existing, highly disparate virtual world user on thousands of platforms across the globe, who exactly is going to use it?

One hypothetical approach is, *a la* OpenSim, to create a reverse-engineered version of a popular metaverse platform (assuming the company behind it approved). But an open source version of, say, Roblox or Fortnite would likely appeal only to dedicated players in each platform. It is hard to convey the fierce loyalty metaverse communities have to the virtual world and the culture that emerges from their chosen metaverse platform—they can even be affectionate and proprietary about its *user interface*.

In any case, despite buy-in from many major tech companies, OpenSim was largely abandoned by them. "There was an appetite to do it from certain parties," says Frisby. "But not from the business-minded people."

In fairness, Frisby sees interoperability's value not so much for being able to bring magic swords from one virtual world to another but for how it would standardize the development of future metaverse platforms.

Up to now, every virtual world has had to build every key component of a metaverse platform—the 3D engine, the networking layers, and so on—from scratch.

"Every single [platform] reinvented the wheel for 30 years," as he puts it to me, "building them again and again. Interoperability would solve that problem." The goal he sees is to follow the path of web interoperability, where websites made as far back as the '90s still more or less work.

Adam will get to test his thesis on interoperability firsthand. As I write these words, his startup Sine Wave Entertainment is planning to open source both its client software *and* server architecture. (Second Life, as noted, only open sourced the consumer-facing client, to the great detriment of OpenSim.)

"Enough people are interested in the Metaverse," Adam tells me, explaining his reasoning, "but you have two choices: You can go with Meta or another walled garden—and Meta definitely will be a walled garden—or you put up a platform anyone can work with."

He sees this move akin to the trajectory of WordPress, the open source content management system that began in the early 2000s as an indie operation developed by a small team, but due to its openness and versatility, attracted a growing wave of developers and content creators. Upwards of 70 percent of all websites on the Internet now use WordPress.

I am fairly biased on this point, having known Adam since his OpenSim and Second Life days (all the way back when he was a teenage real estate baron), along with consulting for Sine Wave a few years ago. If interoperability is going to happen, he is among the best candidates to make it happen.

My fear is that the WordPress analogy is misplaced, because (as stated before) a web page is not an immersive virtual world. And a virtual world that is so open-ended as to have no unified branding, narrative, or meta game mechanics will face enormous challenges.

Hopefully we'll have a sense of who was right in the next edition of this book. And in the face of Adam's dream of a universally shared creative space open to the entire world, something he's yearned for these last 25 or so years, I hope my misgivings are proven wrong. But without a unified and growing user community to accompany it, I believe any interoperability project is destined to remain an abstract goal.

Because finally (and most key), interoperability as an end in itself misses the core realization that *people and the communities they create*, not any technology stack, make metaverse platforms meaningful and worthwhile.

Interoperability as generally understood runs counter to a core principle of successful metaverse platforms: Community Creates Value. No matter how expensive or hard-earned, virtual items detached from their original social context tend to quickly lose their luster.

I'd suggest a corollary to that: **Only Community Must Be Interoperable**.

As long as denizens of one metaverse platform are able to export contacts to their friends and colleagues there, most other interoperability questions fall away.

In any case, a level of community interoperability already exists, with little or no oversight by metaverse companies— virtual world friends tend to quickly connect with each other on Discord, and often go on to spend as much time with each other there as in the actual immersive virtual world—or more.

Speaking with me last year, Matthew Ball suggested this could even be a focus of government regulation. Recently Senator Elizabeth Warren and other politicians have called for standardization of device charging ports. "If that's important," as Ball put it to me, "then the portability of core user data, your social graph, is even more important."

Social interoperability also protects users from the worst consequences of everything else on a platform *not* being interoperable —if virtual content becomes too costly, inefficient, or restrictive for the user base, they can simply threaten to take their friends and move to more welcoming platforms. (Relatedly, in Chapter 9, Ball discusses how different metaverse and game companies can leverage this variety of interoperability to protect their user communities from toxic players.)

Myth: The Metaverse is for everyone!

Variations of this assertion abound, especially among my colleagues in the evangelist wing of the industry. I sorely wish it were true. Twenty years of increasingly frustrating experiences around this topic, however, strongly suggest otherwise. With nearly every technical and financial hurdle eliminated in recent years—by this point, even owners of entry-level smartphones can, if they truly want to, access a freemium, mobile-centric metaverse platform—usage is confined to a significant minority of Internet users.

This is why, when I shared my forecast of the Metaverse's addressable market with Forrester Research in 2022, I pegged the immediate audience to one in four of the world's online population. Forrester branded these the "Digital Immersives," who already play multiplayer games, use a VR headset, or use Discord to communicate with friends, or a combination of all three.

That said, recall that 1 in 10 of the globe's Internet users, 500 million+ people, are already active users of a metaverse platform. That suggests quite a lot of room remains for metaverse platforms to grow—certainly to well over 1 billion people. (As to whether they can grow beyond that number, see Chapter 11.)

Underlying any "Metaverse is for everyone!" assertion is the premise that new advances in technology supplant older forms; but in practice, this is not always true. As our screens become more central to our lives, it seems even less the case. Some believe the Metaverse is the successor to the mobile Internet, for instance, and that may be true for some kinds of content and some use cases. But smartphones have not replaced previous devices; PCs continue to be sold at a fairly strong pace and even saw a 10-percent growth spike during the pandemic, according to Gartner Research.

What is more typically the case is this: New technologies *expand* our possibilities and enhance our existing tools—but those tools that still serve a purpose do not go away. Fifty-plus years after its invention, we still send emails.

Metaverse platforms are already following along this path, with users often spending as much time if not more enjoying Metaverse content on social media or messaging platforms like Discord (essentially an enhanced and updated form of Internet Relay Chat, invented in 1988) than in the virtual world itself.

(Recall again Syrmor in VRChat, whose passionate fans engage with him most not in VRChat per se but on his YouTube page.)

At the same time, it's difficult to conceive of a scenario where the Metaverse supplants the entirety of our digital experience. There are far too many technologies that are far more useful to use as they are deployed now than how they might be deployed in the immersive context of the Metaverse. (More on that in Chapter 10.) It's unlikely we'll regularly read our email in the Metaverse.

Consider the Spouse Test, something I've formulated after years of hearing excessive hyperbole by assorted metaverse colleagues and evangelists:

After listening to their grandiose pitch, I'll eventually ask if their spouse/partner/significant other/etc. is also passionate about the Metaverse. Every single time I've asked, the answer has been Not Really. (And in fairness, this also applies to my own awesome wife!)

But a more plausible future is just as inspiring: where selected instances of Metaverse creativity and practical use cases regularly jump the divide to become popular or common across the culture, even among people with no interest in directly engaging with the Metaverse itself.

Myth: There is only one Metaverse

Here I have to depart from most of my colleagues and even perhaps Neal Stephenson himself. There's no substantial evidence of metaverse platforms converging to become the singular Metaverse that Stephenson imagined. There are many good and impressive people and groups such as The Metaverse Standards Forum advocating for that endpoint, planning for the infrastructure to make that possible. But what is still sorely lacking is interest from actual metaverse platform users, creators, and most telling, corporate owners.

Founding Second Life CTO Cory Ondrejka, reflecting on his 20+ years in metaverse-related technologies, shares my skepticism:

"Looking back to the notion that you'd want, you know, a first-person shooter to come climbing through your business meeting is just not sensible. And yes, we also said that would be funny 22 years ago. But then we built it. And three minutes later said, 'Nope, that's not what we want.'"

So Ondrejka finds it surprising to see that so many metaverse pundits in the current era are once again clamoring for a singular, interoperable platform:

"There's no data to suggest that's actually what people want. And even some sort of softer version of those plans, like a singular identity across worlds with the same avatar—there is plenty of evidence that they don't want that and no evidence that they do. Nor do you want art assets that don't match to be forced in different worlds because they're incongruous and don't work."

My own sense is that "The Metaverse," as the technology becomes even more successful, will take on a meaning like "social media" does today, broadly referring to multiple platforms user networks and content strongly overlap but where each still enjoys its own unique identity and functionality. Similar to the way LinkedIn is for business colleagues and Facebook is for staying in touch with older family members, we should expect to see metaverse platforms mostly popular for gaming and hanging out with friends, lightly overlapping with others for business meetings and events.

If this is roughly the state of things to emerge, it should not be taken as a flaw in the Metaverse vision. With over 500 million active users across many metaverse platforms, there are *already* at any given moment twice as many people using them as there are people in New York. (Which, again, is Stephenson's milestone figure for use of the Metaverse in *Snow Crash*.) At some point, a single platform alone will boast this level of activity, while other metaverse platforms will continue to thrive. It's quite possible two or more will reach these heights of usage in the near future.

In other words, the Metaverse is already more popular and pervasive than even Neal Stephenson ever imagined.

Sex, Abuse, and the Eternal Content Moderation Challenge

"The Metaverse is wide open and undefended, like airports in the days before bombs and metal detectors, like elementary schools in the days before maniacs with assault rifles. Anyone can go in and do anything that they want to. There are no cops. You can't defend yourself, you can't chase the bad people. It's going to take a lot of work to change that—a fundamental rebuilding of the whole Metaverse, carried out on a planetwide, corporate level."—*Snow Crash*, 1992

In the context of the novel, the hero muses these thoughts after a deadly computer virus begins spreading through the Metaverse. But so far the most virulent infection in the Metaverse is basically human nature.

And in a virtual world, human nature at its worst can burst out in unexpected ways.

Philip Rosedale often tells the story of how, in Second Life's early days, he and his development team gave the beta users creation tools that were powerful enough to remake the virtual world however they chose. They expected to see it become a strange alien reality—especially since all avatars can fly at will.

They were surprised to discover how it actually evolved. As Hunter Walk told me for *The Making of Second Life*:

> "They immediately started building—homes!" And not even fantastic otherworldly homes, but realistic houses, for the most part, fully appointed McMansions with utilities of no conceivable necessity. ("Why would you build *bathrooms and dining rooms?*")

While a substantial minority of early users did create castles, steampunk cities, and other fantastic realms, Second Life on the whole quickly began to seem like a fever-dream version of California at its most stereotypical. Giant suburbs sprang up everywhere; nightclubs, casinos, and shopping malls were digitized into existence; and all along the virtual world's waterfronts came homes with picture windows and sundecks.

"It quickly became Malibu," as academic and game industry analyst Nick Yee observes. "A very consumer, materialistic-oriented world."

None of this was consciously planned or encouraged by Linden Lab. (Recall again that Second Life itself was inspired by Burning Man, a proudly *noncommercial* communal arts festival.)

How did it happen, anyway?

The core reason is an early decision the company made that is so standard, most virtual world developers don't even think to do otherwise:

Second Life's only default avatar options were realistic humans. They were highly customizable, to the point where someone could, say, turn their avatar into an orc-like monstrosity, but the default setting for each adjustable feature started with a conventionally attractive male or female human.

With that in place, Malibu quickly followed.

"Once users are presented with a believably human template," as Yee explains, "you want chairs and furniture and cars where your bodies can sit and drive around, and you need large virtual closets to put all your virtual clothing in, and people are building these beautiful cantilevered houses by the beach because that's what people do in the real world."

While Linden Lab may have hoped Second Life users would define reality according to their wildest imaginations, the realistic human avatars shaped how much of the world would evolve, and with them came all the social problems typically associated with wealthy beach enclaves in the real world.

"[That's] where the racism and the sexism comes from," as Yee puts it. "Because when the avatars are sufficiently human to make human assessments upon, our inherent human biases come clawing into the digital world. . . . It's almost unavoidable, because once you have bodies that are anywhere near realistic, people feel the need to dress up their bodies, and to look cooler than the next person. And suddenly you have this whole economy based around selling bodies and hair and body parts." (The problem worsened, as I explained in the previous chapter, when Second Life avatars became ultrarealistic.)

To be clear, Second Life is overall an endlessly creative community that for the most part is highly positive and supportive. At the same time, Linden Lab making attractive humans the default was (and is) a conduit for much player-to-player abuse.

I began noticing that as an embedded journalist very early on. Female avatars that were poorly customized often got roundly ridiculed by many in the user community; people who adjusted their avatars to look fat or disproportionate (because in a virtual world, why not?) were jeered at and harassed.

Worse still, avatars that weren't white regularly received racist comments and trolling. In *The Making of Second Life*, I write about a woman, white in real life, who customized her avatar to look like an attractive Black woman—and was instantly hit with racist jibes, even by people she thought were her friends.

In the same way that Nick Yee's early Stanford studies suggest that users unconsciously bring the unwritten rules of eye contact and social distance with them in these virtual worlds, "a lot of racial norms, gender norms, and sexual harassment follows us in," he tells me. "We shouldn't be surprised by it now."

(Many of these insights, by the way, are featured in Yee's seminal 2014 book, *The Proteus Paradox: How Online Games and Virtual Worlds Change Us—And How They Don't.*)

A metaverse platform is inherently a virtual world, but as Yee's book title suggests, any assumption that a virtual world will offer a complete escape from our daily prejudices and cruelties is sorely shortsighted.

In retrospect, Linden Lab could have prevented much of this problem by making nonhuman avatars also (and equally) available to new users by default, helping to nudge them to consider other avenues and cultures of expressiveness beyond conventional humans—and making it clear that human avatars were only one option among many, no one type more of a "right" choice than another.

Instead, the problem persisted and continues to this day. Kavya Pearlman, an award-winning cybersecurity expert, herself experienced this while still at Linden Lab. Because she was a convert to Islam, someone kindly created a traditional headscarf for her Sansar avatar, so she could express her personal faith in the virtual world.

One day as Kavya was attending an event there, someone said out loud, "Oh, is she bringing Sharia law to Sansar?"

"So I then stopped using that avatar," Kavya tells me now. "Because people literally perceived me as this threat that was coming to their culture."

"I think a lot of people have this assumption that when you create a VR world, you're creating a clean slate utopia," as Yee puts it. "My research, and the point of the book, was always no, you carry all this baggage, and you need to be very conscious of that baggage because people just revert back to the behaviors that our biological brains are hardwired to learn."

The other hardwired human behavior, of course, is horny.

At the peak of Second Life's media exuberance, as former Linden Lab PR head Catherine Smith recalls, "I got a call from a German reporter who had—this is quite a story—who had found a young woman who was using her mother's Second Life account to augment her monthly allowance by having cybersex."

Catherine Smith soon faced a barrage of bad PR when stories around Second Life's extreme sexual content emerged. But it was a foreseeable outgrowth:

"If you're gonna give people freedom to do things, how are you going to moderate it? There's so many intricacies with opening up an environment like this, that you've got to just be prepared—whatever you're dealing with in real life, you're probably going to be dealing with in a virtual space as well. I don't think people understand how complicated and how multifaceted it is."

Rampant virtual sex was another inevitability set in motion by Second Life's human avatar default. An online game where the player characters are (for example) squat, spherical robots will also have its share of juvenile players humping and grinding into each other, but because it doesn't appear explicitly sexual, they will soon get bored with that activity.

Failing to deal with this content and behavior immediately can deeply tarnish a metaverse platform's brand, and worse—as Meta learned the hard way in 2022, when female users of its Horizon Worlds were immediately beset by virtual sexual assault.

Second Life learned that around 2006. "It did not help Linden to get branded as a freak show, particularly through the decade wandering the desert," as cofounder Cory Ondrejka puts it now.

I tell these stories to illustrate how a simple design decision early on in a metaverse platform can lead to enormous unforeseen social/content moderation consequences, many of them bad. Go with human avatars by default at start, reap an enormous community management and PR whirlwind.

"The thing that people forget when designing virtual worlds . . . [is] every decision you make about bodies and social interaction is a really important decision," as Nick Yee puts it. "All these variables that you code create spontaneous unpredicted events that have interesting social psychological consequences."

Perhaps more than for any other online platform, community management of a metaverse platform is a vexing challenge, as difficult, nuanced, and constantly demanding as governing a real country. (And recall again that the leading metaverse platforms have populations that are numerically larger than those of most nations!)

Ever-Perennial Metaverse Problems: Sex, Trolling and Harassment, and Underage Users

While no perfect solution exists to deal with all community management issues in the Metaverse, there's much wisdom from the last 30 years to follow, to keep the abuse tamped down to a dull roar. But first let's dive deeper into three key challenges.

Virtual Sex and the Inevitable TTP Problem

It's an unresolved paradox: Metaverse platforms promote themselves as the successors to social media while also prohibiting activity that's essential to human socialization. Which is to say virtual sex—in every possible variety that frisky avatars can pull off together.

So far, most strategies to preempt this problem are comically Victorian: Roblox bans avatars from even holding hands, and Meta's Horizon Worlds restricts its users to avatars that resemble floating hand puppets with no legs, reportedly for technical reasons—but which, by a nice coincidence, also means they come without even the possibility of having genitals.

But freely allowing unrestricted virtual sex, as Second Life learned, is fraught with its own hazards. The company's openly *laissez faire* approach implicitly invited depictions of violent or just plain bizarre sexual fetishes; confronted by video and screenshots of this content in the media, button-up organizations once interested in Second Life as a platform were belatedly sent scurrying.

So the paradox remains: No evangelist can honestly promote the Metaverse as the next great leap in social technology without acknowledging the inevitability of virtual sex, both between consenting adults and—just as key—the inevitability of attempted abuse, where virtual sex is *not* consensual.

This problem has existed for so long, game developers many years ago gave it a cheeky name: TTP.

That's the amount of time it takes players to figure out how to use the content creation tools to create a virtual penis. (Hence, Time To Penis.) It usually happens during the first day of launch.

How to deal with virtual sex even plagues metaverse platforms dedicated to enabling free user creativity. Most people may not be interested in having pixel porn, or even having to see it, but at the same time, some fiercely are.

Linden Lab wrestled with pleasing both sides and focused their solution on defining rules for public and private spaces in the virtual world.

"There's a reason that you have public and private citizens in real-world societies and the rules are fundamentally different for each of them," as Cory Ondrejka explains now. "There are certainly worse starting points than that, I think. Deciding to have a very strict set of rules everywhere in the universe is probably limiting."

This approach also had limited success. Most reporters who depicted Second Life as a wasteland of sex perverts did not base that perspective on actual visits to Second Life; social media and discussion sites like Reddit are effectively the Internet's public space, and photos and videos of Second Life at its raunchiest were everywhere there, even becoming snarky memes. The practice continues to this day, with assorted smartass YouTubers airdropping into the virtual world in search of cheap gibes.

It's easy to chortle mockingly at avatars engaged in pixel sex, but an important point should not be lost: Many people turn to virtual sex for deeper reasons than simple interactive porn: young LGBT people, for instance, who want to safely and anonymously explore their sexual orientation in a virtual world, or individuals severely isolated and alone in real life for any number of reasons, still yearning for intense human connection.

Trolling and Harassment

The essential power of a multiuser virtual world is also its greatest liability: the immersive sense that you are really there with other people, which is usually thrilling and engaging.

Except when some of those people turn out to be cruel provocateurs or worse. Hateful or trolling words on social media can already be scarring to the target; when abusive words are said by someone in voice chat or even expressed with 3D building tools, it's almost as if the troll is invading the victim's personal space, making the stress and anxiety even more heightened.

Oftentimes this even includes physical attacks on avatars, and thus they become even more invasive. In the infamous sexual assault that happened in Meta's Horizon Worlds, for example, a woman's avatar was surrounded by male avatars who virtually groped and thrusted at her.

"It's like you're giving a megaphone to a baby boy," says acclaimed game designer Jenova Chen. "They will test the boundaries. Or they will say something kind of disturbing and anger-inducing to see how much response they get. So that's why to me the Internet by default is not neutral, the Internet by default is kind of toxic."

Female avatars and avatars who appear as racial minorities tend to bear the brunt of the worst harassment in virtual worlds. Gamergate proved this was not simply casual churlishness, but also a concerted, highly political effort to drive women, LGBT+ people, and other vulnerable groups out of online games and other virtual worlds.

"How I personally think about online bullying today is different than how I thought about bullying 20 years ago," as Cory Ondrejka puts it to me. "I have a lower tolerance today. I have more empathy for what it feels like to be on the receiving end of it. And I would build systems from the beginning that enable less random bullying. The public norms I would set at a more restrictive place than where Linden Lab started. Because we've got way more evidence, frankly, of how people are able to channel their hatred into online spaces and be terrible to each other."

Player-to-player abuse can even metastasize into the real world to the point where it becomes a national security issue.

This is not hyperbole. We saw a variation of this in the early days of Second Life, which were the years after 9/11. Back then, Rohan Gunaratna, an expert in Islamist terrorism, informed me that Al Qaeda–affiliated jihadists were experimenting with Second Life as a near-anonymous Internet platform from which to communicate with each other as avatars, potentially using its 3D creation tools to plan future attacks. Criminal or state-sponsored money laundering within metaverse platforms, via its virtual currency, is also an ongoing concern.

So I was not surprised to learn, via the Snowden leaks of 2013, that NSA agents had also gone under virtual cover as Second Life avatars.

All this happened even though Second Life was (and still is) a niche platform of some 600,000 regular users. It's unlikely that bad actors affiliated with various authoritarians have missed the strategic opportunities inherent in far larger platforms, like Roblox and Fortnite—especially when millions of their own citizens are already active users themselves. At minimum we should expect subtle disinformation and discord-sowing campaigns, the kind wrought by Russian intelligence during the 2016 U.S. election, to play out in the virtual world.

Children

As I touch on in Chapter 4, metaverse platforms are still dominated by users who are minors.

When it comes to crafting metaverse platform policies for kids, however, solid reference data is difficult to come by, digital education expert Anya Kamenetz tells me. The companies themselves refuse to share their internal data with researchers, while social academics do not move at the velocity of the Internet—and tend to be biased against kids playing online games/immersive experiences.

"There's a bias in the world of researchers that is hung up on moral panic," as Kamenetz puts it, referring to studies on the media's impact on ADHD and anxiety, for instance, along with the perennial games-and-violence question. "They're always trying to tie into worst-case scenarios."

As I discuss in the Introduction, there is research to suggest that playing in metaverse platforms is overall a positive experience for children. But then again, in some cases it can contribute to antisocial and self-destructive behavior. The lack of definitive data on this topic, even when at least one in two children are active in a metaverse platform, is a smoldering crisis.

"How do we actually safeguard children in these ecosystems where they are going to exist? We need to enable trust," Kavya Pearlman tells me. "There needs to be custom engineering of that experience, so that the impact on the child's brain is not net negative."

We have barely begun to address the behavior algorithms on our social media platforms for *adults*. But metaverse platforms loom above them with similar unaddressed problems, except that here, teens and children still comprise the majority of the total user base.

"The National Institutes of Health should already be doing this kind of research, to study the impact on children's brains so we can enable these technologies," Kavya Pearlman tells me. "But we don't have those answers. Because we didn't allocate the money to study them. We just let Roblox run wild."

Building a Better Moderated Metaverse

If bad behavior is inevitable to human nature, so is a desire to create and enforce rulesets that minimize and curb it.

Protecting Kids

As a design reference for metaverse platform developers, Anya Kamenetz suggests visualizing the ideal playground that parents would feel safe letting their own kids roam free in:

There's a fun variety of places to explore and installations that encourage fun and creativity; there are many other kids to play with. At the same time, the parents also want to be able to see what their kid is doing at a glance; they also want to see the entry and exit points of the playground and be assured that their kid will not leave the area without their knowledge. The parent also wants to know there are responsible adults actively monitoring the playground, and that they have a fair and consistent escalation system for resolving disputes when arguments break out among the kids. Just as key, the playground monitors should have an identification process for *other* adults entering the playground, to ensure they are not bad actors.

While the concept of a soccer mom has long ago become cliché, Kamenetz advocates for a new role: Minecraft Parent. Someone who engages and encourages their kid's metaverse platform activity, even getting involved directly. (It's fairly common for parents to play Roblox and Minecraft with their kids.)

Platform developers could do more to actively incentivize parents to take an active role in their kids' virtual activity—for instance, by offering discounts on parent/child subscriptions. Or what if a parent is given rewards for regularly logging in, such as power-ups and special content they can then pass on to their kid?

In other words, give parents special protective and fostering powers in the virtual world that echo a child's elevated vision of them. Kamenetz broadly agrees with the idea, citing the beloved online education resource Khan Academy, which has a "coach mode" that parents can take on, creating shared pedagogical quests for their kids to fulfill.

XR security expert Kavya Pearlman doesn't believe the core problem can be solved without some government oversight. "That's where regulation starts to come in. We will say, 'Hey, you will not code for engagement because we already know children can get addicted, so we cannot do that for immersive technologies. Otherwise, they'll just stay there.'

"So we need to put our foot down as a regulatory measure, and say that you will not advertise and code for engagement— you will code for well-being.

"You will code for well-being, and prove to the court, prove to the regulators, that you're coding for well-being. And it's possible." Somewhat ironically, Chinese regulators are taking a more hands-on approach to protecting their children's safety, forbidding algorithms in apps that encourage excessive and negative usage.

As head of the XR Safety Initiative (XRSI), Kavya is also drafting self-policing standards for metaverse platforms to adopt. She believes companies will ultimately want to adopt them out of self-interest—and self-preservation.

"We're trying to build that measuring stick and so if they don't do it by themselves, we're going to tell regulators. And then we're gonna ding them on all the things that they're not doing right. And then they will be forced to retrofit all this regulatory stuff that comes after. So this is their opportunity or window to be proactive, to change their business tactics."

Allowing Virtual Sex but Prohibiting It in Public Spaces—Including Outside the Virtual World

VRChat, as I discuss in Chapter 7, has an extremely open and powerful toolkit. Users can (and surely often do) use it to create virtual porn of all varieties. But you will rarely see any of it posted as videos or screenshots on social media.

VRChat's founders Graham Gaylor and Jesse Joudrey decline to say much on that topic except to suggest any porn that does exist is overshadowed by so much other content. "My guess would just be that most people coming to VRChat are the sort of folks that are interested in making and building things, and so that's the type of content that tends to have the most reach," as they put it.

But the other reason is emblazoned in VRChat's Community Guidelines:

Live-streaming, advertising or publicly sharing content that is sexually explicit in nature or simulates sex acts is not permitted. Doing so may result in moderation action being taken against your account up to (but not limited to) banning of the offending user account depending on the severity of the act in question.

The wording expresses a precise subtlety: Simulated sex in and of itself is not prohibited—it's just publishing screenshots and video of it on social media and elsewhere that's forbidden. Do whatever you like in your VRChat world with other consenting adults, in other words, just don't blemish VRChat's brand by posting it in public.

It's an elegant solution to the Metaverse's sex paradox. Fighting against the inevitability of consensual sexual activity in the virtual world is a lost cause; preventing it from *defining* the platform is not.

Enforcing and Cultivating Norms of Positivity

Veteran developer Jim Purbrick, who vainly warned Meta to prepare for virtual sexual assault, likens the online moderation challenge to keeping the peace in the offline realm:

"If everyone in a real environment decided to riot tomorrow," as he puts it, "no police force would be able to deal with that situation. It relies on most of the people most of the time acting well."

On the highest level, that does require laying down specific, easy to understand rules.

"You have to be super clear about that stuff. Especially because we have an environment where people have been growing up playing video games since they were tiny, where video games they're playing, maybe they're the only actual human being [in it] and everything else is an NPC."

Enforcement of rules also has to be done in real time. This runs counter to how social media platforms are run, where a user can be flagged for toxic content but the issue is adjudicated days or even weeks later. "If you got strangers meeting each other in real time," as Purbrick puts it, "you have to have real-time ways of responding to bad behavior.

Finally: "You want those laws to permeate the environment and become norms." This, and not virtual world policing, is what ultimately keeps a virtual world's (relative) harmony.

Anil Dash, a veteran Internet thinker and CEO of Glitch, a web app development platform, has advice applicable to online communities of all kinds: Actively promote social norms around good positive behavior, through simple adages and memes as well as stated policies. Once inculcated, the community itself will then enforce those mores among each other and new users.

"They tell each other 'we don't do that [trollish behavior] here'," says Anil. "That has more power than banning or any policy things we can do . . . we don't want to be in an arms race of bad actors, and [community norms are] super powerful."

But those norms take time to establish and can't be imposed on a code level or through automation. They're grown during the early beta phase of a metaverse platform, as the company's community management cultivates and rewards norms, and those norms are passed on by the user community to new members.

Another way of putting it: Hire humanities graduates to run community management. They tend to be best attuned to the nuances of social behavior and have the skills to communicate and encourage good behavior in a clear and fun way.

Interoperability Against Abuse

In his book *The Metaverse*, Matthew Ball briefly touches on a concept of interoperability that's different from how it's generally understood: not to enable 3D asset transfers but to address metaverse platforms' broadly shared desire to tap down on racism and other antisocial behavior by trolls—the small but incredibly radioactive subset of users whose main goal is (with an impressively dedicated, sociopathic zeal) to abuse these platforms and the players, until they are finally banned from a particular world . . . after which, typically, they migrate to another platform and once again fire up their special feedback loop of assholery.

In cases like this, Ball suggests, interoperability on the user account level would be a powerful way to identify and blacklist this.

"So what you're talking about is interoperation of data and identity," he tells me. "This is much easier technically. And I think it's a lot more powerful.

"The classic example is credit score systems. Banks used to believe that their credit information on customers was the single most important thing that they had, because it allowed them to make the best judgments on who to lend to. The problem is no one benefits from default. And so there were customers who would have poor credit with Bank A and go to Bank B to get a loan. So they opened up their credit systems to the benefit of all.

Major metaverse-facing companies are beginning to hammer out a similar shared system, but directed at trolls.

"We are seeing with Epic, with Microsoft, with Sony, and myriad different startups, an effort to say, 'Let's interoperate not just our communication suites, but cross-reference, corroborate, and integrate our player information.' So that someone who behaves poorly on Game A or platform A can't just shift to game B or platform B. Because no one, not players, not publishers, not platforms, benefits from toxic behavior." Airbnb and VRBO are already doing this with their own data, "because bad hosts and bad renters hurt everyone, including the commissions that need to be paid by good users."

As I hint in Chapter 8, this specific version of interoperability definitely has value (if carefully managed to avoid false positive trolls identification). It's also a corollary to my principle "Only community must be interoperable."

Call it "Only tools that support community must be interoperable."

Designing for Positivity: A Sky Model

This chapter started with the story of how a standard design decision—conventionally attractive human avatars—biased a virtual world's community in a very consumerist direction, while also indirectly leading to a small but steady amount of toxic behavior.

But if bad design choices can lead to negativity, good ones can encourage positivity.

Or as Nick Yee puts it, referring to toxic behavior: "The way to get around that is to break reality in productive ways."

Jenova Chen's upcoming metaverse project may be the most ambitious in that regard, drawing from the design of Sky: Children of the Light, his highly successful virtual world (which will be incorporated into his company's upcoming metaverse project).

"So when we approached our metaverse design for the society of Sky, we wanted to simulate what reality is. In reality, we are social animals by nature, and there's social consequences."

Chen sees those consequences emerging from our evolution as a species, when ostracization from hunter-gatherer tribes did not mean being banished to 4Chan but being abandoned in the wild to defend oneself. "And so, to me, it's: how can we simulate that evolutionary biology?"

"[Designing] how people socialize is so delicate that I feel like if people who design the Metaverse do not pay attention, they could easily create a very tricky situation." After 20 years of writing about the chaos and drama eruptions from poor social design, I'd call this an understatement.

Chen's innovation is to change the game structure, so it's not based on defeating opponents (a la Fortnite) or earning achievement badges (a la Roblox) or leveling up as in traditional MMORPGs.

"We don't have role-playing-game leveling—but we have leveling for relationships." Only at mutual level two, for instance, can you share your name with another player or even share a hug. While this might seem artificial, Chen suggests it models how strangers become friendly only after several random street encounters; it takes a while for a level of trust to develop.

These mechanics, he adds, do not come with a reward beyond the activities you share with a friend—there are no "karma points or other benefits," as is common in many virtual worlds and social platforms. ("That's like the worst way to start a friendship," says Chen. "We learned that human relations cannot be meddled with any gamification.")

FIGURE 9.1 Avatars in Sky: Children of Light
Courtesy of Thatgamecompany

Following Yee's insights, the avatars in Sky are humanoid but genderless, evoking Studio Ghibli characters, and are intentionally without race—their skins are a dark-grayish hue.

"We don't really care about gender either because a lot of people, their gender in their mind and the gender of their body is different. And it doesn't really matter if they are a man or a woman in real life. As long as they are who they are in the virtual world."

Chen's team also minimizes class bias through its monetization system as a free-to-play virtual world. Where most metaverse platforms will have a sliding scale of avatar enhancements based on quality and price—so, as in real life, it's fairly easy to spot a wealthy person with a single glance at the finery of their clothing—Sky's system is based around gifts you can buy for other players.

"Half of our design is about how you buy things for other people," as Chen puts it, "rather than buy things for yourself. So it's altruistic spending. Yeah, I think right now, about half of the players who use our season pass, they're getting a season pass from a friend."

Often this is done by players across countries as a bridge between economic disparity, with (for instance) relatively well-off people in Japan and the United States gifting friends in Sky based in the Philippines.

Over 22 percent of Sky's revenue now comes from player-to-player gifts—a truly impressive number and proof that Chen's approach is working.

As is Sky's success as a virtual world: In 2022, it boasted some 20 million monthly active users, with 600,000–1.5 million con-current players. A global online community with a population the size of Taiwan, architected around friendship.

A better metaverse can be built.

10

Metaverse Real-World Use Cases—Separating Substance from Hype

The very best use case for the Metaverse is the Metaverse itself: a real-time immersive virtual world for entertainment, socialization, and creativity on a mass scale. Despite this, I am often asked by reporters and analysts to discuss "real-world" use cases for metaverse platforms. It is somewhat strange to look at a technology with at least half a billion engaged users and creators on platforms run by highly profitable companies, and effectively say, "But this isn't useful until it does something *I'm* interested in."

Any successful real-world use case for the Metaverse will be an extension of what it already excels at: immersion, fun, and creativity in a shared social space. The best and primary audience for those use cases will be the people deeply comfortable with

225

immersive spaces, in either metaverse platforms themselves or 3D games/virtual worlds. Several of these applications have already proven themselves well enough to believe they'll be sustainable for the next few decades—not perfectly and not universally, but well enough to grow and sustain real companies and organizations built around them.

Understanding Real Metaverse Use Cases: A Checklist

Before going further, it's important to first address some frequent misunderstandings that often confuse this conversation. To hopefully make this a helpful guide, let's arrange them in the form of an advice checklist.

Avoid the Allure of Unscalable Anecdotes I've been bruised too many times by the seductive promise of real-world applications of metaverse platforms that, while powerful as anecdotal examples, subsequently failed to scale.

In Second Life's first decade, for instance, I'd write about acclaimed, award-winning architects using the virtual world as a prototyping and demonstration tool in their practices, and would come away convinced that the profession as a whole would soon follow suit. (I said as much in a talk to a professional society of architects, and they sure seem convinced too.) Then a year or two later, I'd wonder why that handful of architects in metaverse platforms hadn't grown into thousands.

I gradually realized what was at work: By and large the people creating real-world uses for metaverse platforms are already personal enthusiasts of the technology. They were not there, in other words, because an immersive virtual world was necessarily the best solution to the practical problem they wanted to solve.

They personally enjoyed the experience and brought along their professional interests into this new realm.

Eschew Use Cases Only Compelling in Isolation of Everything Else   There's a recurring temptation to promote a powerful metaverse application with little regard to how it might (or might not) integrate with the rest of the economic infrastructure.

A common belief is that metaverse platforms will combat climate change. With the argument going roughly like this: The sense of social immersion in virtual worlds is so transformative that we'll find less need for air travel, since we can conduct business meetings and conferences in the Metaverse.

While I do suspect we'll see *some* adoption of metaverse-based meetings as a standard use case (more on that later in this chapter), I believe it's a mistake to argue that this will have any substantial impact on climate change.

The COVID-19 era gave us the most compelling counter-example to date: Under quarantine lockdown, we did indeed suspend most air travel and instead conducted business meetings via Zoom, Slack, and the occasional virtual world.

When the quarantine ended, however, air travel came roaring right back—if not for business, definitely for tourism and reconnecting with family and friends. Indeed, as I wrote much of this book during the summer of 2022, many of my interviews with various metaverse developers and experts were rearranged to accommodate their vacations in far-flung places.

Also: With the notable exception of Second Life and VRChat, many metaverse companies still place a heavy emphasis on work conducted . . . in their real-life offices. As I mention in Chapter 3, for example, developer Jim Purbrick left Meta in part because the company kept demanding that he make arduous work trips from London to San Francisco to work on their metaverse platform there.

If the Metaverse is such a great solution to air travel and on-site work, why do metaverse companies rarely put that into practice for themselves?

It's likely we will see some adoption of metaverse platforms for business meetings, but as far as addressing the climate crisis, it's much more plausible that we will see other applications do that, such as by prototyping and marketing electric vehicles and undertaking green urban architecture projects.

Beware Self-Refuting Evangelism   The limitations of real-world applications for the Metaverse went into the very writing of this very book. Whenever possible, I conducted interviews for it within VRChat and other metaverse platforms, or at the very least, had them in Discord, which has effectively become the communication bridge for all metaverse platforms.

By and large, however, most of my interviews with metaverse developers about the Metaverse were conducted, instead, in Zoom or Google Meetings. Or even, radically enough, on an actual phone. It's strikingly similar to how the most avid and widely shared conversations about the Metaverse are conducted among people on Twitter and LinkedIn—or via webinars.

If we're all so enthusiastic about the Metaverse, shouldn't we be talking about it on, well, a metaverse platform?

When I bring this contradiction up with various metaverse evangelists, I'm told that existing technology is not yet ready to handle a conference-like meeting experience. This is demonstrably untrue. In 2021, for instance, I hosted a conference in Break-room, a metaverse platform architected for enterprise use, with *The Metaverse* author Matthew Ball and the *Washington Post*'s Gene Park; about 100 attended live as avatars, and many more thousands watched the recorded event on YouTube.

In my experience, many or most evangelists interested in the Metaverse as a business opportunity are not personally interested in or familiar with the experience themselves. They may protest this by saying it takes extra time to learn a new virtual world's UX or customize an avatar, but these very activities are supposed to be part of the technology's appeal.

So this suggests a good rule of thumb for judging the plausibility of any metaverse evangelist's over-bold prediction. To frame it in the form of a question: If you really think this is the next generation of the Internet, why aren't you using it as much as you can?

Distinguish Between Metaverse-Adjacent and Metaverse-as-Such Applications When asked to describe a major metaverse use case, many technologists will describe an immersive 3D application that is actually *metaverse-adjacent* but not a Metaverse-as-such use case. The more valuable the use case, the more likely it will involve a platform with *some* metaverse qualities, but is not a metaverse application in the full sense of the definition.

Let me explain one way to distinguish a metaverse-adjacent application:

I have helped pitch metaverse technology to several major organizations and companies. The first serious question they inevitably ask is: "Can we put this behind our firewall?"

And if you are creating an application for an organization with incredibly strict standards around privacy and security, that question will keep coming up.

But a metaverse platform that's completely behind a firewall is not really the Metaverse at all.

The firewall requirement exists with most all enterprise-facing applications of virtual worlds: simulations of city infrastructure and architecture design, national defense/military training and prototyping, and so on. Applications like these already exist, but by and large they *are* behind a firewall, architected for security over usability. And being firewalled, they are regularly used only by a small group of people. The considerations and tooling also tend to be so different from consumer-facing, broadly used metaverse platforms, they deserve to be put into a related but decidedly different category.

At the same time, Metaverse-adjacent applications are unlikely to be widely adopted *unless* consumer-facing virtual worlds/metaverse platforms continue gaining users. An enterprise-facing pitch that runs, "It's a bit like Fortnite but for prototyping city streets," will become less compelling if Fortnite is no longer popular.

Or to put it another way: The best way to grow real-world use cases for the Metaverse is to first grow the general user base for it.

Acknowledge and Address the Limitation of For-Profit Use Cases

In technology we often only see solutions framed by the commercial needs of a company's product, and so we miss all the possibilities that would exist were that same technology not tied to an immediate profit motive. This is very much the case for the Metaverse.

I have seen proposals, for instance, where bedridden hospital patients, often confined and usually alone, would be able to share a virtual world space with their loved ones and other patients. In this unique situation, most of the practical impediments that help make VR a niche technology would be overridden by the patient's desire for social connection and an escape from the hospital ward. With over 35 million hospital stays per year in the United States averaging nearly five days per stay (according to pre-COVID government data), a shared virtual world for patients and care workers in the American healthcare system would be incredibly valuable.

Unfortunately, medical experts have also laid out to me how difficult all this would be to implement with existing VR and metaverse platforms, both of which have processes around personal data collection that run wildly, wildly awry of HIPAA/ patient privacy laws. Further, the virtual world itself would need to be extremely easy to navigate and use (for both patients and already-busy hospital personnel), likely on simplified, easily sanitizable devices, all of which would need to be created in close participation with stakeholders across the entire healthcare industry, including government and patients themselves.

I am hopeful such a metaverse application can be made, sooner rather than later. There's at least one proposal I'm familiar with, where a virtual world would be customized to benefit kids in hospitals across the country undergoing chemotherapy and other difficult hospital procedures. It would be a relaxing and creative social space to comfort these children through a time of unimaginable loneliness, fear, and pain. This is a metaverse application worth fighting for.

I am also frustrated that this kind of use case is rarely if ever discussed by people in the metaverse industry, who are too dazzled by the excitement of brand deals and corporate synergy to confront the Herculean challenges of bringing a product like this to market. I dearly hope my skepticism here is proven wrong.

With that checklist established, there are several real-world use cases of metaverse platforms that are showing genuine promise now. Here's an overview of three, with an assessment of their usefulness over the long term.

Use Case: Live Music/Entertainment— Pros and Cons

In early 2020, at the pandemic's peak, when most everyone was trapped at home in lockdown, the future of live music seemingly appeared in the form of a 100-foot avatar resembling rapper Travis Scott, striding the world of Fortnite like a colossus.

Performing to 28 million users over a single weekend, Scott's Fortnite performance would have been impossible to replicate in real life, full of dazzling, reality-altering visual effects painted across the canvas of Fortnite, while fans scrambled like ants beneath Scott's heavy stride.

Immersive and dreamlike, the show felt like an experience that seemed superior to a real-life concert in many ways. (And that's even before factoring in the porta-potties.) At the time, I estimated Scott's Fortnite show generated over $10 million worth of branded virtual merchandise (avatar enhancements and so on), all without the costs and logistical nightmares associated with managing a real-life concert. Surely, many people (including me) thought that this was going to be a central aspect in the future of music performances, even after the COVID lockdowns ended.

This may still be the case, but in subsequent years the number of metaverse platform music performances to meet the standards set by Travis Scott's show has been roughly zero. There have since been many virtual concerts featuring pop stars, to be sure, but the shows themselves have been far less extravagant. By and large, most of these "concerts" consist of a 2D video stream broadcast on a screen in a branded space, with little or no direct avatar-to-avatar audience engagement with the actual performer.

There are several reasons why live music events have not managed to scale into the Metaverse yet. To name just a few barriers:

At the moment, no major metaverse platform can host a mass live event attended by thousands; local concurrency limits tend to cap out at around 500 users, but often much less.

And while metaverse platforms already attract tens of millions of people, only a few hundred or a few dozen can share the same contiguous space at exactly the same time. Consequently, the Travis Scott performance—along with most others on current metaverse platforms—are not actually "live," but prerecorded and preinstalled on an update of the software and played back on thousands of virtual world servers, or shards.

The Perils of Live Events in the Metaverse

Hosting a *truly* live performance in a metaverse platform is not only technically difficult to scale, the financials are also questionable. Blocked by concurrency caps from hosting an audience of more than a few hundred in a virtual venue, artists face the costly option of developing a prerecorded version of the show that can play to millions—or performing to an audience of under 500 in a virtual space the size of a small theater.

Barring a corporate sponsor for the event, the economic questions quickly get vexing: The artist can charge a high ticket price to a small number of audience members, the most passionate fans who'll pay up in the hopes that they'll get a chance to interact virtually (and in close proximity) with their beloved star. (And in a metaverse platform context, even the $10 equivalent of the platform's virtual currency is typically considered to be premium.)

And in exchange for paying a high premium, the attending fans will likely expect far more than just seeing a 3D avatar re-creation of their star—they'll expect close-up interaction, best achieved by rigging up the star to a full VR rig, so that their hand and body gestures are mapped onto their avatar and play in real time. There are very few recording artists of any renown willing to strap themselves into such an apparatus simply to perform "live" to a small audience of anonymous avatars. So far, at least, no startup or management company has to my knowledge attempted to do all this.

I've not even delved into the licensing and IP challenges of live music on a metaverse platform. Is it truly a live event, requiring a public performance license, or a glorified Internet stream, requiring another kind of permission system? Little of this contractual infrastructure has been built out. Unsurprisingly, I know of several projects in recent years backed by major labels to build their own metaverse platforms, so they can fully control and monetize their IPs; also unsurprisingly, none have really gone anywhere.

Admittedly I'm somewhat jaded on the live music question. Having helped produce many live events and music performances on various metaverse platforms, I can say this with hair-pulling, scream-at-the-monitor surety: The logistics and preparation it takes to stage one is almost as time-consuming and complex as staging it in the real world—and becomes vastly more so when the featured artist and their team has limited experience with immersive virtual world events.

I think back warmly—so, so, *so* warmly—to my time attempting to produce a live performance on a metaverse platform that would star a platinum-selling singer. While the star himself was completely game to do it, he also refused to let it interrupt his real-life concert tour. Then his record label nixed the idea of him singing live in the virtual world—since doing so would allow audience members to record (and perhaps sell?) a bootleg recording of the concert.

After much back and forth with his management, the proposed concert would have been a sad affair: Instead of performing live, we would be allowed to *stream* just two to three recordings of songs from his library, while his avatar performed onstage with prerecorded gestures. And far as appearing "live" in the virtual world, it would have required me lugging my laptop to his touring bus when it was in a nearby city, so I could puppeteer his avatar while he spoke and chatted with fans. (To my relief and probably the pop star's, the whole project faded off our collective radar.)

Best Practices for Metaverse Platform Music Events

All these considerations to one side, many indie artists *have* carved out some success in the Metaverse. In Second Life alone, hundreds of performers put on regular shows that tend to be in smaller, coffee house–type venues for an audience of dozens, earning tips and building their fan base (including bluesman Mr. Charles Bristol, whom you meet in the Introduction). I'm heartened to see a number of live performers emerge in VRChat, amplifying their in-world shows with live streams to their YouTube/Twitch channels.

Rafael Brown, CEO and founder at Symbol Zero, produced 2020's Lil Nas X event in Roblox. With a reported 33 million in the Roblox audience, the event ranks just behind Travis Scott's Fortnite performance in terms of largest attendance. Brown worked directly with the artist, planned out the concert and choreography, and worked with Nas to motion-capture the performance that his avatar would perform.

Very little (nothing, really) of most major concert events on metaverse platforms is "live" in any way comparable to a concert in the real world, Rafael affirms to me:

"This is basically photogrammetry and mocap and music stems that are then brought to a real-time in-game cinematic and run for the players paired with scaling so it runs simultaneously on every server," as Brown puts it. The performance is essentially a 3D music video, played on several thousand servers to small groups of online avatars.

With major label music experiences on metaverse platforms, Brown argues, the crucial factor is not that the artist performs live in-world—it's the audience's own live experience together that matters. And when it is convenient for them. ("Do you want to tell little kids' parents who want to watch Nas X that they have to do it at 2 a.m.?")

"Indie artists should be live, but if you're going to put Beyoncé into a thing, you don't want to be, 'Hey Beyoncé, we're going to expect you back at 6 a.m. for the next show.'"

In any event, Brown believes a music event that makes use of real-time motion capture probably won't be feasible anytime soon without a considerable loss of quality.

"The fidelity is shit," as he puts it. "You get jitter." When South Korean mega group BTS performed in Roblox, Brown tells me, they built that motion capture jitter into the performance, adding visual effects to make it seem part of the performance.

In smaller venues such as Second Life and VRChat, successful indie artists build a following by creating a connection with their loyal fans—not just by performing for them but by palavering with them in between songs, calling out to their avatar names and replying to questions and requests sent via in-world text chat.

While this kind of direct engagement isn't feasible for a label artist performing on a platform like Fortnite or Roblox— "There's a limit to who she can view and understand when there's millions watching her"—Brown recommends alternatives that maintain controlled live engagement—for instance, a phase during the event when the artist speaks to the fans on livestream, answering a number of questions sent to it beforehand.

But fundamentally, says Brown, these experiences are basically stuck for the time being at the stage of prerecorded music videos that play out in 3D. "That's kind of where live music in the Metaverse has to be now." Five to ten years from now, he believes, the technology for genuine real-time live music on a mass scale may be possible. Until then, he adds, "We need to buy them that time."

But those technical caveats aside, when it's done well with artists like Nas X who have maximum appeal to the Metaverse's Gen Z core demographic, the major music experience is a scalable use case now.

Little Nas X's merchandise sales—branded avatar enhancements, emotes, and other items—paid for themselves within a *week* after his Roblox shows and continued selling long after. From March 2020 to March 2021, Brown tells me Nas X's Roblox merch generated $15 million in revenue with no further work.

Direct virtual world ticket sales, by contrast, remain unproven and difficult to scale. Were users to pay an entrance fee costing the virtual cash equivalent of $10 or more, they would probably expect special exclusive content, likely including truly live shows or VOIP interaction. This might very well be feasible for artists who genuinely enjoy metaverse experiences and are willing to make appearances multiple times (perhaps from the comfort of their home studios), but as of this writing, that possibility largely remains untested waters.

"Your biggest payback is the merch," Rafael tells me. The event itself is free-to-play; a percent of attendees buy the merch, and the event producers cite the high attendance numbers to immediately justify its ROI: "The number that attend the concert becomes the viability of the concert, and selling merch over time pays for it."

All that to one side, I should also add that contemporary metaverse platforms have largely failed to meet the potential suggested by early music experiences in Second Life.

In one, branded as "Musimmersion," the world would change around folk singer Grace McDunnough as she performed, morphing to fit themes or lyrics mentioned in the song—a rainy bayou at one point, a giant birdcage in another, beneath the wings of a dragon, and so on, imagination seeming to endlessly unfurl. In another, called Parsec, created by experimental musician Robert Thomas, spheres of light and tonal melodies would be triggered whenever members of the audience spoke through voice chat.

Both of these previous examples happened well over a decade ago. With some exceptions, next-gen metaverse platforms have yet to realize the medium's full potential.

This may quickly change. In December 2022, Jenova Chen's game studio, Thatgamecompany, unveiled a full-length concert in Sky: Children of Light, featuring popstar AURORA. Over 1.5 million players attended. More important, by optimizing player avatars (minimizing detail and not displaying avatars at a distance), Thatgamecompany was able to host 4,000 of them in the same concert venue/server shard. This is impressive in itself, but Chen and team also created (with AURORA's input), an entire interactive experience only possible in the virtual world. As Chen recapped to VentureBeat's Dean Takhashi:

> [In the show's climax] everybody dies and is brought back to life. They're like butterflies. This is 3,000 butterflies, and the sun rises, which brings back Aurora, who represents Mother

FIGURE 10.1 Popstar AURORA performing in Sky: Children of Light for 4,000 simultaneous avatars in the local audience; total audience, 1.6 million

Courtesy of Thatgamecompany

Nature. A lot of people were crying. You can see the emotes from the players. Then we have this giant version of AURORA. Instead of just jumping around, she reaches out and touches you and holds you, like your mother. A lot of the players, when they played this part of the concert, they were crying. It reminds them of their mothers, the love they have.

This technology, Chen tells me, will be available in his upcoming metaverse platform.

Use Case: Real-World Meetings/Conferences—Pros and Cons

As I show in Chapter 2, Second Life's fate was partly sealed in 2010 by a futile and costly attempt to make it feasible to host real-world professional meetings in the virtual world.

Since then, however, a generation raised on immersive games has moved into the workforce, and the technical capacity has nudged this use case into the realm of feasibility. Interest was accelerated by the worst possible circumstances, as the COVID lockdown pushed people into remote meetings and they yearned for anything even somewhat less aggravating than Zoom.

Though it's unlikely that metaverse platforms will minimize long-distance geographic travel overall (for reasons I went into previously), they do have an opportunity to supplant work-related conferencing, especially when the specific destination offers little beyond the conference itself, or when the attendees are constrained by a limited travel/accommodation budget.

Learning from Breakroom

Founded in 2020 at the height of the pandemic, Breakroom is an enterprise-facing metaverse platform from UK-based Sine Wave Entertainment. I did some consulting for Breakroom, so I can share some firsthand best practices based on that.

I hosted two Breakroom-based business conferences, one with the *Washington Post*'s Gene Park and Matthew Ball. (It's not all the time that you get to talk with the author of *The Metaverse* inside a metaverse platform.) As we chatted in a beachside auditorium, Breakroom staff instantiated a delightful hodgepodge of 3D objects around us on the stage (a Japanese garden, a giant blue frog, and so on). Prior to that, I hosted a chat with Philip Rosedale and an audience gathered around a roaring bonfire in the mountains under a breathtaking star-filled sky.

Of the two, I think Philip's event was more immersively successful. The primal draw of the bonfire naturally drew the audience closer, to the point where the flame glowed on our avatars' faces, encouraging a more intimate, truth-telling kind of

FIGURE 10.2 Cohosting a conference with Philip Rosedale (avatar in the black T-shirt) in Breakroom

conference. I felt myself sinking into a warm intimacy, to the point where it really did feel like I was speaking to people around a roaring flame, as opposed to people logged in from San Francisco, London, Australia, India, and all points in between.

But these meetings were about Metaverse-related topics, for participants who are Metaverse enthusiasts. Would they work just as well for standard business engagements?

The best data point to prove a virtual conference's effectiveness, Sine Wave CTO Adam Frisby tells me, is how much attendees spend in it. For Breakroom, he says, the average time hundreds of attendees spend in a Breakroom conference "has been in the five to six hour range per day." (Webinar engagement rates tend to fall below 30 minutes.)

And while you might expect a virtual conference of game developers or other 3D-friendly industries to engage the longest, a major international banking institution had the longest session times of any Breakroom client.

Adam tells me of a Fortune 50 company planning to deploy job fairs on Breakroom, where recent college students can meet companies in a virtual world space. Up to now, a fair like this is hosted in a convention center or on a college campus—costly to set up and attend. "This lets them do it remotely," says Adam, "but they're also able to interact socially." Each virtual world job fair is planned to hold a maximum of 500–1,000 people at once, enabling attendees to socialize and network with each other.

These are encouraging figures, though as the pandemic's memory fades, I'm still not convinced regular metaverse-based conferencing is sustainable. For occasional meetings between people who work remotely? Quite possibly. But my strong sense is that virtual conferencing on a frequent basis will not be feasible or desirable until launching them is as at least as simple and seamless as initializing a Zoom call from within Slack.

I'm also convinced that virtual world conferences as they're currently deployed need to be better designed to scale.

Nick Yee's advice, "break reality in productive ways" to overcome prejudice in virtual worlds (see Chapter 9), also translates to this context, offering ways to make metaverse-based meetings *better* than what we have in the real world.

"We know that there are some people who, by virtue of their personality or their appearance or gender category, age, or whatever, tend to dominate the discussion," as Nick puts it. So what if people's avatars virtually get bigger in a meeting room, the more disproportionately they speak? Then you can literally see someone who is disproportionately dominant in conversation."

A similar approach could encourage attendees to identify and encourage those who don't tend to participate in meetings: "[P]eople who haven't spoken for a while, their avatars literally start fading away . . . the visual cues help balance a conversation."

So far, no metaverse platform is attempting to do anything like this with real-world conferencing, instead relying on standard human avatars. But as I discuss in Chapter 9, a conferencing solution that offers only human avatar choices will inevitably encourage some level of harassment, toxicity, and other HR problems. In a work context, requiring personnel to take a meeting in a metaverse platform can cause anxiety to some, since it puts them in an unfamiliar medium they're often not comfortable with. Women in particular can sometimes consider the very request to be uncomfortable. ("I'm already judged by what I wear at work," as one woman told me. "Now I gotta be judged as an avatar, too?")

Until we see the kind of innovations Yee is proposing, metaverse meetings can only offer a somewhat-more-fun alternative to Zoom, which also introduces a new set of problems.

Use Case: Marketing/Brand Extension—Pros and Cons

Second Life's hype period was driven in great part by the arrival of Coke, Reuters, Armani, and other major real-world brands, setting up official headquarters and marketing experiences in the virtual world. This hype bubble largely burst when reporters finally noticed that very few people in Second Life were actually engaging with these brands. (A 2007 *Wired* magazine cover story title summed it up well: "How Madison Avenue is wasting millions of dollars creating ads for an empty digital world.")

This criticism, once valid, has largely been defeated by next-gen metaverse platforms. Major real-world brand experiences, especially deployed in Roblox and Fortnite, can and often do attract heavy user engagement.

For instance, the U.S. restaurant chain Chipotle launched a 2022 campaign in Roblox, offering free real burritos for the first 100,000 people to play Chipotle's virtual burrito builder game in the metaverse platform. According to RoMonitor Stats, a web service that tracks Roblox metrics, the Chipotle Burrito Builder attracted roughly five million visits in its first month.

This is extremely strong engagement. Traditional digital ads on the Web and mobile, even for major big budget brand campaigns, rarely bring in these kinds of numbers. Other brands appealing to the primary metaverse audience of teens and early 20s, such as Nike and Vans, have also done well.

One ROI lacuna, however, remains: Does brand engagement in a virtual world lead to actual engagement with the brand's products and, well, increased sales?

"I tend not to address it, because there's so many intertwined business models," Nic Mitham of the consultancy Metaversed tells me. "And there's just not enough data. I'm less interested in

'Does a virtual world campaign do something in the real world?' I'm more interested in 'What's the behavior of the consumer when they interact with that brand in a virtual space?'"

Mitham has worked with numerous major brands across multiple metaverse platforms. Instead of dealing with traditional ad metrics, he emphasizes direct engagement:

"[We] had fans of L'Oréal Paris, and all fans of cosmetics, almost demanding to run a competition where they could showcase their creations and then have them judged by L'Oréal Paris. That's golden for a brand that you've got someone who's inside a virtual world who's spending hours and hours trying to create [an avatar] skin underneath the umbrella of their brand."

For instance, a recent Mitham client is a brand selling hair extensions; his firm launched a virtual world competition where users vied to create new design styles, making it "a virtual competition to give them new product development ideas for real-world products. Super smart."

These are all positive signals for an experimental campaign, but *tracking* the customer's journey (as the marketing expression goes) from a fun virtual world experience to a real-world purchase remains difficult some 20 years after Second Life's first real-world marketing campaign.

"Most of them don't," Justin Bovington tells me. "The reason for that is it's just an issue of the interoperability of that data. You can't really punch out of those worlds into the Web."

Bovington should know: He was one of the very first people to bring major brands into Second Life, perhaps most prominently with the classic UK band Duran, which, with the help of Justin's studio, Rivers Run Red, deployed a whole fantastic island.

Now a creative marketing strategist with PVH Corp. (corporate owner of Calvin Klein, TOMMY HILFIGER, and other top fashion brands), Bovington has set up campaigns in Roblox and other metaverse platforms. As he did back in his Second Life days, he emphasizes the entire ecosystem around the virtual world activation itself—the social media reach, mainstream media coverage, word of mouth, and so on.

"Eighty percent of [the marketing campaign] is happening outside of the metaverse," as he puts it. "Twenty percent is happening inside."

But virtual marketing that leads to actual sales remains a thorny challenge.

"What about a simple coupon code that avatars could get in a metaverse experience for a brand," I suggest, "to redeem at the brand's store or website?"

Bovington is skeptical:

"When you're talking about back-end e-commerce systems, like using Salesforce or whoever, integration with those particular systems will probably take six months to a year to do. They don't move very fast."

Which makes me skeptical that marketing in the metaverse is (as yet) on solid enough footing for the long term. During Second Life's 2006–2008 peak, there was enough excitement around the virtual world to subsidize a dozen or so firms creating marketing experiences in the virtual world, led by a "metaverse big three" (as I called it back then) of Rivers Run Red, Electric Sheep Company, and Millions of Us, founded by fellow Linden Lab alum Reuben Steiger.

And then the full effect of the housing crisis finally devoured the corporate world's experimental marketing budget, and without the audience numbers *or* the ROI, most of that went away. My fear is if metaverse marketing ROI still can't be established, this cycle will once again repeat.

Untapped Opportunity: Classic IP Extension

Adjacent to marketing, major media brands have been slow to experiment with their back catalogs of intellectual property.

Fortnite has seen many promising cross-promotions of *current* IP, from Marvel and other Disney-owned franchises. Missing in this equation are decades of beloved *back* catalog IPs.

"They've got IPs in the form of movies that they own completely," Nic Mitham points out. "And, sure, you can stream it off your smart TV, Netflix, wherever. But by and large, these are intellectual properties that are making little to zero money now that have got massive brand equity and brand recognition."

By way of example, Nic mentions *Jaws* and *The Shining*, classic movies from the '70s still regularly watched but with a declining long tail of revenue. "How much money does *The Shining* make them every year? What if you could go inside a virtual version of that hotel?" (This is actually depicted in Spielberg's adaptation of *Ready Player One*, but perhaps lost in the forward momentum of the plot is the opportunity for the IP owner, Warner Bros., to actually create something like this.)

It's worth noting that with the exception of the *Star Wars* franchise, there have been several single-player games based on classic movies like *The Godfather* that have, at best, garnered modest success. What's unique about putting them in a metaverse platform, however, is that the immersive version can be experienced and enjoyed socially with a group of friends. They can also exist as virtual soundstages for grassroots creators to shoot their own movies or create unofficial spinoffs of the underlying IP.

And this shouldn't just stop at re-creating classic movie backdrops, but props and practical effects, re-created and made available in multiple metaverse platforms. Deckard's gun from *Blade Runner*; Julia Roberts's thigh-high boots from *Pretty Woman*; Oh Dae-su's hammer from *Oldboy*; thousands of items like these and more are cherished by millions of movie-loving metaverse users across the world and across generations.

The possibilities are exciting to consider. Brands can expand into the Metaverse, while metaverse content can seep into traditional media platforms.

Imagine an avatarized TikTok, where most video diaries are delivered not from the disheveled bedrooms of emo teens but in fantastic castles or underground fortresses, many drawn directly from classic movies and TV shows, where the latest school drama is shared, with more anonymity and therefore less drama, by voluble baby dragons and other fantastic avatars.

Picture a Metaverse portal for Netflix and Disney+, where instead of simply watching the latest hit streaming series in 2D, some can choose to be active participants, entering into select scenes that are digitized sufficiently to transform into fully immersive 3D scenes, and where some can even take on cameo roles. ("Remember that romantic scene in *Andor* season 5? I was the purple alien bird thing in the background.")

Consider a future presidential campaign online—for the sake of public awareness, politicians are also brands—catapulting from what we saw with Joe Biden's Fortnite island in 2020 (see Chapter 5), where many of the volunteers organize not in fluorescent-lit calling banks but in the candidate's official HQs across multiple metaverse platforms, and instead of texting and calling prospective Gen Z voters on their phones (long ago discarded as a spam-choked cul-de-sac), engage with them person-to-person in virtual spaces across multiple platforms.

For now, most of these use cases remain conjectural, niche, or yet to be proven for the long haul. Before we can seriously engage in a conversation about practical use cases for the Metaverse (beyond enjoying the Metaverse itself), two serious challenges need to be confronted.

But that's for Chapter 11.

11

Overcoming the Metaverse Age Cliff and the Immersion Funnel

▐▌ I tried installing and running Second Life and now my whole laptop screen is black!", the technology reporter with National Public Radio told me on the phone, somewhat panicked.

And now *I* was hyperventilating. I had just arranged an interview about Second Life and the metaverse in general with this reporter, who covered technology issues for a major news outlet. (This was during my days as a contractor for Linden Lab.)

But instead of getting the opportunity to show them all the potential of the virtual world, we now faced the likelihood of a PR disaster. A reporter specializing in high-tech news, surely savvy around computers, had just experienced a major client crash, suggesting Second Life had major show-stopping flaws. (A bug? A hack?)

I escalated this issue to a senior Linden Lab engineer who scrambled to a phone so they could walk the news correspondent through some troubleshooting checks. Meanwhile, a team of developers in the office attempted to replicate the "screen goes black on client startup" bug.

After some back and forth dialog, we finally realized what was happening.

This technology reporter for the United States' most reputed news radio outlet had launched Second Life . . . and then somehow tapped on the laptop keyboard until their avatar walked into a nightclub and careened into a black marble pillar at the edge of the dance floor.

The viewer camera, which usually hovers just above the user's avatar, simply follows along, displaying what was currently in front of the avatar.

And because the avatar was currently face-planted into a pole, the national correspondent only saw darkness.

I tell this story not to embarrass anyone at NPR, but to illustrate a common theme that's often missed by metaverse evangelists, who have typically loved and played 3D games and virtual worlds since childhood.

There are vast swathes of the global population—the majority really—who simply do not have the first-hand experience, the muscle memory, or, frankly, the personal interest to participate in metaverse platforms.

This is why I expect that metaverse platforms will attract only one in four people within the Internet-connected consumer base.

I attribute this to two related factors, which I'm dubbing:

- **The Metaverse Age Cliff:** Consumers' interest in metaverse platforms tends to drop off sharply after their mid-to-early 20s.

- **The Immersion Funnel:** Consumer interest in interactive 3D graphics tends to attenuate as it becomes more immersive.

They simply reflect what the data, as best as we can tell, shows us. Only a subset of people show highly active interest in regularly interacting in 3D game worlds and experiences; most of them are people in their teens and early 20s. Neither challenge is insurmountable, but they do require some closer understanding.

Aging Out

The Metaverse Age Cliff is not due to a disinterest in video games per se. Every smartphone owner is almost by definition a gamer on some level, and the number of smartphone gamers is estimated in 2022 at around two billion people. However, most of these mobile gamers do not prefer highly immersive experiences with first-person 3D graphics and enveloping stereophonic audio optimized for earphones, but casual 2D games, designed to be played in short, blooping, time-killing bursts.

This is true despite the fact that metaverse platforms and immersive 3D experiences are hardly new concepts. *World of Warcraft*, the first U.S.-based MMO to gain active users in the many millions, was launched in 2004; *Grand Theft Auto: San Andreas*, the immersive sandbox game intended for an adult audience, was launched that same year and went on to sell nearly 30 million copies. In nearly every case, however, the player base for titles like these almost always ages out.

I am among the relatively small coterie of Generation X geeks who fell in love with immersive 3D worlds as kids in the '90s, and continue to play in them. For the most part, however, the rest of my peers have moved on. Above all, immersion requires extended time and extreme focus, something that

Metaverse User Age Profile %

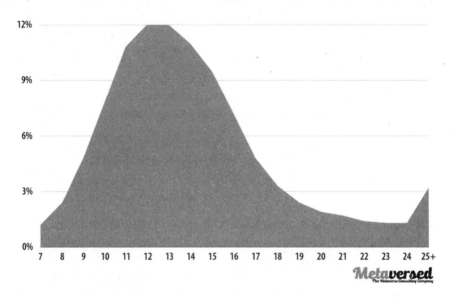

FIGURE 11.1 The Metaverse Age Cliff: From Metaversed's 2023 Q1 Demographics Profile

From the Metaversed consulting agency's Universe Chart, Q1 2023

steadily erodes in the face of romance, social life, family, work—essentially, adulthood.

You can see this in Metaversed's 2023 Q1 age profile, with the sharp cliff or steep hill hitting at age 13, and just 3 percent in the 25+ cohort:

I suspect Metaversed's estimate is a bit too bearish, and that it's likely 10–20 percent of total active metaverse platform users are 25 and above. But even then, usage still rapidly declines into users' 30s, 40s, and beyond.

"Roblox still has not crossed the age gap yet," as acclaimed game designer Jenova Chen tells me. "People seem to just retire and graduate to Fortnite after they reach 12 years old because you leave your middle school and go to high school—it's like, 'Oh, you're still playing that game? That's not cool anymore.'"

Here again, Second Life is both an exception and an aspirational role model. Back in 2008, Linden Lab reported that a full one in three members of the active user base were in their 30s and 40s; this user base has largely remained with the platform, so that with its 20th anniversary in 2022, much or most of the user base is in its 40s, 50s, and older.

As Philip Rosedale put it to me, "Second Life still exists, in part, because nobody's replaced it."

There are likely reasons for this resiliency that can be replicated in other metaverse platforms, which I'll come to later in this chapter.

The Immersion Funnel, however, may be even more challenging.

Inside the Immersion Funnel

Many or even most people only want immersion in small doses, for the simple reason that immersive 3D graphics tend to give them motion sickness. In a 2012 study published in the National Library of Medicine, 67 percent of adults and 56 percent of children reported feelings of motion sickness after playing a standard console video game with 3D graphics for up to 50 minutes. (It has been dubbed "simulator sickness" because the condition was noticed decades ago when military pilots first began training in full-motion flight simulators.)

As I mentioned when discussing Meta and VR, researchers led by danah boyd have also observed a tendency for women to experience more motion sickness than average in 3D simulation.

Just as fascinating, there also seems to be a racial component to motion sickness. Han Chinese, and potentially other Asian ethnicities, have been observed to tend in this direction (documented in the academic papers "Chinese hyper-susceptibility to vection-induced motion sickness," 1993, and "Effects of ethnicity and gender on motion sickness susceptibility," 2005).

Virtual world researcher Nick Yee, who shared those papers with me, saw this phenomenon firsthand when advising the developer of a first-person shooter game:

"They were getting a lot of churn in their tutorial," Nick tells me. After going through the data, "what it ended up being was that a lot of their Chinese players were literally getting sick because of the specific kind of gameplay in the tutorial that was really bad for motion sickness."

Apple prototype designer Avi Bar-Zeev saw similar reactions when developing what came to be called Google Earth, the fully 3D mirror world. Different humans, he found in tests, do not process 3D graphic spatial representation in the same way:

"There's a group of people who map the space in three dimensions," he says. "They can picture wherever they are three dimensionally, and can mentally rotate that picture and have a sense of their position in the world relative to some cognitive map. And then there's a whole group of people, 50 percent of the population, who map by landmark. So they don't necessarily have a sense of where they are in [the 3D virtual] space, but they know 'When I see this, I turn left.'"

Women, he found, tend to navigate by landmarks:

"What we learned was that skews a little bit more towards women in terms of the perceptual mapping, versus the spatial 3D mapping, [which] skewed more towards men. And that doesn't necessarily mean it's genetic, either; it could be that it's a skill that men learn playing video games. It could be that by playing 3D video games, you help [hone] that skill . . . which isn't useful for a whole bunch of things, except maybe playing video games and building virtual worlds."

Here again is another hurdle for full mass adoption of the Metaverse. If the propensity for motion sickness has some basis in genetics (as it seems), it may be insurmountable.

If navigating 3D spaces can be learned through practice, by playing 3D video games, then the barrier is social, and about as challenging. Hardcore 3D gamer spaces tend to be male-dominated and infamously toxic to women and girls. As I discuss in Chapter 3, Fortnite is also a partial exception to this rule; Blizzard's colorful shooter Overwatch counts 16 percent regular female players, more than double the genre average (according to Quantic Foundry). But by and large, for many reasons, most females aren't clamoring for highly immersive 3D experiences.

Widening the Funnel

Moving past the motion sickness caused by full immersion might require changing the very nature of how virtual worlds are displayed—and accepting the extra costs required to make them more accessible to a more diverse range of people.

One possible solution is keeping the 3D camera locked in a fixed position, so that the user enjoys the action as if they were peering into a dollhouse.

This presentation is not unlike what's displayed in the phenomenally popular game franchise *The Sims* (with over 200 million copies sold), where the players typically control characters from a serene God's eye view. (If God were a slightly deranged reality show producer.)

More recently, Nintendo's *Animal Crossing: New Horizons*, a casual multiplayer simulation game that became a runaway hit during the pandemic (over 40 million copies sold thus far), also constrains the camera, mainly keeping it to a diorama position with slow camera tracking to leisurely follow the action.

This, however, introduces another challenge. While a constrained camera appeals to most casual players, it tends to alienate hardcore gamers who feed on the thrill of high-speed, first-person or "over the shoulder" views, and the ability to move their camera eye around the world at will.

A hybrid approach may appeal to both groups, with the option to choose either display setting. This has never quite been attempted. More likely, different parts of the virtual world may have to operate by different rules of gravity and kinetics. Teens may enjoy high-velocity running gun battles in the virtual desert on dune buggies, then drive them over to a neighborhood of the Metaverse where grandma spends time, noticing that when crossing into her zone, their vehicles have been slowed to a putt-putt crawl.

Bridging the Age Cliff

The realization that the Metaverse is still mostly for kids has haunted Philip Rosedale:

"Getting adult users into social, virtual worlds as opposed to just escapist or relaxing video games or something, that remains the big challenge of our time," he tells me. "There's not a lot of proof yet that you can get people who are older than 18 to hang out in a lean forward, socially engaged way with other people in a virtual world or metaverse. We're not there yet, but I remain as enthusiastic from an optimistic-doing-good-for-the-world perspective as I ever was. But it has certainly turned out to be a lot harder than I thought, if you were to ask me in 2006."

My hope, at least, is that the cliff can be turned into a trampoline, with activity slacking into people's 20s and 30s, as they enjoy all the fleshy delights of young adulthood. But as marriage, family life, and financial comfort finally kick in, people who cherished their time in the Metaverse a decade or two ago can find themselves returning back, to reconnect with old friends and make new ones.

Journeying Across the Age Cliff with Jenova Chen

One potential bridge across the Metaverse Age Cliff is being created by a completely new approach to the challenge.

Shanghai-born game designer Jenova Chen has devoted his career to proving that a game can be as artistically accomplished as *Citizen Kane*. Many (including myself) believe he's already succeeded, creating a series of acclaimed titles that expand the possibilities of immersive entertainment.

Chen succeeded most vividly in his best-selling game called *Journey*, in which the player must traverse wild lands and the remains of an ancient city to reach the summit of a strangely glowing mountain. It pairs favorably with the films of Hayao Miyazaki—achingly beautiful and melancholy, but hopeful for humanity. Chen made that last aspect possible by making *Journey* a kind of virtual world in miniature that two people could play together. In a brilliant innovation, the players are anonymous and can communicate only through gestures. Many players describe the profound feeling of emotional bonding they have, wordlessly sharing an adventure with another person in the world they'll likely never know.

When I ask Chen about a solution to the Metaverse Age Gap, his answer is refreshingly unique:

"First of all, you have to create emotional accessibility."

The first challenge to that is recognizing that some emotions tend to be closed off by age:

"You might enjoy some kind of body horror film when you're a kid because kids by nature love to be scared . . . evolution made us want to be scared of some things as a kid because then you know to run, and survive. As you grow older, you don't enjoy that horror film anymore; as an adult, we are scared of something that is more deep, which is a scare of something that is unknown—so like mystery, suspense, thriller is more of the adult version of a scare."

Chen shows me a chart of movie genres and their highest box office popularity according to age and gender, where sci-fi action is most popular among men aged 35–44, romantic comedy most popular among women aged 25–34, animation among teens of both genders, and so on.

"You have to create emotional combinations like cocktails to catch the young and old, and men and women. So if you think about a Disney movie, like for example *The Lion King*, it's animated, it's very colorful and vivid. So young kids will find that attractive. It's in a fantasy land where animals talk and they want to be friends, so it's hyper social. So women and men both are interested.

"Parents need to feel something emotionally, like the beginning of *Up* and the end of *Toy Story*. They have this moment where adults have a joyful tear. They get adopted, meaning after they watch the films they can talk about life using the film as a kind of medium.

"So this is how you catch everybody, parents and kids, women and men: to have that emotional accessibility to all ages."

Chen's breakthrough game *Journey* came with a weave of suspense and drama, targeting the two quadrants of men and women in their 30s. ("This is what I would call the Oscar category.")

His latest game, *Sky: Children of Light*, was designed to appeal to both these groups but also incorporates anime aesthetics appealing to a younger audience, but in a more social context.

"The game right now actually is 70 percent women [players]," who tend to skew younger. "However, we have many 70- and

80-year-old players in their own group, and my mother-in-law is 68 and she plays every day." There's also a small contingent of older men, "because they actually use the game as a tool to connect with their daughters [who play]." (The quadrant of younger males, however, is lacking: "They say, 'There's nothing you can kill here, it's so boring. Why would I play a game only about making friends?' So the young boys are out.")

Chen's metaverse-flavored follow-up to *Sky* will attempt to bring them in, too:

"We are building another theme park. I don't want to miss those hardcore gamers, who I used to be. So the young boys cannot be left behind. *Sky* to me is kind of like the princess castle in Disneyland, kind of for younger kids who're not looking for a thrill and action. They will enjoy *Sky*, but we're building something that will be a nice counterpart to *Sky* that will together be able to attract the rest of the age and gender group." (More on that and its relationship to the future of the Metaverse in Chapter 12.)

Beyond any bridges that artists like Jenova Chen can bring to the Metaverse Age Cliff, it's incumbent on the industry to advocate for itself and elevate the conversation. We know this can succeed because it's already been done before.

Metaverse Mindshare and a New State of Play

Second Life did not become a mainstream media darling in its peak period simply because of its evocative name and its powerful creation and monetization features. And its marketing budget was modest by game-industry standards. There's another reason why politicians, established artists and writers, and academics across multiple fields, among many others, frequently cite Second Life, and not other metaverse platforms, to this day.

What Linden Lab did back then—and what current metaverse platforms are *not* doing now—is create *mindshare* around the technology and culture they are trying to create.

Second Life's mindshare was actively fostered by Linden Lab from the start—first by Linden Lab executives in the early years, as they planned out the virtual world's future.

They reached out to experts "[with] deep backgrounds and a very wide range of areas of expertise," Cory Ondrejka tells me. "We had this army around us of incredibly deeply thinking folks. They didn't always agree with us, they often would just throw grenades at us . . . we had a community around Linden of some of the brightest people in their fields, who we could bounce ideas off of, and we were really never afraid to do that."

We rarely see that kind of outreach emanating from contemporary metaverse platform owners.

"[T]hat's not the norm, especially for really big companies," Cory observes. "It just gets scary to try to operate that way."

But the very act of seeking wisdom from a wide range of experts creates mindshare roots that quietly spread awareness through these experts' own social channels.

This culminated in the State of Play, a conference hosted at New York Law School beginning in 2003. Founded by law professor Beth Noveck (who went on to become a technology advisor in the Obama Administration), State of Play was attended by top academics in jurisprudence and sociology, the multidisciplinary field of game studies, and executives from the game industry.

State of Play is where Philip Rosedale made a landmark Second Life policy announcement. Crafted with the advice of Harvard law professor Lawrence Lessig, and then widely covered throughout the game and business press, he announced that Second Life users would retain intellectual property rights over the content they created on the platform. The policy was immediately and vigorously debated by the brilliant minds in attendance. That the announcement was made there, and not at a self-promotional tech conference (as is usually the case), immediately enshrined Second Life as being on the daring vanguard.

In doing so, Rosedale positioned the virtual world as not just an online game, but a phenomenon that artists, writers, designers, and innovators should engage with. Reporters, noticing this buzz, quickly followed. That interest quickly spread into mass media. So when the second State of Play kicked off the following year, an entire news crew from MTV was there, too.

An academic conference like this is long past due for contemporary metaverse platforms—a venue to reposition these virtual worlds away from merely being games or commercial enterprises and establish them as platforms for creating art, education, and culture.

It will likely lead to difficult questions, and definitely to fairly heated debates. But these discussions are what is needed to help us bridge the Metaverse Age Cliff.

A Metaverse Worth Fighting For

12

Future Paths

I t is foolhardy to forecast with any great confidence the next great leap in the Metaverse's evolution. Even in retrospect, its progress up to now is remarkably unpredictable:

Minecraft was conceived by a handful of indie developers in Sweden, a ridiculously blocky-looking sandbox game that no major game publisher would ever possibly create.

Roblox floundered for years as an also-ran virtual world for kids, dwarfed by much larger platforms.

Fortnite seemed at first like a knock-off of an already popular online combat game subgenre inspired by a cult Japanese novel/movie.

VRChat was written off at launch as a cesspool for hit-and-run video streamers.

Yet together these unlikely products have amassed an aggregate user base larger than the entire population of the United States.

It is also the case that none of them made their first strides into the market with loud and open proclamations to become the Metaverse, but instead marketed themselves as fun games and social spaces. The best contender to become the primary model of The Metaverse (capital T, capital M) may not call itself that now, and maybe never will, even after satisfying all the requirements laid out in Chapter 1.

That said, my strongest suspicion is that this epochal leap is taking shape as I write these words in 2023.

As a thought experiment, consider just four plausible near-future scenarios:

Garena Free Fire: Largely ignored by the Western game industry as yet another knockoff of PUBG and Fortnite, the mobile-based battle royale game from Garena—a game studio/publisher owned by massive Singapore-based conglomerate Sea Limited—already has the early makings of a metaverse platform, with an open toolset for players to create their own worlds, and following in Fortnite's footsteps, cross-reality appearances by music and sports celebrities.

What it also has—far more than even Roblox—are mass numbers of users, especially in South America and South Asia. As VC Julie Young noted on Twitter in late 2021: "Free Fire has 700 million quarterly active users concentrated largely in some of the highest growth regions in the world."

All of this positions Free Fire for marketing and expansion into the United States and EU in the very near future. It may have once seemed implausible that an interactive Internet platform first popular in the "developing world" could then become popular in the United States, but the global dominance of Tik-Tok, first developed and launched for the mainland China market, has torn that assumption asunder.

But whereas TikTok's U.S. viewership is stovepiped and separated from its Chinese user base and divided by a language barrier, not to mention highly incompatible political assumptions, there is little reason to keep Free Fire's worldwide user base isolated by national origin. (Certainly not in social areas of the platform that don't depend on split-second twitch action.) This opens up the tantalizing possibility of Free Fire becoming a truly global metaverse platform, one where the culture would be defined by the non-U.S./EU community that first grew with it.

Grand Theft Auto Online: Already a highly active virtual world platform in miniature, with millions of monthly active users who role play as gangsters, molls, and the occasional popo, the scabrously popular franchise could easily evolve into a full-fledged metaverse platform: a geographically accurate re-creation of modern California (albeit drenched in scumbag perfume), it's the most commercially accessible virtual world, replete with functional stores, nightclubs, even banks.

There's already a massive market for a more open-ended version of GTA Online. FiveM, an astoundingly popular, highly customizable modification of the game created by community developers, is attracting more players than the official GTA Online on Steam.

Google CEO advisor Cory Ondrejka roughly concurs with my sentiment here, and points out other candidates beyond GTA:

"You watch the big FPSes, so whether we're talking about Call of Duty or Apex Legends . . . I think those games will eventually notice that Fortnite Creative is a big deal. And you'll see more creative modes start sneaking their way into some of these games.

"Then you've got a whole other layer, which is the online versions and sort of effectively MMOs of games you wouldn't necessarily expect to have MMO modes. So whether it's Grand Theft Auto, whether it's Red Dead Redemption, Skyrim Online, Fallout, you have all these different games really stretching around different aspects of what is a virtual world, what is the Metaverse."

World of Valve-craft: Valve, creator of *Half-Life*, *Portal*, and *Team Fortress* and the venerable "gamer's game publisher," continues to be the Metaverse dog that doesn't bark. A company possessing all the requisite technology and artistry to make a metaverse platform of its own (including proprietary VR headsets) mysteriously declines (so far) to do anything explicitly metaverse-related.

At the same time, *Garry's Mod*, its mammothly popular sandbox game, already gives players access and customization power to their 3D assets; Steam, its game distribution platform, could easily offer a shared virtual world that acts as a lobby with portals into virtual worlds on the platform. In Chapter 8, I note how most Metaverse visions actually boil down to being Steam with extra steps. So why not just Steam itself, to take the vision further?

Discordia: While Valve has had difficulty creating an active online community on Steam, gamers have flocked to Discord, the social messaging platform. Now boasting some 150 million active users, Discord is also positioned to add an immersive, networked virtual world to its players, perhaps as an optional add-on to server managers.

But again, these are only conjectural scenarios. An actual platform currently being developed by an artist with a proven track record may warrant just as much attention.

Jenova Chen and the Metaverse Theme Park

We first met acclaimed game designer Jenova Chen in Chapters 9 and 11, where he explains how to grow a virtual world based on giving and his strategy for bridging the Metaverse Age Cliff. There is more to that story:

Armed with $160 million raised through his Santa Monica game studio, he has been building what's been described as a "theme park–like" metaverse experience.' This may seem like a contradiction in terms, but Chen says what he is doing is distinct from the ultimate Metaverse depicted in *Snow Crash*—where, as he puts it, "everybody has the power to create and download. It's like a big flea market . . . and people who're really good at making content start to have a brand and then they start to differentiate themselves from each other."

Chen compares that aspect of the Metaverse to America during the boom times after World War II, when makeshift carnivals with rickety rides, dubious freak shows, and games began to spring up in dusty fields across the country. It felt predatory and unsafe. ("Hey, kid, hit three of those three targets and win a prize.")

And in Chen's telling, it's what led Walt Disney to found a theme park that still bears his name.

"He wanted to build a park that treats everybody, not just kids, as first-class citizens." And so the rides Disney created were not just fun for children, but moving and relevant for parents as well.

What he has in mind is an experience like that, building on *Sky: Children of the Light*, his latest game, which currently counts over 20 million active users.

As with Disneyland, he intends this metaverse experience to be for the entire family. Even as a seasoned designer, he notes, "I have yet to play any game which me and my wife can play at the same time, together with our daughter, and then all of us have a good time."

Chen's goal is to make this experience the best *channel* for the Metaverse, whatever platform that ultimately becomes.

"A lot of people are talking about the Metaverse mostly from the infrastructure level," he explains. "'Can people upload their things? Can they make money out of it?' I'm more worried about the content itself. Let the cable company worry about hardware."

His focus is more essential: "Is it emotionally accessible to a wide range of people?"

He's right that most metaverse conversations have circled far too much around technical infrastructure, while missing the fundamental piece that makes any of this worthwhile.

Every successful metaverse platform evokes emotional chords, from the wonder and awe of exploring a new world to the surprise and delight of sharing user creativity. Chen's goal is to create a broadly accessible experience with a wide enough emotional spectrum to appeal across all demographics.

He also thinks it's in the Metaverse that his lifelong goal of creating the *Citizen Kane* of games might be achieved.

"What I like about the Metaverse is people automatically assume that whatever happens there is just an extension of life, and therefore they don't have the kind of prejudice that they have towards games—'only for kids, for the losers.' You don't have that connotation with [the Metaverse]."

Connecting Across Generations

Projects like Chen's leave me hopeful that we will see platforms that can bridge the Metaverse Age Cliff by connecting the very young with the middle-aged and older.

I am a proud member of Generation X, the first cohort to grow up with the Internet and 3D online games. When senior citizen status inevitably grips us by our tattered Nirvana T-shirts, many or most of us (65 million strong) will spend increasingly more of our indoor hours as we always have, immersed in the virtual worlds that still inspire our creativity and imagination. The people we meet and play with in metaverse platforms will tend to be much younger.

We have already seen this microcosm play out in Second Life, where the inquisitive Gen Xers and Boomers who first joined the virtual world in their 30s and 40s are now in their 50s and 60s, among the platform's most active participants. But their social network within the virtual world often skews much younger, as they meet and befriend young gamers, sharing experiences and interests that transcend decades of age difference.

In most parts of the developed world, it is extremely rare—nearly to the point of nonexistence—for people who are not related with each other to regularly and actively socialize with people outside their peer group. It is highly common in Second Life, and an inherently good thing, a mingling of life experiences and aspirations that all can find value in. (The age distance-defying friendship of Second Life performers Charles Bristol, a bluesman in his 80s, and Russ Roberts, an indie musician in his 40s at the time of meeting, is not at all uncommon). As platforms like Roblox and Fortnite begin to show their own age, we may certainly see this trend continue.

Ironically, this may also be the best metaverse use case for Facebook, which was created for college kids in their teens and early 20s but has since become the prime destination for Baby Boomers and older Gen Xers. It will likely look nothing like Meta's original, problematic vision for the Metaverse. Not the high-adrenaline gamer zone for the young strapped into headsets to play with peers, but a place where immersive adventures for all ages (and races, and genders, and nations) can come together.

AI and the Metaverse

In 2022, many years after he had become famous as the Second Life avatar artist known as AM Radio, technologist and artist Jeffrey Berg began playing with Craiyon, one of many generative artificial intelligence applications capable of creating impressively detailed images simply from whatever text a user entered.

Curious, he entered the words, "A wheat field under gray skies with an abandoned train."

In minutes, Craiyon had generated a series of images that eerily looked like The Faraway, his beloved Second Life installation that he had labored so long back then to create.

"I wondered about the impacts it could have on metaverse space creation," he mused to me, after sharing with me Craiyon's attempts to re-create The Faraway. "3D geometry rather than a generated image from plain text input doesn't seem like a huge stretch."

After leaving his role at IBM designing UX interfaces and virtual world experiences, where AM Radio was born, Berg eventually joined Arup, a firm that helped engineer the design of fantastic but quite real buildings like the Sydney Opera House.

It's from that perspective that Berg notes how the design of *physical* spaces is already highly automated:

"Today, engineers use tools such as Dynamo in Autodesk Revit and Grasshopper in Rhino 3D to create designs based on input parameters, often referred to as parametric generative design." Through largely automated processes, "entire volumetric 3D building shapes are determined, taking into account building position, angle to the sun, soil types, and more."

So the technology to digitally blueprint 3D virtual world spaces not only exists but is already in practical operation. Linking it to a text-based AI system such as DALL·E, Craiyon, or Midjourney is eventually going to happen:

"I believe we're just waiting for the moment, not the technology, for someone to ask for an environment, *Star Trek* Holodeck style, and have that environment appear in their headset."

But what happens to creativity and art in the Metaverse, when luminously beautiful 3D environments can be created simply by speaking the right evocative words into a voice prompt?

"I am hopeful that we can transcend the prompts and look for outputs that show us more than what machine learning can do," the artist formerly known as AM Radio tells me, after some thought. "That is as good as an artist can create a virtual space experience, and reimagines the way we experience virtual spaces."

He imagines a scenario where future metaverse artists who come after him will integrate AI with the talent of the human creator:

"Maybe the artist sets up a virtual space for visitors to interact directly with machine learning that provides the visitor with a profound experience about themselves and their interactions with the world around them. In this case the artist constructs a space where machine learning is a visitor to the space as much as the humans who enter the space with it. What can we as artists do in the guiding of those interactions? I am hopeful that experiences waiting to be unlocked will astonish us all, and I can't wait to be there."

At the same time, AM Radio's current successors can probably rest easy awhile. There's likely to be a substantial interim before AI-generated virtual worlds become genuinely scalable.

"That *could* happen, but we're a long, long, long way out from it being feasible," veteran game industry artist Aura Trilio warns me. "Not just because there's a massive lack of training data, not just because nearly all 3D model generation results in extremely unusable topology, but also because retopology isn't in a place where this sort of stuff is worth anyone's time."

It's one thing to generate an impressive-looking 3D vehicle or house, for instance, but in a physics-enabled virtual world, let alone a multiuser world, an unexpected interaction could lead to disaster. I'm reminded of a level designer on the classic game *Skyrim*, who once recounted how a poorly optimized *pebble* on the road unexpectedly caused passing horses to go catapulting into the air.

Or to put it in technical terms, care of Aura:

"There aren't enough 3D models in existence for basically any model to eat and spit out anything usable. Even most bespoke, handmade 3D model generation algorithms spit out models that are completely unusable in games because the logic behind character creation and topology is extremely precise and needs to be carefully thought out."

In the more immediate future, I think it's more likely that we'll see AI-powered chatbots integrated into metaverse platforms. Last year, I spoke about that possibility with artist Michelle Huang. In a viral demonstration, Michelle trained ChatGPT on reams of entries from her childhood journal—and then had a moving, even enlightening conversation with her younger self.

"It illuminated to me how hard I was on myself, but how much I extended understanding to others," she explained. "It felt really rewarding to receive this kindness as well, from a younger version of myself."

Imagine a metaverse platform where you can chat with NPCs directly based on novelists, poets, and public speakers from history and fiction.

"This is the stuff I think that has the most interesting ramifications," Michelle told me, expanding on the possibilities. "More immersive human/computer interface loops, from conversation with virtual therapists to in-game interactions for virtual worlds; given there is user input, AI could be used to train highly customizable responses or generate unique storylines per use."

Streaming the Metaverse in Our Hands

Cory Ondrejka sees a future where cloud streaming of 3D metaverse content might change how we interact with video streaming services like Twitch and Google's YouTube—or even how we stream video in mobile calls.

With cloud streaming, Cory observes, "what starts as video and switches to static or switches to a more game-like experience becomes a very sort of smooth continuum. And it seems inevitable to me that we'll see exploration in what is currently the video chat space around more games and virtual world experiences. Because that has a lot of nice properties—you can make eye contact. You can move around a space where we have a more situated conversation about something."

We now take it for granted that we can instantly bring up an interactive 2D map of our surroundings on our phone within seconds. Ondrejka sees a time where it'll be trivial to stream interactive 3D content from a metaverse platform onto our devices for everyday practical reasons:

"What if it's so easy to use Epic products that when you're meeting people at an event, you don't just say 'I'm meeting you at this restaurant.'" Rather than texting a series of confusing written clues of where your table is located, you could create annotations on a 3D mock-up of the space, and send that as a text."

In Ondrejka's examples, useful immersive apps like these might integrate into our everyday digital lives so that there's no dramatic shift to the Metaverse that suddenly changes everything, but becomes an enhancement to our daily lives:

"All of those are creating these on-ramps to virtual worlds and Metaverse-like experiences, and I think it becomes a more regular part of how we access computing and information, and how we access each other," as he puts it.

As for whether Cory Ondrejka himself might return to this work, taking leave as advisor to Google's CEO:

"It's certainly an area that I still have opinions and interests in," he tells me, grinning. "I love what I'm doing right now, but life is long, time is long, so there are always chances to go back to the Metaverse again."

Ondrejka's current perspective sees the Metaverse gradually becoming a part of the mainstream Internet experience through the side door of various peripheral use cases. To my mind, it contrasts sharply with what Philip Rosedale sees ahead: a nearly insurmountable challenge to create a Metaverse that is not a game, that is enjoyed not just by kids but by people of all ages, and has mass adoption.

Looking for a Lean-Forward Metaverse

"I think sometimes the industry makes a mistake and says, 'We're going to take a leaning back experience, like *Call of Duty*, something like that, and we're going to make it somehow something that a billion people want to do," as Philip Rosedale puts it to me.

"And that design arc, I don't think really makes sense. Because I don't know that a billion people all want to lean back and kind of trip out on the same experience, like chasing people around and shooting at them or whatever.

"I think instead, we have to look at more lean-forward experiences, like Zoom, and ask how we generalize those to get to a Metaverse rather than starting from games."

He cheerfully allows that gamers often do meet each other in real life after playing together online, even forming fast friendships and marriages. But in his eye, that's *despite*, not because, of how the world is designed:

"For the most part, the whole structure of it is to abstract the people into avatars in a way that makes them play a role, where everybody has a pretty good understanding of what the rules are."

Rosedale argues for this approach for both practical and principled reasons:

"I think sometimes we're trying to scale up games, but keep people leaning back and kind of relaxing. And I don't think that's going to work. And maybe, ethically and morally, maybe we don't want it to? We may not want to give everybody SOMA, you know, we may not want to all kind of veg out?" (He means the pleasant hallucinogenic that pacifies the population in Huxley's *Brave New World*.)

This sharply contrasts with John Carmack's oft-stated preference for a mass-adopted metaverse, where the "crass commercialization" of a fun online game will eventually become popular enough that it will attract mainstream crossover users:

"[W]hen people like John Carmack, for example, talk about video games, he talks about it from the mindset of, 'Can't we build an escape from the real world that is incredibly pleasurable and exactly what we want it to be, and nominally single player, right? Like just a wonderful experience.' And I think that's a laudable goal." (But as we'll see in Chapter 13, that goal may come with a high price.)

"Think how different Second Life would be if you just expected everybody to behave the way you wanted them to," Carmack says. "It wouldn't be a very rich experience, if everybody was [like] an NPC that was just really super nice to you. That would be maybe cathartic or relaxing, but it wouldn't be engaging in the way that Second Life is."

I take him to mean all the examples of positive connections between people from many backgrounds that happen daily in Second Life—the very kind of stories I've written about for nearly two decades.

"Are we talking about a moment here when two strangers need to figure each other out and come to an agreement? Or are we talking about an experience like *No Man's Sky* or something, right?" That's the acclaimed game where players get to explore whole galaxies with thousands of flora- and fauna-rich planets— but generally play alone.

"And of course, Second Life can be that way too. But as we know, a lot of the time in Second Life, you're engaging with people very substantially, trying to sell them something, trying to build something."

I believe this can be achieved on a broad scale with a vast user base, and I have advice that may better get us there.

But first, some last warnings on the dangerous snares ahead.

13

Future Pitfalls— Manipulation, Takedowns, and the Experience Machine

Whatever transpires with Meta's plans for the Metaverse, it's also worth noting another, little known goal that's been rumbling beneath the surface across Silicon Valley from the very beginning.

Back in 2014, shortly after Meta announced acquisition of virtual reality company Oculus VR for $2 billion, the firm's very young founder, Palmer Luckey, appeared onstage at the Computer History Museum in Mountain View, at a conference devoted to VR and creating the Metaverse. Someone in the audience asked Luckey why he spoke of a "moral imperative" to bring virtual reality to the masses.

"This is one of those crazy man topics," Luckey began, "but it comes down to this: Everyone wants to have a happy life, but it's going to be impossible to give everyone everything they want."

Instead, he went on, developers can now create virtual versions of real experiences reserved only for the wealthy. By which he meant people sitting in the room with him.

"It's easy for us to say, living in the great state of California, that VR is not as good as the real world," he concluded, "but a lot of people in the world don't have as good an experience in real life as we do here."

Instead of providing the poor of the world with a better material life, in other words, we might provide them with virtual versions.

"VR can make it so anyone, anywhere can have these experiences," as Luckey put it to me later.

Luckey has since left the Metaverse industry, unceremoniously defenestrated by Mark Zuckerberg after the 2016 election, when it was revealed that Luckey was secretly funding a pro-Trump troll group. (Which is somewhat ironic, because after Luckey helped elect Trump, many miserable people really did yearn for an escape to a better world.)

But he is far from the only person in the VR/Metaverse space who has said similar things. It was actually John Carmack who first spoke about a "moral imperative" to develop the Metaverse, and as far back as 1999. The term doesn't allude to Kant, but, as Carmack once told me by email, is a line from the '80s movie *Real Genius*. ("So don't take it too terribly seriously.")

But he is quite serious about the moral part:

"There is no technical reason why a VR headset needs to be much more expensive than a cell phone," as he put it to me. "These are devices that you could imagine almost everyone in the world owning. This means that some fraction of the desirable experiences of the wealthy can be synthesized and replicated for a much broader range of people, and that is a reasonable characterization of the positive aspects of a technological civilization."

I tend to think a future where billions of the globe's most destitute queue up to enter Internet cafes in smoggy, sunbaked megalopolises so that they can briefly enjoy a virtual beach on a tropical island in the Metaverse seems somewhat dystopian. But then again, many making VR and metaverse platforms would strenuously disagree with me.

As I cover in Chapter 1, it's a mistake to assume that simply because *Snow Crash* takes place in a dystopian future, the Metaverse itself is dystopic. Stephenson himself denied that interpretation even before cofounding a metaverse company himself.

But as the 21st century (if not the 20th century) has taught us, a full-blown dystopia need not emerge for us to still witness a low-pitched but constant level of preventable suffering and cruelty.

The most likely and imminent pitfalls for the Metaverse will not involve pacifying the poor with virtual experiences.

The far more plausible future will simply expand on what is happening now: people enjoying metaverse platforms and the possibilities in them—but not being treated fairly or openly by the companies who profit from them.

The Dangers of an Unregulated Metaverse

Starting in 2022, officials and staffers with at least two major world governments reached out to me, asking for advice on regulating metaverse platforms. Their findings may become public before you read this book. I was impressed by the level of knowledge they already had about their underlying technology.

All of which is a roundabout way of saying: Government regulation is coming.

So if you're a metaverse developer—or for that matter, if you consume, create, sell, or market content on metaverse platforms—you should anticipate that legislation directly targeting your interests will soon be up for serious consideration.

This should not be too much of a surprise. Nearly half of the United States Congress are Gen X or Gen Y, people who grew up with games and online virtual worlds and are often personal users of them. As just one notable example: Alexandra Ocasio-Cortez is not only an avid gamer but uses platforms like Twitch and the virtual world Animal Crossing in her political outreach.

As for the specific regulation, I'm pretty sure (or know for a fact) that U.S./EU government bodies are looking into the topics below, framed in terms of five starting questions:

- Are metaverse companies doing everything possible to prevent harassment of their users, especially women and vulnerable minorities?

- Are metaverse platforms that are predominantly used by children fully informing these children's parents about all the risks and costs involved with creating and selling content, mostly on behalf of a for-profit company—along with the risks of interacting with other users in general, especially adults who might be predators and other bad actors?

- Should metaverse platforms officially allow users to form labor unions, so that they may collectively bargain with companies for a fair revenue share, not to mention having a say about the use of their personal data, especially if they are minors?

- Are blockchain-based metaverse platforms accurately communicating all the risks involved with NFTs and virtual real-estate speculation?

- Should the government impose restrictions on VR headset manufacturers to protect user privacy and data?

From my view the answer key is currently: No, No, Yes, No, Yes.

Meantime, metaverse platforms themselves seem amazingly slow to confront these issues, let alone acknowledge them. Then again, they could always wait for Congress to subpoena their CEOs to face the flinty glare of AOC.

Several concerns soon to be scrutinized deserve an in-depth look:

User Manipulation Through Avatars

When Meta's potential to cause harm to metaverse users is discussed, most experts point to the way the company tracks and records user activity while wearing a Quest headset—giving Meta incredible, unprecedented (and easily exploitable) insights into the user's interests and desires, with the power to literally see what each consumer sees and what they gaze at most.

That is certainly a deep and valid concern, though the VR industry is fairly aware of it—and any danger this might pose is limited by the Quest's slow sales and relatively low user activity. If Zuckerberg's ultimate goal with the Quest and the company's metaverse technology is to create the ultimate consumer behavior tracking technology, it's falling short due to a notable shortage of actual consumers.

Less known is how *avatars themselves* might be abused to manipulate our behavior, even for decisions with global consequences. And the use of VR is not even required.

Between 2004 and 2008, Stanford academics led by Jeremy Bailenson and Nick Yee were able to alter a group of volunteers' preferences for the upcoming U.S. presidential election.

They were able to do that simply by showing these volunteers photos of what appeared to be the candidates' faces—Hillary Clinton, George W. Bush, John Kerry, and so on—that

FIGURE 13.1

Jeremy et al., 2008, Oxford University Press

had been altered in photo editing software. The researchers subtly combined the faces of presidential candidates with photos of the volunteer test subjects themselves.

Yee publicly reported the terrifying results in the run-up to the 2020 election, when there was concern that Putin's Russia was once again manipulating U.S. social media on behalf of Donald Trump.

"We found," Nick announced then, "that people are more likely to vote for candidates that look more like them (even in high-stakes/information races like the 2004 Kerry/Bush election), and this photo manipulation was largely undetectable."

Doing this changed the volunteers' aggregate vote preference by up to 9 percent, Nick told me—more than enough to change the outcome of most elections.

Worse, very few volunteers were even aware of this manipulation.

"With lesser known candidates," as Nick recounts to me now, "volunteers said, 'This guy kind of looks like my pastor or my uncle.' But very few of them said, 'Oh, you took my photograph and you blended it with this political candidate.' Because at a 20 percent [morphing] ratio, it really was not detectable on the conscious level. . . . For a lot of these manipulations, they can be so subtle, and yet still have a measurable effect."

It's a dark application of the Proteus effect that I discuss in the Introduction:

If an attractive avatar unconsciously encourages the user to be more confident, an avatar that seems to resemble a blood relative can unconsciously encourage the user to trust it more—even when that trust can be exploited.

This experiment was conducted nearly two decades ago. Since then, new morphing technology (and its sophisticated, AI-powered cousin, the Deep Fake) has become even more powerful, with an ability to convert a user's photo onto the appearance of a virtual world avatar. (And Meta, it need not be said, likely has the greatest repository of people's photos—voluntarily uploaded to Facebook and Instagram—in the entire world.)

"[It would be] really easy for them to take the photographs stored in Facebook and then reuse them in the VR platform," Nick Yee tells me. "So we're living in this very different age . . . [it potentially] opens an interesting door to them, dynamically creating virtual salesmen that adopt 25 percent of your facial structure. They look similar to you but not identical to you."

This concern still holds with Meta's current approach to avatars, which are designed to resemble the user in a cartoon form. Even though the overall look is nonrealistic, these avatars still maintain a core resemblance to their user. And the fact that they are cartoonish opens up another potential vector for manipulation:

"Once you move into the more cartoony faces," Nick tells me, "you're more likely to come up with attractive faces." This kind of avatars tend to resemble babies in their attractiveness: "Your eyes are wide, your skin is smoother . . . so that sets into motion other kinds of psychological effects."

Manipulation of User Data and a New Glass-Steagall Act

All this potential for abuse is careening toward us at a time when social media algorithms have already created an alternate perception of the world where, say, a teeming mass of rioters is encouraged through Facebook to storm the U.S. Capitol.

"Reality's being warped for a lot of people even without VR," as XR technologist Avi Bar-Zeev puts it to me, "but as soon as you are literally able to warp people's reality and change [it], all bets are off in terms of manipulations."

Bar-Zeev has been a relatively lonely prophet on this point, as Silicon Valley embraced VR and then casually shifted its obsession to the Metaverse, rarely discussing the implications of a technology that can track the windows to the soul, collecting data on what items and people a VR user looks at for the longest time—and then alter *what* is being looked at, according to their soul's desire.

"So if a company wants to cycle through 100 iterations of cars to figure out which is the exact car that I really like, I just need to spend time in the [virtual] world. The more time I spend, the closer the system comes to showing me the exact car that I want. And I accidentally give them feedback that lets them know when they're ready.

"They don't know what thoughts you're having, but they can tell what you're paying attention to and how you're reacting to it."

Dire warnings of impending doom can get tiresome without a specific call to action, so I ask Avi what he would say if a leading senator asked him to frame his concerns in terms of an enforceable law.

"We need a Glass-Steagall Act for data," he tells me immediately. That's the former U.S. law that prohibited banks from also operating as investment firms. "We repealed it, and we regret it, right?"

Largely eliminated in 1999, the law's expiration was a core cause of the financial crisis of 2007–2008 that nearly led to a global depression.

So, yes.

"What we need," Bar-Zeev goes on, "is a separation from the parts of the companies that collect the data and use it for practical purposes like improving the quality of the world."

He means VR/virtual world user-interaction data that helps a company track down performance problems and system bugs.

"So that part of the company has access to data. And maybe it needs to be a whole other company that sells all the ads. They shall not talk. They shall not share information. That's the way I would write it: The information must be firewalled so that the ads can't use it."

It's not enough, he adds, to ask that metaverse companies strip the user's names from the tracking data.

"A lot of people make this mistake. They say, well, as long as we anonymize it, we're fine. But no, it's not about anonymizing it. It's about how effective it is. You don't have to know who I am, if you can build a profile of me on the fly in 10 minutes."

So does that mean breaking up Meta from its XR division?

"I would be okay if they can technically prove that the data does not flow between the biometric collection and the advertising [division]," Bar-Zeev speculates. "If they can firewall it in such a way that literally the user has the keys to the encrypted data for anything that's saved, and the company does not have the key, and it's never sent to the cloud. And there's no possibility of that data leaking over to the other part of the company. That would be a good start.

"But if they can't prove that, I think you have to separate the financial concerns just like we did with Glass-Steagall."

Corporate Encroachment on User Creativity

While I was researching VRChat for this book, an interview subject decided I should upgrade my avatar and instantiated a purple teleport portal in the air.

It instantly transported us to an underground complex displaying custom-made avatars free for the taking—but since nearly every option is a replica of characters from Disney and Warner Brothers' cartoons, it might as well have been called "Joe Bob's Copyright Infringement Emporium." (Recall also the hundreds of user-made re-creations of Netflix's *Squid Game* in Roblox.)

These are just brief glimpses below the surface of the IP infringement iceberg bearing down on the Metaverse across multiple platforms.

By definition, a metaverse platform enables user-generated content. By the inevitability of human nature on the Internet, much of that content will actually be fan tributes or outright knockoffs of highly protected intellectual property owned by Disney and other giant conglomerates.

To put it another way: The lawyers are coming for the Metaverse, and they're bringing avatars.

This is not hyperbole. Due to Second Life's prominent public profile back in the day, lawyers regularly scanned the virtual world, often sending terse cease-and-desist messages to everyday users. In 2009, for instance, lawyers for the Frank Herbert Estate sent takedown orders to a small user community that had created a virtual desert to engage in roleplay based on Herbert's *Dune* novels.

The mystery is why the IP lawyers have not yet struck in concerted force already.

To some extent, I imagine they are largely looking the other way while their media clients consider partnerships with or even outright acquisition of these metaverse platforms. At some point, however, this benign neglect will end, and the DMCA takedown requests will start flying.

Brands should always keep this in mind, whenever planning their content strategies. User creators should also learn their rights—and begin engaging with organizations like the Electronic Frontier Foundation.

"We're definitely very adamant about fair use and fan-made content to be protected as a form of expression," Rory Mir, Associate Director of Community Organizing at EFF, tells me. "If someone wants to make an Iron Man avatar—yeah, that's something that should be protected."

My hope (and it may be in vain) is that metaverse companies preemptively work with major media holders to carve out fair use principles that allow fan-made tributes to their favorite IPs under reasonable parameters.

Media companies themselves should consider enlightened ways of offering official editions of their work to metaverse creators—and encourage fair use creativity around their IPs.

Before Disney acquired Marvel, for instance, the comics giant did indeed distribute copies of an official Iron Man avatar outfit in Second Life, part of the promotion for the first *Iron Man* movie in 2008. And rather than release a static version, the marketing company made it fully editable, so users could create their own customized versions and take them on zany adventures in the virtual world.

To judge by the results, this gamble has paid off, leading to a large number of *Iron Man*–related screenshots and machinima shared on social media, amplifying promotion for the movie.

"The challenge for lots of corporations and established companies is whether they end up defaulting to the controllable level of where the user can modify the outfits but can't really create [with them]," VC Hunter Walk observes. He recommends the *Iron Man* route, "as opposed to some of their inclinations around protecting and extending the IP rights."

Those are just three areas that deserve immediate attention. At some point, however, we will need to squarely face the Experience Machine problem.

Confronting the Experience Machine

When he was still an engineer at Linden Lab in the mid-2000s, Jim Purbrick would often give presentations about Second Life at various European tech conferences. He began to hear the oddest response from attendees:

"On more than one occasion," as he put it to me, "I was left flat-footed by enthusiastic [SL users] thanking Linden for building Second Life. So that they would have a virtual world they could upload their consciousness to.

"It was pretty mind-blowing and more than a little terrifying, given that I'd seen the code."

I have also spoken with people like this in Second Life and other virtual worlds—confidently telling me that they hope these digital realms can become realistic and immersive enough that before they die, they'll be able to hook electrodes into their brain and digitize themselves into this artificial afterlife.

In an influential thought experiment from 1974, Harvard philosopher Robert Nozick argued against hedonism by asking readers to imagine an "experience machine":

Suppose there was an experience machine that would give you any experience you desired. Super-duper neurophysicists could stimulate your brain so that you would think and feel you were writing a great novel, or making a friend, or reading an interesting book. All the time you would be floating in a tank, with electrodes attached to your brain.

"Would you plug in?" he asks the reader. After all, "What else can matter to us, other than how lives feel from the inside?"

To Nozick, it was patently obvious we would reject this vision. He believed our rejection proved there was something besides mere experience that is fundamental to human existence.

"We learn that something matters to us in addition to experience," wrote Nozick, "by imagining an experience machine and then realizing that we would not use it."

But some 50 years later, Nozick's device is no longer a fanciful thought experiment. Many leaders in metaverse development believe they are now building what is, for most intents and purposes, Robert Nozick's Experience Machine.

And strikingly, many of them explicitly reject Nozick's conclusion that there is more to a happy life than pleasing simulation. And not just as a philosophical stance but as a serious business proposition targeting billions of consumers, backed by some of the world's largest corporations—either to give the poorest of us the simulation of a better life or to create immortality, or both.

If they are right, the implications for our culture, economy, even the world itself promise to be profound in ways we have barely begun to contemplate.

In fairness, VR and the Metaverse are only the latest technologies that simulate human experience.

"I think you are making a false distinction between real and virtual life," as John Carmack put it to me once. "Activities in VR are aspects of your real life, just like the movies you watch and the books you read. If your experiences in VR are soothing and happy, they contribute to a better 'real' life.

"If people are having a virtually happy life, they are having a happy life. Period. If someone wanted nothing more in life than to read books, providing them with a massive library is not doing them a disservice, even if that means that they are less likely to be involved in other activities."

This strikes me as well-meaning sophistry, since no one is also arguing that books in themselves can or should be a sufficient replacement for material and social needs they are lacking.

Carmack and Luckey are hardly alone among pioneers of the virtual reality/metaverse business who well and truly believe that their technology is an adequate pacifier for the underprivileged.

"In a sense some of the things he's saying are mild in relation to what some of my friends in Silicon Valley say," as VR pioneer Jaron Lanier once told me, when I asked for his thoughts on Palmer Luckey's vision of a virtual utopia for the poor. "I hear a lot of talk that people who are rich and successful will be immortal and everyone else will get a simulated reality. And that's the kind of thing that's really evil that might lead to a violent reaction."

To judge by the heavy sigh when I bring up this topic with Matthew Ball, *The Metaverse* author has also heard similar pronouncements many times.

"I think that's a depressing and sad argument to make. There are so many ways in which we can understand 3D simulation and the Metaverse as solving or helping to solve current problems—access to opportunity, to jobs, to education. But those who believe that it *is* the solution, that it's sufficient . . . I really do find it offensive, insensitive, and ignorant.

"And that's because these are societal problems; they're human problems. They're questions of me-versus-them or us-versus-you. And the idea that, 'well, we've now got technology that's good enough for the real thing, and thus, let's give it to them and move on,' is disrespectful and wrong."

On this question I have a decided bias, having grown up in Hawaii. By day, the sun marinates the earth, creating heat waves infused with the scent of hibiscus, a humid perfume that follows you even into the most urban areas of Honolulu. Outside my family's home at night, a warm, softly fierce wind swaddles you, bringing with it the ambient distant roar of ocean waves, gently crashing forever.

I've experienced many simulations of my island home on multiple metaverse platforms. While many are visually impressive, none come close to approximating the lived essence of Hawaii. No simulation of the empirical senses can capture it. There is no haptic platform capable of replicating *aloha*, a concept far more resonant to islanders than tourist brochures suggest, and there is little corporate impetus to re-create the pangs of past colonialism and moral debts yet unpaid. So it is not even conceivable for me to imagine a desirable Metaverse whose moral imperative is to simulate paradise for the world's poor. (Many of whom, sad to say, are themselves native Hawaiian.)

Far better, I believe, to fight for a Metaverse that benefits all of us now, connecting us across borders and accidents of birth to *other people*. Because in the end, the simulations of the world itself only matter if there is a community to share them with.

That future is possible. But only if we draw from the often harsh lessons we have learned so far.

14

Metaverse Lessons for the Next 30 Years

We cannot completely know how metaverse platforms of the next few decades will grow and evolve. But if the past is any guide (and it always is), and we are dedicated to making the best possible Metaverse, worthy to be The Metaverse not simply because it satisfies the core technical requirements but because it thrives on maximum human flourishing, we do have some fairly reliable rules to go by.

Learning from the debunked myths explored in Chapter 8, we know some of the fundamentals: The Metaverse must be multiplatform and mobile-facing, and not fully orient itself around XR devices; its user community must be interoperable across platforms; its avatars and graphics should not be hyper-realistic, but expressive, responsive, and highly customizable instead. And web3 aspects will probably not be involved, except perhaps on an experimental basis.

Positive principles for the Metaverse are more nuanced and subtle and include:

Community Creates Value—Not the Other Way Around

The failure of Decentraland and other blockchain-based metaverse platforms, as covered in Chapter 6, illustrates the limitation of virtual worlds that begin with virtual real estate sales and other speculation. The users attracted to them tend to be there in search of easy riches and rarely become active participants in the virtual world itself.

By contrast, one rule of thumb for judging whether a metaverse platform is successful is this: You will find a subset of content creators who create not primarily for profit but for the benefit of the user community, and social recognition by that community.

We have seen that in powerful examples across many metaverse platforms, from a professional game artist creating free games in Roblox, to an unemployed developer creating and then open sourcing a C# compiler to help VRChat creators, to a technologist with IBM creating transcendent works of immersive art in Second Life simply for the sake of sharing that vision with others.

This social spirit is not simply about idealism. Second Life founding member Hunter Walk, who left Google/YouTube to become an influential venture capitalist, sees this community-centric approach as fundamental to its sustainability as a platform.

As he puts it in a rhetorical question: "Is this a space that feels owned by the people or does it feel owned by companies—where the business model was set before the creative model? My belief is that parts of a successful metaverse will be more open and jazz-like—creative model first, business models second."

A related realization is that getting community correct first and foremost matters most of all.

"If you invest in creating a positive environment up front," as Linden Lab/Meta veteran Jim Purbrick puts it, "you can get a positive feedback loop. If you don't set that up up front, you end up with a toxic environment; it's super difficult to turn that around later on."

When VRChat was besieged by YouTube trolls, it very nearly ran the risk of being branded as a troll haven, and then being abandoned when those trolls became bored. By creating a karmic trust system that rewarded active users who contributed positively to the community, VRChat instead grew and thrived.

Accessibility Isn't Optional; It's Fundamental

When VRChat was wracked by a user protest (Chapter 7), part of the outrage was driven by the removal of some user-made modifications that helped players who were color blind and had other challenges. It's part of a phenomenon I've seen over two decades: people with various physical and mental disabilities finding deep and lasting value in metaverse platforms. The very elderly and physically disabled; the housebound, seeking a portal into new possibilities; veterans with PTSD, connecting with each other through the anonymity of avatars across far distances; those for whom in-person social interactions for various reasons are excruciating, but who still yearn for human connection; those with severe vision impairments, who rely on a virtual world's audio cues and text-to-audio options to create a place for themselves in the community. For people like these and many more, creating a metaverse platform with maximum accessibility for everyone is not simply a matter of satisfying regulatory requirements or even just out of ethical obligation (though it is also definitely that): Accessibility is essential to a metaverse platform's success.

A Game First and Foremost

Every metaverse platform that's been launched without game mechanics has failed to gain mass adoption; every metaverse platform that has gained a large audience was first launched explicitly as a game, or is embedded with game mechanics. That ludic framework may be as explicitly game-like as Fortnite or as meta as VRChat's karmic trust system, where continued good behavior earns greater access. Second Life, as we see in Chapter 2, squandered its early success by frustrating new users with a lack of game structure or goals. As we also saw, a game structure is not an artificial imposition to a platform but a recognition that a virtual world with avatars is inherently a game-like play space, dependent on rules of shared imagination.

As it happens, games are also the most proven way to satisfy Philip Rosedale's ultimate goal for the Metaverse to be a platform as openly convivial as Burning Man. For the 80,000 or so souls who attend the Black Rock festival yearly, it may be easy to meet anyone there (most of whom, by a happy coincidence, happen to be various levels of stoned, attractive, and naked). For the rest of the world, it might be a good idea to first play a game together. It's no coincidence that most third spaces, from pubs and bars to parks and beaches, also center games as a primary social lubricant.

Collaborative, In-World Creation Remains the Gold Standard

Something magical was lost when our focus in metaverse platforms moved away from live, immersive social creation, and we resigned ourselves to offline editing in 3D software programs. While I hesitate to call this a hard and fast principle, because there are several exceptions, I'm dedicated to the belief that it remains the most unique and profoundly exciting feature of metaverse platforms: the ability to instantiate objects from nothingness into the virtual world, and in real time—while working with other avatars around the world—and then together shape these disparate pieces into a jaw-dropping 3D experience.

Founding Second Life CTO Cory Ondrejka agrees:

"Focusing on approachable in-world tools would be where I start; and make sure that the act of using in-world tools is so much fun, and showing people how to use the in-world tools is so much fun, you can really build your hook there to begin with."

But where Second Life and Minecraft enabled prim-based creation, Ondrejka believes the future is enabling users to dynamically build with high-definition 3D objects:

"I think I'd be very focused on holding hard constraints that what you can build in-world is as high quality as what your core developers can build. You can't have an escape hatch like, 'Oh, here are the cute little tools we gave for the audience, but when we really want to build, we go off and use [a professional offline 3D editor].'"

With its steady growth in monthly active users (from 40 million in 2016 to upwards of 170 million in 2022), Minecraft remains the shiniest testament to the power of multiuser collaboration, contributing new content—and new social/community bonds—to the virtual world with a speed and diversity of creation to make the platform feel endlessly fresh. (According to Minecraftservers.org, there are well over 30,000 private servers set to Creative Mode.)

Among current metaverse platforms with a strong VR-centric focus, Rec Room probably has two to three times more monthly active users than VRChat. It too enables live, collaborative creation:

"In Rec Room, you're doing it with up to 40 people across almost any platform, voice chatting and co-building and hanging out the entire time," as a dedicated creator on the platform told me. "You don't have the friction of needing to go download Unity or Roblox Studio and learn all of this dev-tool stuff on your own. Plus other Rec Room users will teach you how to build in real time."

Time Shifting and Social Media Are Essential to the Metaverse

What we do in a virtual world unfolds in real time. That's key to the power of the Metaverse, and also among its chief hurdles, since the most fun or interesting activity is destined to be missed by most members, if only by dint of the world's different time zones. As I note in Chapter 4, it was the early metaverse communities of Minecraft and later Roblox and others that embraced YouTube and Twitch to share their activity in a time-shifting context. (Or even enjoying the latest event as passive viewers, without having to make the full, attention-consuming leap into the virtual world.)

Due to this need, Discord also rapidly grew among gamers and metaverse denizens, giving them a place for asynchronous conversations and content sharing, as well as a channel into their favorite virtual world community that they can access while multitasking.

To this day, most metaverse companies miss this insight, treating social media as a kind of afterthought as opposed to deeply integrating it into their platform from the start and treating it as a *part* of their virtual world.

On a broader level, a metaverse platform deeply integrated with social media extends its reach from the immersive space, acting as a draw to new users. On a still broader level, a social media ecosystem devoted to more virtual creativity and fun, and less real-world toxicity and outrage, amplifies the moral force of the Metaverse.

Avatars Shape Culture

We have explored how ultrarealistic human avatars can negatively shape the culture of a metaverse platform, arguably shifting Second Life in its later years from a highly imaginative creative platform to a heavily materialistic, often-toxic consumer-driven experience (with some creativity still persisting on the sidelines). This variety of avatar definitely did not grow Second Life's user base. And once again, human avatars were only one of many types in *Snow Crash*, with its virtual world shared by avatars of all species and varieties.

What's also clear is how much nonrealistic, heavily stylized avatars have succeeded instead:

Roblox and to a lesser extent Fortnite created avatars ideally suited to their target core demographic: the former, simple, blocky avatars evocative of LEGO characters, most appealing to young kids; the latter, semirealistic human avatars with a expressively cartoonish aesthetic reminiscent of characters from a *Star Wars* animated series or the hit video game *Team Fortress*—IP highly popular with teenage gamers.

While VRChat launched with semirealistic human avatars as its default option, the openness of avatar customization encouraged players to expand the actual spectrum of avatar appearance to include *anime* characters, furries, and avatars based on popular film and TV cartoon characters. This wide range of creativity went on to influence the kind of content created in VRChat in general, moving far beyond environments where human avatars organically "fit."

The challenge, as discussed in Chapter 11, is presenting a selection of default avatar options with aesthetics that are broad and diverse enough to attract nearly *all* demographic groups, and can grow the community in a positive direction. This remains a goal for the metaverse platforms of the future.

Jenova Chen's heavily stylized sylph-like avatars for his upcoming metaverse experience offers us one promising avenue.

Beyond that, the creative space remains wide open. As Nick Yee points out, in the history of virtual world/metaverse platforms over the last few decades, roughly 95 percent of them have been centered around human/humanoid, one-to-one embodied avatars.

It's likely that the Metaverse cannot keep growing without addressing this largely unchallenged assumption.

"There's this whole separate evolutionary branch of what are other ways we could be doing work and play and social interaction if we weren't forced into this one user, one avatar and embodied assumption," as Yee puts it. "What if you could control multiple avatars at the same time? What if multiple people had to control the same avatar?"

The main goal, Yee writes to me, is "to look at the 'social architecture' (i.e., the hidden parameters and rules) in virtual worlds (and that includes the design and affordances of avatars) *intentionally* rather than as arbitrary/accidental outcomes or simply replicating reality. Or put another way, to think about the goals of a specific virtual world and to make sure the social architecture supports those goals."

In Chapter 10, for instance, Yee mentions how changing the size or visibility of avatars would help make metaverse-based meetings more productive "because we know that group discussions are typically unbalanced if left to their own devices."

In a similar way, Yee argues, setting limits for avatars up front so that they can't easily evolve into the Malibu curse that hampers Second Life to this day:

"[W]e might consider what goal we're trying to reach (or lean towards). For example, if the goal is to discourage hyper-consumerism/materialism, then less realistic/blocky or simple/uncustomizable avatars may be more productive—if there is literally no way to make your avatar look better or different, then you stop spending time doing so, and you spend your creative energies elsewhere (e.g., early Minecraft)."

As a thought experiment—and hopefully an inspirational starting point—Nick Yee asks us to consider how a metaverse platform might evolve if the avatar choices don't follow the traditional path of humanoid and one user-one avatar, and instead, the designers make some dramatic departures up front:

"Consider also the possibility of breaking the current assumptions of what having an avatar means and the potential social consequences of:

1. You are given a random avatar, and you can't change it.

2. Your avatar changes every 24 hours, and avatars don't have persistent handles/IDs when this change occurs.

3. You are randomly paired with another user, and the two of you must share an avatar and figure out how to do so."

Some of these suggestions may seem radical to virtual world/ metaverse platform colleagues, but variations of them have been implemented in online games with some success.

"I think once we start brainstorming how differently we could be doing avatar design/control," as Nick Yee puts it, "it becomes clear very quickly how unimaginative virtual worlds have been and how large the potential design space actually is."

Community and Company Must Grow Together

We saw in Chapter 2 how, when Linden Lab open sourced its Second Life viewer software too soon, it permanently isolated the existing community from new users, permanently hurting its growth.

It also illustrates the need for a metaverse platform's corporate owners to gradually evolve with its most dedicated users.

"The economic impact of potential changes was a really, really strong emergency brake on everything we were trying to do," as Philip Rosedale puts it. A user-created innovation, once it becomes popular with the active community, cannot be removed without serious consequence.

Or as Rosedale puts it: "Creative economies can't be changed very much after they're initially released."

And we see in Chapter 7 how VRChat embraced something like this principle, incorporating a user-made tool into its development kit, then hiring the user who created it.

To say metaverse companies and communities must grow together implies that they must *thrive* together, sharing in the success that they make possible together. This means treating community creators as cherished collaborators and offering them the best possible revenue share.

Following something like this principle, Linden Lab shares its revenue from Second Life about equally with its community creators. It is a key reason why that virtual world still hums with life, even after nearly 20 years of existence. As I show in Chapter 4, however, leading platforms like Roblox still fall short of that ideal.

At some point soon, however, the community creators who make metaverse platforms possible will understand their power and advocate for themselves. Enlightened companies will embrace them as collaborators and flourish together.

A Metaverse that matters undermines the corrosive power of social networks to depress, anger, and divide us further by amplifying our offline outrage and envy.

A Metaverse that matters offers a creative platform where anyone, especially grassroots creators, can create content and experiences that are as appealing as what legacy media has to offer or more so—enabling them to thrive on the love of the user community, build a business for themselves, or both.

A Metaverse that matters affords us the ability to simulate nearly any experience in a shared immersive space, empowering a variety of applications from education and training to prototyping and marketing and beyond.

A Metaverse that matters will enable billions of people from many countries to interact with each other in a virtual world where offline identity and the prejudices based on it become secondary in a shared immersive space, a space where creativity, community, and fun matter more.

A Metaverse that matters is now in our hands to build.

Afterword: Where in the Virtual World the Platforms and People from This Book Are Now

Philip **Rosedale** continues to advise Linden Lab on the future of Second Life, though lately he's set his sights on a somewhat more ambitious goal: using what he's learned from the economies of metaverse platforms to solve global economic inequality in the real world:

"I want to give people something like the Linden Dollar but just as an iPhone app that they basically can use to buy and sell anything from each other," as he put it to me in a February 2023 call.

During the COVID-19 lockdown, Rosedale created an economic simulation that showed him a frightening thing: "Even with people in a small community trying to look after each other, you will basically end up with a kind of a natural, almost a thermodynamic problem, where some randomly chosen people will basically just end up getting more and more money."

He sees that in the state of the real-world economy: "If you recognize that the economic system we have is so broken, the only safe assumption is we're going to have a violent revolution, as has been had many times throughout history."

Some metaverse platforms might help with inequality, he believes, but then again, others will not: "Roblox is a lottery you're not going to win," as he puts it, echoing concerns raised in Chapter 4. "You can't go into Roblox and say, 'I'm gonna make my living in here.' Maybe you can go into Second Life and say that."

His new project, called FairShare (www.fairshare.social), aims to solve that by offering people who sign up a universal basic income modeled after one that's helped keep Second Life's economy thriving for 20 years:

"You have some kind of tax that drains money out of the system—a sink, in Linden Lab terms. But then you also have a faucet that puts money into the world. But the money always goes in equally for everybody."

Unlike other UBI programs, distribution would be done among friend groups through their own digital currency. And Philip Rosedale believes he can massively scale FairShare (still in an early phase when we spoke) to millions:

"It's something where when you signed up, found a group of friends, you suddenly got $50 a day for the rest of your life," as he puts it. "That would be pretty viral."

It's one of several ambitious projects he's working on from Linden Lab's Second Life office, which once housed hundreds of employees but is still fairly empty, as the company largely remained remote, post-COVID.

"From this point in my life," Philip Rosedale tells me, he's going to work on projects like this. All of them "have the property that they're attempting to use technology to do something very good for people, generally focusing on inclusion and connection."

He is still striving, in other words, to bring his dream from Burning Man decades ago in the desert into a broader reality.

Cory Ondrejka continues in his role at Google as VP of Product Management and Tech Advisor to Google's CEO. From that vantage, he sees a major leap in metaverse technology ahead: "As crypto fades, generative AI takes off, and wearables keep plodding along," he tells me. "I think we're only a few years away from an entirely new generation of virtual worlds taking entirely new approaches to rendering and simulation."

Meta: In February 2023, *The Wall Street Journal* published a memo from Meta's vice president of Horizon, outlining that year's goals and strategies for its metaverse platform. After nearly $16 billion spent by Meta's Reality Labs in 2022 alone, they were disarmingly modest:

The company has set 500,000 monthly active users as the unit's goal for the first half of 2023, with one million as the goal for the full year, according to the memo.

500K MAU, as you may recall, is a bit less than the number of users a small startup called Linden Lab attracted to its own metaverse platform. In 2007.

Roblox announced strong quarterly revenue and user growth in February 2023, with its average daily active user rate up to 65 million in January, growing from 58.8 million in December 22. As a result, its stock grew by 25 percent, making it more valuable than traditional AAA game publishers such as Take-Two Interactive and Electronic Arts.

In February 2023, a small team of community developers released the latest version of Frontlines, their attempt to create a Call of Duty–level multiplayer FPS game on Roblox with comparable graphics and gameplay quality. With backing from the company's Game Fund, providing support for indie teams, they succeeded: Frontlines rapidly went viral among gamers and major gamer publications, eliciting responses that were uniformly in this vein: "I can't believe this is Roblox." In doing so, it also offered a shining example of how Roblox could overcome the Metaverse Age Cliff and even become competitive with gamer platforms like Steam.

Fortnite: At GDC 2023 in March of that year, Epic unveiled the long-awaited Fortnite Creative 2.0, directly integrating Unreal with Fortnite, enabling multi-user, multiplatform live editing along with many other powerful tools. Even more key, Epic announced a revenue sharing deal where community creators would receive 40 percent of items bought in the Fortnite store commensurate with the popularity of their island. With these and other moves, Fortnite Creative became far more of a full-fledged metaverse platform.

Epic's Tim Sweeney capped these announcements with a galvanizing speech in which he rejected Silicon Valley's narrative that failed web3 metaverse platforms, and Meta's stumbles with Horizons and the Quest headset, meant that the concept as a whole was moribund. Pointing out that Fortnite, Roblox, Minecraft, and other platforms had continued growing, with "over 600 million active users in these virtual worlds," he said:

"[The Metaverse is] on a growth trajectory that'll put it at billions of users by the end of this decade, so we can set aside the crazy hype cycle around NFTs and VR goggles. These technologies may play a role in the future but they are not required. This revolution is happening right now."

VRChat continues adding updates and new features for its developer community, and in March of 2023 announced the imminent release of a VRChat app for Android mobile devices later in the year, with a VRChat for iPhone coming soon after.

Somewhat ironically, VRChat's entrance into mobile was made possible by Meta: "Since the Meta Quest runs Android," as the company explained on its blog, "any world or avatar that works on Quest loads just fine on Android mobile." So even if Meta's ambitions to build the Metaverse had fizzled, it still empowered those of VRChat.

Lamina1 in early 2023 announced that its first phase was live for testing to the public—the first step for launching its revenue solution for creators on multiple metaverse platforms. Former Magic Leap executive Rebecca Barkin was appointed CEO, with Neal Stephenson continuing to be Lamina1's chairman—and presumably he will continue in that role to develop his THEEE Metaverse project—the placeholder name for Stephenson's own plans to build the Metaverse from *Snow Crash*, just as he had reportedly tried to do as far back as the mid-90s.

Second Life continues adding features and updates to serve its existing community, most recently with the beta launch of physically based rendering (or PBR), a feature that would largely bring Second Life's notoriously out-of-date graphics closer to a modern standard. Most notable, in March 2023 Linden Lab finally and officially announced "with joy and trepidation" (as a Linden staffer put it) the imminent release of an iOS/Android app for Second Life running on Unity—bringing the venerable virtual world kicking and screaming into the modern era.

This was not the only project to update Second Life to Unity. In January 2023, when I was briefly in Second Life to do a quick errand for this book, a longtime developer who remembered me from my Linden Lab days casually IMed to say she was launching a somewhat ambitious project dubbed Crystal Frost, a new third-party Second Life viewer that runs on Unity:

"Having a modern graphics engine that's multithreaded, easier modability, implementing ray tracing and proper VR is super easy," the dev, known as "Berry Bunny" in Second Life, explained to me. "I have ideas about how to implement VR and make it feel like VRChat."

Just as notable (and on brand for the platform), I first learned about Crystal Frost through a casual, serendipitous encounter in-world—and it's an innovation put forward by a Second Life community creator, not the company itself.

A Metaverse that matters is one that helps transform the people in it for the better. So this book should end with the people we met at the very start, in the Introduction:

Gizem Mishi continues to head her Blueberry brand. In 2021, after Second Life was acquired, Mishi saw buzz around user-generated content flowering in multiple platforms. "I realized, okay, it's time to scale this company," she tells me.

Through 2022, exactly 10 years after Mishi stumbled as a college girl in Istanbul into Second Life, Blueberry began expanding its brand into Roblox and other platforms. House of Blueberry, Inc. now has over 12 employees and has been featured in *Vogue*, *Women's Wear Daily*, and beyond.

"All of our management team is made of women, and I want this side of the metaverse to be shaped by women," Mishi tells me. "It's very important for me that it be represented by women. We set the standards, we set the tone, and we become almost like the Disney of the Metaverse. I think we're in a good position to do that."

Nick Yee continues to co-lead his analytics firm, Quantic Foundry (quanticfoundry.com), giving top game industry clients deeply researched insights into what motivates people to play and enjoy games and virtual worlds. Lately he's been experimenting with AI image generators like Midjourney to create highly stylized and glamorous avatars based on users' real-life photos. Nick believes this application of AI could transform the Proteus effect, the phenomenon he co-discovered in which our avatars influence how we see ourselves, ideally for the better:

"It opens the door to much more fine-tuned and tailored interventions once avatar customizations can be dialed/modified more precisely," as he puts it to me. "E.g., stepping-stone avatars

FIGURE A.1 Fran Swenson/Fran Serenade
Photo by Tom Boellstorff

to slowly guide someone through a longer arc of development/transformation, like iterative Invisalign trays." He is referring to the clear mouth braces that people wear to gradually perfect their teeth. "Although," Nick acknowledges, "that might be the least sexy metaphor possible."

Fran Swenson, known by thousands around the world through her avatar "**Fran Serenade**," died at the age of 91 in 2019. In her last few years, Fran helped pioneer the use of virtual worlds for physical therapy—a tremendous potential achievement that could benefit millions in decades to come.

A memorial service was held for her in the Savoy Ballroom of Second Life, where Fran enjoyed watching her avatar twirl. Many attended from around the globe, including Tom Boellstorff, the UC Irvine anthropologist who first told me Fran's story:

"It was fitting to remember Fran in Second Life, since she brought so much strength and joy to so many there," Tom tells me. "I met Fran many times in the physical world, but she always felt she was just as real in-world, and her ability to bring people together in Second Life was as real as it gets. Behind that gentle laugh was a fierce will to love and support without judgment. For that I, like so many others, will be forever thankful."

After his stint as AM Radio in Second Life, **Jeff Berg** learned to model data in 3D and transitioned from IBM to an architecture firm, leading development of a software application that helps urban planners understand the environmental impacts of their designs in an online collaborative 3D environment. So the artist who created nostalgic metaverse experiences meant to evoke our relationship to nature went on to enable designers to do that better, but for cities of cement and steel.

The leap from metaverse imagination to real-world design was direct, Berg tells me:

"I literally went from the creation of virtual spaces to the real world using skills I had gained as AM Radio." He does that now at ARUP, an internationally renowned firm that creates sustainable designs for clients like NASA. "I'd still be working on traditional browser experiences had I not had the chance to be AM Radio."

He sees echoes of his artistic creations as AM Radio in his work today:

"For example, helping, even in a small way, an entity such as NASA to study the psychoacoustic impacts of drone designs on society helps ensure that the real places that inspired The Far Away continue to exist," he tells me. "And I mean a less tangible use of the word 'exist,' but persist with the intangible qualities that inspire others to explore the mysterious gestalt in our interactions with our environment and the places we build in it that haunt human perception."

Berg tells me he'd love to go back to creating transcendent experiences in a metaverse platform. But he adds, "I think there are so many things that need to be just right for such a wonderful moment to even happen. Maybe that's the most important ability

FIGURE A.2 Jeff Berg/AM Radio

of the Metaverse. It's to provide a place where such an amazing and rich moment could ever happen."

Then there's a brief pause in his answer to my question.

"I've just come back to writing it, leaning again towards my desk, towards this digital glow. While I was paused, I heard my daughter's footsteps through the open window in the hallway. I leaned back in my chair in my little apartment to see better down the hall to admire the flow in her hair as she arrived home. Suddenly I understood the wind in the trees more than I did a moment before."

This moment prompts Jeff Berg to picture his beloved avatar with a cane and top hat, often seen in a rustic cabin, looking out at the digital snow:

"Now I think of AM Radio leaning back in his own chair, to see a serene view, one of his own, and then as he leans forward at his simple desk in his little apartment, he knows that wonderful moment is gone."

In the spring of 2018, at the age of 96, **Mr. Charles Bristol** played his last gig in the Metaverse. After their virtual shows together, Charles often slept at the home of Russ "Etherian" Roberts, his drummer. Russ would drive the old gentleman around on errands, and then back to his dilapidated home.

"Charles lived in a poverty I never understood," Russ tells me now, as we stand near a soundstage in Second Life. "I grew up in New York City as a teenager and had never seen anything like that."

By then, they'd been jamming together in the virtual world on Sundays once a month for about 10 years. Through that time, as Russ remembers, Mr. Bristol seemed to believe that the audience displayed on the screen in front of him was real, as if on a video feed. He had cataracts the size of raisins in both eyes, and peering at the foggy world ahead, Charles told Russ he saw in it the lake near his home:

"Charles, this is a game," Russ would try to tell him. "It's not real."

But for Mr. Bristol it was real enough. Peering at the screen, he'd often fall in love with the pretty lady avatars from everywhere in the world, who came to dance to the blues riffs that he played.

Then one day, Charles Bristol did not show up for their regular Metaverse gig.

After a search around town, Russ found him in a hospital, recovering from pneumonia—but also diagnosed with stage four dementia.

Charles was transferred to a nursing home. Russ visited his friend weekly, insisting that the staff care for him well, even as Charles himself faded in and out of lucidity.

Until one visit, Charles was no longer there.

Mr. Charles Edward Bristol died on September 12, 2018. His family arranged his "Home Going Celebration," at Harland

Church of God, for September 22. By design, that would have been his 97th birthday.

Well over 150 attended, including Russ, who was (as he casually noticed after arriving) the only white person in the entire church. Russ doesn't recall ever telling Mr. Bristol's family about the gigs they played together in a digital world called Second Life, but the picture on the memorial flier hints at that connection.

On it, Charles Bristol wears a Panama hat and a showman's stylish shirt, triumphantly holding up two of his prize guitars. One was a gift from Von Johin, a fellow blues guitarist who also found success playing in Second Life.

The other guitar, electric and lacquer black, is one in the "Lucille" style made famous by blues legend B.B. King, a gift from another admirer. But Russ Roberts made it more special still.

After sending out advance emails to his entourage, Russ arranged to have B.B. King himself sign Charles Bristol's guitar and even have a short chat after one of his concerts. (This was very shortly before the music icon himself passed away, in 2015.)

Russ remembers watching at a distance the two bluesmen talking. We do not know what they said, but I wonder if Mr. Bristol mentioned these strange and otherworldly gigs he'd been playing for the last decade. I wonder what Mr. King would have said, he who had transformed so much of modern music and had gigged across the world. What would B.B. King have said about this new venue where people around the globe could quickly come to digitally twirl, enjoying the music that he played?

And then Mr. King signed the guitar that Charles would go on to play for his audience in Second Life.

As it happens, it is the very same guitar I heard when I randomly logged into Second Life in 2008. And realized that there was still so much of the story of the Metaverse left to be told.

That story is still unfolding now.

Glossary

3D engine Sometimes "game engine," the visualization software undergirding metaverse platforms. Unity and Unreal are by far the leading 3D engines. (See also *Unity* and *Unreal*.)

augmented reality (or AR): The layering of virtual/digital input on top of the user's view of the real world, typically through a head-mounted display or smartphone. (See also *mixed reality*.)

avatar From the Sanskrit for "godly incarnation," the onscreen character that a virtual world user controls.

blockchain A distributed online ledger (somewhat akin to Google Docs) that anyone can access to track payments in cryptocurrency or create "smart contracts" with others.

concurrency A key industry standard metric of user engagement, counting the number of users logged into the same Internet service (that is, a metaverse platform) at the same time. Peak concurrency, typically reached during special events, is a helpful metric for measuring the overall health of a platform, both technically and as a virtual community. Peak *daily* concurrency is a good indicator of average user activity, especially on the weekend, when metaverse platforms tend to be busiest. (See also *monthly active user* and *local concurrency*.)

core (or hardcore) gamers A subset of gamers who primarily enjoy 3D games with an emphasis on action and "twitch" (fast reflex) interaction, especially those played on video game consoles or high-end PCs. Traditionally and typically young men, though this is starting to change in places (see Chapter 5 on Fortnite).

cryptocurrency A form of virtual currency that generates its value by complex computer processing (proof of work) or contributions to the system (proof of stake).

Epic Games Store   Leading game distribution platform. As of early 2023, it reportedly has over 62 million monthly active users. (See also *Steam.*)

Discord   An extremely popular community messaging and communication system among gaming and metaverse platform users. (Think Slack for game geeks.) As of early 2023, it reportedly has over 150 million monthly active users.

framerate, frames per second, or FPS   Very broadly speaking in this context, the metric for determining how visually immersive (see below) a metaverse platform will be. At this date 60 FPS is optimal for PCs, while for VR headsets, which demand higher graphics, FPS should be closer to 90.

furries   In the metaverse context, avatars customized to resemble adorably cartoonish anthropomorphic creatures (typically cats, dogs, squirrels, and other fur-forward animals) similar to those you'd encounter at a theme park. A subculture unable to thrive before the Internet, furries have always been on the vanguard of metaverse platforms, which have creation tools powerful and open enough to convert avatars (typically human by default) into users' "fursonas" of choice. In interviews with furries over the years, they describe to me a feeling of discomfort with their real-life bodies, matched by a desire to be embodied in an avatar with animal cuteness. Typically friendly, tech savvy, and highly quirky.

immersion   The subjective "you are there" sense created by a VR headset or by navigating through a high-definition 3D graphics/audio virtual environment on any digital screen.

interoperability   In the context of metaverse technology, the ability to seamlessly move and use content (3D assets, user identity, and so on) from one virtual world/metaverse platform to another, or within them.

local concurrency   The number of users able to be online and represented as avatars in the same virtual space—for instance, in a concert hall, nightclub, or game space. (See also *concurrency.*)

machinima   Narrative videos created with action and imagery captured in a game/metaverse platform. Not to be confused with streaming. (See also *streaming.*)

The Metaverse versus metaverse platform/startup/company/etc.   How this book distinguishes between the core original concept and the many individual attempts to realize it. The Metaverse (capital M) is the original vision depicted in *Snow Crash*. It also refers to the industry as a whole that's attempting to develop it as a product; "metaverse platform/startup/ etc." (lowercase), by contrast, can refer to a startup like Core, a public company like Roblox, and so on.

mesh   In 3D game/virtual world graphics, the amalgam of vertices, edges, and faces that comprise an object. In the context of Second Life, an additional creation option introduced to the platform in 2010 that largely supplanted prims (see also *prim*) as the primary creative canvas.

mixed reality   In the context of metaverse platforms, the blending of virtual world data with external real-world devices/data, or vice versa. (See also *augmented reality*.)

MMO   Massively multiplayer (or multiuser) online world—typically with a role-playing game structure (it's often referred to as an MMORPG); for example, *World of Warcraft*, *Elder Scrolls Online*, and so on. To metaverse evangelists, MMOs are often considered training wheels for The Metaverse.

monthly active users (or MAU)   A key industry standard metric of user engagement on metaverse platforms and other online services. Not to be confused with "registered users," a number that often includes discontinued accounts. (See also *concurrency*.)

prim   Short for "primitive," the original creative canvas for Second Life—highly modifiable, connectible building blocks, similar to blocks in Minecraft. Supplanted to a great degree by mesh. (See also *mesh*.)

Proteus effect   First coined and researched by Nick Yee and Jeremy Bailenson at Stanford, the phenomenon where a user associates characteristics of their virtual world/metaverse platform avatar with aspects of their real-life identity. (See Chapters 9 and 10 for both positive and hazardous applications.)

Raspberry Pi   A small, affordable single-board computer often used by hobbyists for mixed reality projects. (See also *mixed reality*.)

scripting language   A programming language used to change, customize, and automate interactions on an existing system—in this case, a metaverse platform. For instance, Second Life's original scripting language is LSL (Linden Scripting Language), and VRChat's is Udon.

single shard   In the context of MMOs (see also *MMO*) and virtual world/metaverse platforms, refers to an online world where every user is online on the same server that hosts the world itself. Most MMOs have multiple shards—that is, copies of the world—that only a select number of players can share at the same time (typically several thousand). The original Metaverse conception implies a single shard virtual world, but very few worlds have been able to accomplish this successfully—the science fiction MMO Eve Online and the metaverse platform Second Life are rare exceptions.

Steam   An online game distributor and marketplace owned by Valve Software. As of 2021, it reportedly had over 120 million monthly active users. See also *Epic Games Store*.

streaming Live footage recorded and broadcast directly from a game/metaverse platform broadcast on a video platform such as YouTube or Twitch.

Unity A leading 3D engine used by Avakin Life, Garena Free Fire, Rec Room, VRChat, and other metaverse platforms. (See also *Unreal*.)

UGC User-generated content. On a metaverse platform, UGC ranges from high-quality 3D assets and shaders to skilled socialization.

Unreal The other leading 3D engine, used by Fortnite, Core, and other Metaverse platforms. Developed by Epic, publisher of metaverse platform Fortnite Creative. (See also *Unity*.)

virtual world (versus the Metaverse) A self-consistent simulation of an alternate reality, accessible by one user or many people. The simulated reality itself can be anything—a medieval fantasy world, the most popular context for MMOs (see also *MMO*), or a completely blank immersive space (think the empty, all-white "Desert of the Real" in *The Matrix*) that can be adjusted and customized by the user or developer. Most popular virtual worlds do not have all the features of a metaverse platform—MMOs, for instance, typically do not allow users to cash out their virtual currency for real money. A virtual world is not necessarily a metaverse platform, but a metaverse platform must always be wrapped around a virtual world.

Appendix A: Rules for Avatar Radicals and Reformers

The Metaverse is made by imperfect people with conflicting interests, but more than anything, it exists because user *communities* make it real. Rarely, however, do these communities act in solidarity to improve their own virtual world for the good of all.

Angry YouTubers often post rants complaining about a platform's new policy change or feature update, but they are usually ignored, or not even noticed amid the Internet's constant churn.

Small disorganized groups of users sometimes lash out at the platform's corporate owner in a way that doesn't help their cause but does threaten the overall health of their own community. We saw that with the Steam review bombing of VRChat featured in Chapter 7. While the startup's cofounders moved quickly to address the protest's legitimate concerns, the protesters' use of unfairly poor reviews hurt VRChat's growth and reputation on the world's largest game/VR distribution platform.

The need for focused activism by metaverse communities on *behalf* of metaverse communities has never been greater. User creators devote much of their lives to laboring on user-generated content that disproportionately profits the company owner; everyday users are often preyed upon by trolls and predators and don't feel sufficiently protected by the company. (Just to name a few of many concerns.) Government bodies or class action lawsuits may eventually step in to force change, but not usually before tremendous damage has already been done.

There's a better way to be an activist in the Metaverse. I've seen it play out myself.

Also, it was pretty hilarious.

Twenty years ago, at the start of my metaverse career, I witnessed a user uprising that changed the shape of Second Life and, by extension, the future of metaverse platforms to come. Second Life being Second Life, it was led by a humanoid cat abetted by a pro-wrestling supermodel and a teenage kid with a gang of dancing rats.

In its earliest period, Second Life operated on a monthly subscription model, with users getting a weekly stipend of Linden Dollars, a land allotment, and an allotment of objects they could create on their property. Create more prims than range allowed, and the company deducted some L$ from that user's account—in effect, a "tax" on excessive building. By doing so, the company hoped, it would discourage poorly optimized construction that contributed to server lag, which hurt everyone's enjoyment of the world.

These intentions backfired with beautifully catastrophic results.

Because as the tax policy was imposed in the late summer of 2003, a group of dedicated Second Life users were already hard at work creating "Americana," a kind of sprawling immersive theme park dedicated to iconic American locations: Fenway Park, Route 66, the Washington monument, and so on. But because the "prim tax" did not offer any exemptions for collaborative, group-based building projects, the Americana group suddenly found itself volunteering to create interesting content that benefited Linden Lab—and being taxed for their efforts.

So when I visited Americana after a barrage of frantic, late-night messages, it was already in open revolt.

The Route 66 gas station had been set ablaze by an insurrectionist midget in giant shoes, who stood there at 2 a.m., gleefully shooting off seditious fireworks while several flag-waving rats danced at his feet. And everywhere, giant tea crates: the Washington Monument had been buried by a stack of giant tea crates; the center of Fenway Park, buried under a pyramid of crates; Washington Monument, barely peeking out behind a pile.

The metaverse-based Boston Tea Party did not end there. Across the world, signs and billboards took up their cause; emblazoned on signs and billboards bristling from homes and lawns and cyberpunk alleys were the words "Born Free—Taxed to Death!"

While no one enjoys paying their monthly subscription fees, what bolstered the revolutionaries' protest was their charge that Linden Lab had failed to keep the vision it promised on its website and ads, and above all in its official slogan, "Your world, your imagination." What the tax system offered was not a world of freeform imagination, but a platform where stringent limits were set on that creativity.

The tax revolt frittered away after some weeks of protest, gently smothered by the embrace of Linden Lab, which took pains to publicly praise the protesters. But the uprising inadvertently exposed a near-fatal flaw in the company's operations: Its revenue model was so unfair, it provoked an organized revolt with virtual arson and gratuitous tea crate stacking.

But the revolt also indirectly encouraged the company to move away from the subscription model, and take what was a radical leap for the time: End monthly subscriptions, and instead, sell Second Life users plots of virtual land and charge usage fees for their regular maintenance. It led to the first sustained virtual real estate boom of any mainstream metaverse platform, and continues to be influential to this day. Consciously or not, the blockchain metaverse platforms I cover in Chapter 6 bear the DNA of this policy move, and therefore, to the Second Life community tax revolt.

This policy protest is among the earliest (and the most visual) to convulse a metaverse platform, but it's far from the only one.

Most of these later protests, however, quickly fall beneath the social media churn, unnoticed, and don't lead to actual platform change.

Following are lessons I take from Second Life's 2003 tax protest that dedicated user communities might want to draw from today.

Engage the Outside Media Ecosystem

Second Life's tax protest hit before the advent of Twitter, but it did occur during the rise of blog networks (the Twitter of the time), enabling news to quickly spread to a relatively small but often influential following. Had my reporting on the uprising not been featured by the Yale Law School blog and on Terra Nova, a group blog popular with virtual world/gaming academics, developers, and reporters, it would have likely fallen far beneath the surface of wider attention.

Since then, the scale of attention has completely changed. Metaverse platforms are no longer projects for niche technology startups, but massive companies worth billions of dollars, most of them publicly traded on the stock market.

This makes any significant uprising of community members a potential news item both for technology and business reporters, both of whom treat Twitter as their virtual news desk and tip hotline. Drawing their attention could make all the difference. A virtual tree falling in the forest doesn't make any sound in the Metaverse if no one's on the same server, and a metaverse platform controversy doesn't exist until *The New York Times* asks the corporate owners about it.

Attack the Policy, Not the People Who Enforce It

The Second Life revolutionaries' declaration was directed against "Mad King Linden"—decidedly not any actual, specific individual with Linden Lab. This was partly done (as its leader told me later) to prevent the protest from seeming like a personal attack against Linden's employees. This also made Linden Lab far more likely to fully listen to the grievances, without defensiveness or suspicion that the movement was really just an aggregate of personal grudges against them ginned up to seem like a revolt.

Make Revolution Fun for All— Including the Victims

With the giant tea crates and exploding rockets, the Tax Revolt was very much a Second Life phenomenon, fully leveraging user-created content and the improvisational play inherent in a metaverse platform. It's why so many SLers were eager to participate, or hang back as amused but still-engaged spectators— and why many Linden employees happily joined in the fun.

Mix Your Revolutionary Reality

In 2003, Second Life's population was mostly from the United States, so modeling the virtual tax revolt after the American colonists' resistance to British taxation had a unique emotional power for most of the community—and for most people reading about the revolt on technology news sites. And because it was directly associated with a major real world historical moment, anger over what was fundamentally a subscription policy suddenly took on an epic, transcendent appeal.

Hold the Platform Owner to Its Stated Ideals

What ultimately drove the revolutionaries, and led them to essentially succeed, was their belief that Second Life's tax policies were betraying its own vision as an improvisational, collaborative, community-minded world. Most other metaverse platform companies have similarly high-minded mission statements with lofty ideals—check their websites, I promise you it's somewhere there.

Declare Victory Before It's Too Late

Weeks after it started, the Second Life tax revolt began to generate a backlash (some users even dubbing themselves "Linden loyalists"), while infighting among the activists was threatening to undermine its general goals. But public statements by the company acknowledged that their message had been received. That was enough for the activist leaders to present their followers with a verifiable win and wind down the protest with dignity.

It occurs to me, having written this based on a protest that happened on a metaverse platform, that these guidelines probably apply equally well to real world activism. Your reality mileage, however, may vary.

Appendix B: Advice for Metaverse Reporters

I dearly hope the major news outlets assign beat reporters to the leading metaverse platforms, a need that's long overdue. At the risk of advising the competition, here are some of the practices and guidelines I've developed over 20 years on the Metaverse beat.

Fiercely Ferret Out and Report Unique, Engaged User Numbers and Concurrency Rates

It's easy to be swept up in a startup's grand vision, but a metaverse platform stands or falls on a growing, engaged community. ("Yes, this may be interesting," as my then-editor Om Malik once told me, "but *where's the fucking user growth?*") The hype wave over crypto and NFTs and the disastrous crash that followed would not have happened, had enough journalists maintained their focus on user metrics.

Leading Metaverse Community Creators Are as Important as Company Executives

Their stories are not only more interesting and inspiring, their insights into the platform that helps provide for their livelihood tend to be more brutally honest.

Related to that: Also *join* the metaverse platform you're reporting on it as a user, not necessarily to do embedded reporting (though that's highly recommended) but to get a firsthand view of how it works (or as is often the case, doesn't).

Please Stop Putting Photos of People in VR in Your Articles about the Metaverse

This one is more a note for your outlet's editor, but it definitely reflects poorly on you. Roughly 80 percent of features in mainstream media about the Metaverse feature photos of gawk-mouthed people in VR headsets. In the original depiction of the Metaverse, only the elite use standalone VR to access it, while the vast majority of people who use metaverse platforms in the real world do not access them through HMDs. Worst of all journalistically: Illustrating a metaverse story with headsets implicitly promotes Meta's VR-centric strategy at the expense of its many competitors who do not.

Acknowledgments

Much mahalo to my agent, David Fugate of Launch Books, who steadfastly steered this book's proposal through the rocky shores of a skeptical publishing world to the safe harbor of Wiley. Thanks to my Wiley editor, Jim Minatel, who ran with it from there and helped elevate it beyond what I originally imagined.

Copious gratitude to longtime friend and colleague Vanessa Camones, founder & CEO of AnyContext, a boutique marketing agency, for making my there as her editorial content lead the best "day job" a technology writer could have. It's through Vanessa that I met some of the experts and companies who provided insights throughout this book.

All thanks to everyone I spoke to for this book, many of whom I am not able to name but whose insights still ring throughout. Extra cheers to Nic Mitham, metaversing since back in the day and whose consultancy, Metaversed (www.metaversed .consulting), provided a key infographic and source in this book.

Thanks to Rick Chen at Blind (www.teamblind.com), the anonymous messaging app, for his assistance generating the metaverse platform employee survey data featured here.

And, as always, many thanks to all the regular readers of my blog, *New World Notes*, where much, if not most, of this book was germinated. (Doubly so to Cajsa Lilliehook and a host of columnists who've helped me keep the blog alive since 2006.) I'm grateful for all their feedback and commentary through the years, helping evolve my thought to the point you are reading now here.

About the Author

Wagner James Au is the author of *The Making of Second Life* (HarperCollins, 2008), based on his experiences as the first journalist officially embedded in a metaverse platform, telling the surreal, tragic, inspiring, and fundamentally human stories of its user community.

James continues covering virtual world culture on his blog *New World Notes*, the longest-running site devoted to the Metaverse, at nwn.blogs.com.

He is also the author of *Game Design Secrets* (Wiley, 2012) and has written about virtual worlds and gaming as an emerging cultural force for *The Wall Street Journal*, *Wired*, the *Los Angeles Times*, *Harper's Magazine*, *GigaOm*, *Salon*, *Polygon*, and *Kotaku*.

Along with helping launch and grow several metaverse-related platforms and technologies over the years, James is also Senior VP of Editorial & Content Strategy at AnyContext, a marketing and communications agency with clients in AI, VR, health-tech, gaming, web3, design, and future forecasting.

He spends far too much time on Twitter @slhamlet and on Discord as WJA#3523, and as an escape from the virtual world, lives and adventures in Los Angeles with his wife.

Index

335